Responsive Collaboration for IEP and 504 Teams

This book is dedicated to the God we seek;

our husbands, Glenn Johnson-Mussad and Chris Peltier;

our siblings, Emir, Peter, and Alissa;

our children, Wren and Elijah;

our parents, Edward and Samiha, George and Darla;

our extended families;

and the many students, families, and educators we know.

You have inspired us.

You have encouraged us.

Your love and support gave us this opportunity.

Your stories, strategies, and your amazing gifts are the heart of this book.

We offer this book

with love, gratitude, and joy!

Responsive Collaboration for IEP and 504 Teams

Albert Johnson-Mussad

Laurel Peltier

FOR INFORMATION:

Corwin
A SAGE Company
2455 Teller Road
Thousand Oaks, California 91320
(800) 233-9936
www.corwin.com

SAGE Publications Ltd.
1 Oliver's Yard
55 City Road
London EC1Y 1SP
United Kingdom

SAGE Publications India Pvt. Ltd.
B 1/I 1 Mohan Cooperative Industrial Area
Mathura Road, New Delhi 110 044
India

SAGE Publications Asia-Pacific Pte. Ltd.
18 Cross Street #10-10/11/12
China Square Central
Singapore 048423

Printed in Canada.

Library of Congress Cataloging-in-Publication Data

Names: Johnson-Mussad, Albert, author. | Peltier, Laurel, author.

Title: Responsive collaboration for IEP and 504 teams / Albert Johnson-Mussad, Laurel Peltier.

Description: Thousand Oaks, California : Corwin, 2022. | Includes bibliographical references and index.

Identifiers: LCCN 2021059522 | ISBN 9781071854624 (paperback) | ISBN 9781071854617 (epub) | ISBN 9781071854600 (epub) | ISBN 9781071854594 (pdf)

Subjects: LCSH: Children with disabilities—Education—United States—Evaluation. | Children with disabilities—Education—Law and legislation—United States. | Individualized education programs—United States.

Classification: LCC LC4031 .J54 2022 | DDC 371.90973—dc23/eng/20220302
LC record available at https://lccn.loc.gov/2021059522

This book is printed on acid-free paper.

22 23 24 25 26 10 9 8 7 6 5 4 3 2 1

Contents

Visit the companion website at
https://resources.corwin.com/responsivecollab
for downloadable resources.

List of Illustrations, Figures, and Tables

Preface

Over the past 30 years, we have had the marvelous privilege of working with children between the ages of 3 and 21 in public and private schools in New Jersey, Connecticut, and Massachusetts and Vermont. Because our teaching careers focused on English learners and students with disabilities, our work as educators involved deep relationships with families. As district-level leaders, we have also been blessed to work closely with teachers, principals, directors of special education, instructional assistants, and many state-level policymakers.

Again and again, we have been amazed at the creativity, compassion, and resilience of so many committed people involved in public education. Thanks to the advocacy of teams that include students, parents, caregivers, community advocates, educators, and legislators, the doors of public schools are open wide. Classrooms are places where children from many backgrounds, cultures, and experiences meet, learn, and grow together. And we continue to push the boundaries that divide us as we bring our children together in our nation's public schools. We have also seen more students than we can count make gains beyond their wildest hopes as the result of the love, encouragement, and outstanding education offered by the team of adults surrounding them.

We have also seen good people become lost and discouraged when partnerships give way under the strain of long-standing differences. We have watched beautiful young people strive against the belief that they are not good enough, not capable, not welcome at the seat of learning. We have seen families weeping and raging at the lack of progress their children are experiencing. We've sat with educators, shoulders bowed and hearts burdened by the demands and limitations of broken, biased systems and intractable, unsolved problems of teaching and learning.

In this book, we want to offer you, the people who care deeply about children with disabilities, an invitation to the responsive teaming community. We're inviting you to consider the possibilities for teaming with one another in more mindful, more supportive ways. We're inviting you to look with us at research about how to be a team. We're inviting you to reflect with us about new ways to navigate the referral, evaluation, eligibility determination, and planning processes. We're inviting you to use data to make your teams stronger. We're inviting you to join us in trying new tools and to tell us what you discover: What works? What doesn't work?

This book is an invitation to you to bring a spirit of inquiry to your teams, to approach team meetings as an opportunity to build strong relationships and networks of support. As you approach the people who join you at the 504 or IEP team meeting table, we're inviting you to respond to them as human beings, as partners, as valued members of your community.

Come. Join us in responsive teaming. Let's keep working toward connection, trust, and relationship.

Acknowledgments

PUBLISHER'S ACKNOWLEDGMENTS

Corwin gratefully acknowledges the contributions of the following reviewers:

Christopher Brum, PhD
Assistant Professor
San Diego State University
San Diego, CA

Edward Palmisano
School Psychologist
Brookwood School District #167
Glenwood, IL

Otistine T. Williams
Special Education Supervisor
Verona Area School District
Verona, WI

Whitney Schexnider, MEd
Statewide Instructional Coordinator
Idaho Special Education Support and Technical Assistance
Boise, ID

About the Authors

Albert Johnson-Mussad holds a PhD in applied linguistics (language teaching, testing, and learning) from Georgetown University. He has worked in PreK–12 schools for 30 years as a teacher, professional development facilitator, and instructional leader. He currently consults nationally to provide professional development, coaching, and technical assistance in PreK–12 schools. Albert's interest in language, culture, and responsive practice began as a child of immigrants from Egypt to the United States. Albert lives in Greenfield, Massachusetts, with his husband Glenn.

Laurel Peltier holds an EdD in special education leadership from the University of Massachusetts Amherst. She has worked in public schools and postsecondary colleges and universities, teaching English and special education courses for the past 33 years. Laurel is trained and has experience in facilitating person-centered planning, educational advocacy, and mediation. Her interest in disability advocacy and education began when her youngest child was diagnosed with autism at the age of 2. Currently, Laurel lives in Amherst, Massachusetts, with her husband Chris and her son Elijah. She also has an amazing daughter, Wren, who has fled the nest and lives in the Midwest.

CHAPTER ONE

Introduction

"If he's not speaking by now, it's not likely he will speak."

These are the words the team heard about Elijah when he was 8 years old. Elijah has autism and a learning profile that easily fits into the federal disability definition for intellectual impairment. Members of his school team—including his speech and language pathologist, his special education teacher, the school principal, and a behaviorist—joined Elijah's parents for the evaluation at a very reputable clinic. We all wanted what was best for Elijah.

As a team, we struggled with the results of this evaluation and recommendations for services and placement. And as a team, we rejected the recommendations for a substantially separate school with a program focused solely on "functional" vocabulary and life skills. While we all respected the expertise of the evaluator and his team, our vision was about inclusion, membership, and an enviable life in the community among people with and without disabilities.

Along the way, Elijah's team discovered that his full-scale IQ is <1st percentile, with subtest scores at the highest in the 1st through 3rd percentile across the board. Achievement testing showed similar results, particularly in reading comprehension, writing at the single-word level and basic computation in mathematics. Middle school came and brought opportunities for inclusion in community-based settings, chorus, and science classes because these fit with Elijah's strengths, interests, and preferences. High school offered opportunities for volunteer work and internships, as well as a new interest in art classes with nondisabled peers. Seizures, severe aggression, and a long-term absence from school were also part of the journey through high school, as were some amazing relationships with community fitness and recreation networks and with employers.

Fast forward to postsecondary life: Elijah has paid employment. He actually has his dream job: working on a farm with animals, being outside every day, and being part of a crew of people of all abilities—many of whom are young people, all of whom help each other do what needs to be done. He does speak, though not often, and sometimes about things that are silly or, in Michelle Garcia Winner's language, "unexpected." He reads and writes well enough so that without any instruction he recently ordered $300 worth of Gatorade and $150 worth of strawberry Mentos on Amazon. He also read from the Advent liturgy in church last Sunday, prompting a flood of emails to us from excited parishioners.

This is one story. There are many, many stories like this one. They are about one child, an individual, who was found eligible for special education at a young age. There are children all over our nation whose story includes, at some point, a journey through the referral and eligibility process. These children are accompanied on this journey by the adults who are caring for them and educating them. And what this group of adults, this team, decides can change the course of these children's lives.

HIDDEN FACTORS THAT IMPACT TEAM DYNAMICS

At the point when a child is referred for a special education or Section 504 evaluation, a team of people is formed. This team of "parents, teachers, other school staff—and often the student—must come together to look closely at the student's unique needs . . . and decide whether the child is a 'child with a disability' as defined by IDEA" if the referral is for special education (U.S. Department of Education, 2000). The team plays a similar role during consideration for eligibility under Section 504 of the Rehabilitation Act. The reason for having such a diverse team is to "pool knowledge, experience and commitment to design an educational program that will help the student be involved in, and progress in, the general curriculum" (U.S. Department of Education, 2000). The child's trajectory toward a life of optimal outcomes rests on the success of the team. Teams succeed when decisions are made as the result of a compliant and collaborative process.

When team members meet, there are some very real barriers that can impact effective partnership. IEP and 504 teams have a common purpose: finding a fit between the learner and schooling that results in effective access to schooling and progress in the general curriculum. Yet there are many hidden elements that can impact team collaboration when making the decisions that are required by law. For example, Figure 1.1 shows a few of the factors that team members may not share but that can have a significant impact on team dynamics.

Figure 1.1 • Factors That Influence Team Dynamics

ANXIETY
CULTURE
DEFICIT-BASED MINDSET
What will the other kids think of me?
What if I don't have time in my schedule?
What will happen when school ends?
What if the goal isn't met?
What if someone gets hurt?
How can we meet everyone's needs?
TEAM DYNAMICS

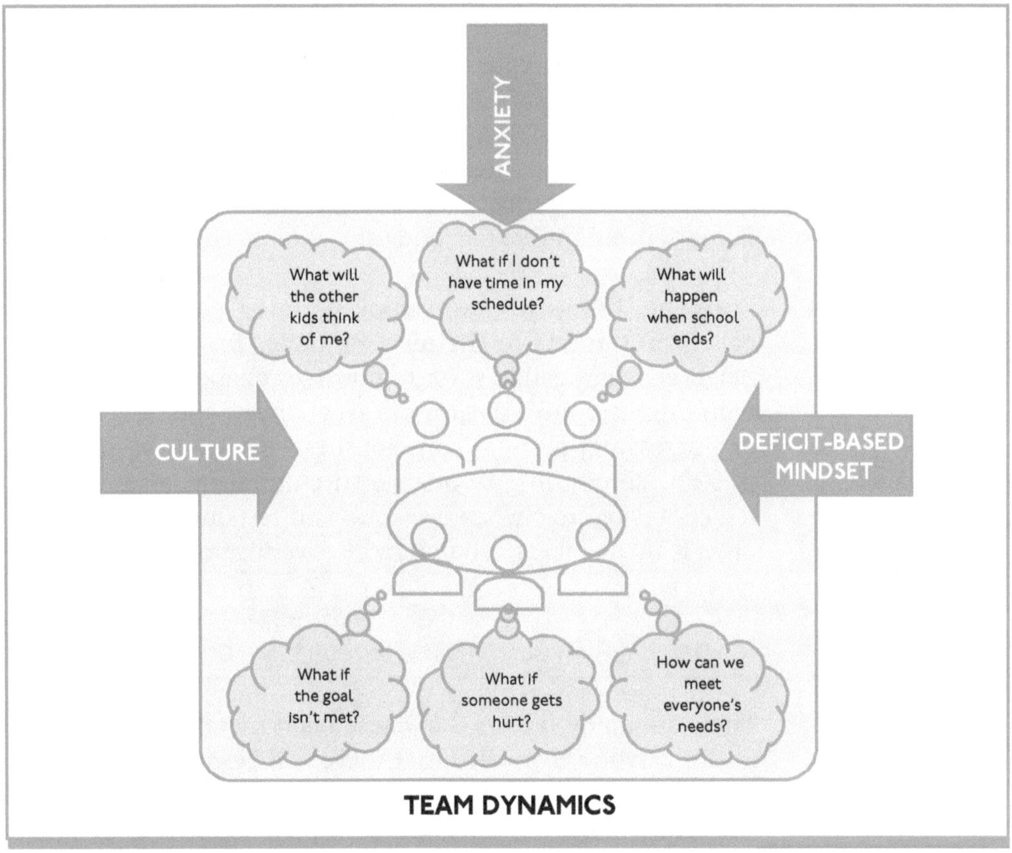

Impact of Culture on Team Dynamics

Team members bring their multiple cultural identities to the table. Culture refers to the diverse ways we understand and engage with the world, other people, ourselves, and institutions like families, schools, and other service agencies. People who work together on 504 and IEP teams are operating at the intersection of multiple cultures.

It is critical that team members understand the impact of these cultural differences on team decision-making. One model of culture that teams might use to understand this impact is presented by Zaretta Hammond in her 2015 book *Culturally Responsive Teaching and the Brain.* This model recognizes *surface culture*, *shallow culture*, and *deep culture* ("Culture Tree" illustration by Aliza Maynard, in Hammond, 2015, p. 24). While it may be easy for team members to understand and accommodate surface culture, such as differences in native language or differences in physical ability, it is harder for team members to understand and accommodate deeper differences, many of which are not visible. How team members experience and respond to conflict—and express conflicting perspectives and wants—reflect elements of *shallow culture*. At this level, unspoken rules (e.g., being honest, ways of handling emotion, the nature of relationships) carry high emotional impact. Elements of *deep culture* include unconscious beliefs and norms (e.g., notions of fairness, decision-making) and carry intense emotional impact.

Everyone brings these unspoken rules and unconscious beliefs and norms to the meeting table. Team members can heighten their readiness for responsive collaboration by "[self-reflecting] on cultural beliefs and experiences" and "[developing] or [increasing] cultural consciousness" (Rossetti et al., 2017, p. 330). Responding to one's own cultural beliefs and experiences related to the team's work, and responding to those of other team members, can start by discovering potential anxieties.

Impact of Anxiety on Team Dynamics

There are many factors that cause team members to feel anxious. Everyone is worried that there will be conflict. Different perspectives and priorities about time and money can impede the team's work. The laws are complex. Team members' familiarity with the laws and regulations differ. The team meeting is serious business. It's no wonder that the process of teaming can be filled with confusion and can provoke anxiety.

When anxiety is at play, brains flood with cortisol, frontal lobes shut down, and people can fall prey to blaming and judging one another, further damaging relationships and the ability to partner. So everyone who comes to the table is facing a situation in which there is tremendous potential for connection as well as considerable anxiety surrounding our relationship with a particular child and with other team members. We know from research regarding the brain and emotion that fear and anxiety impact brain function and decision-making

(Crespo et al., 2015; Grupe, 2017). The strategies for responding and supporting one another described throughout this book offer ideas for leaning against the emotions that come into play when working as a team on behalf of a child with disabilities.

Impact of Deficit-Based Mindsets on Team Dynamics

Another condition faced by 504 and IEP teams is the deficit-based approach to eligibility determination. This approach is strongly rooted in the history of educating people with disabilities. If you're not familiar with this history, one excellent resource that is being used by history educators across the United States comes from the Emerging America Project. This project offers professional development funded by the Library of Congress (find more information at www.emergingamerica.org.).

If you are familiar with the history of educating people with disabilities in the United States, you know that institutionalization and segregation on the basis of disability-related needs is a prominent feature of our approach to educating this population. Messages about disability and a tendency to address people who think, learn, and behave differently by separating them from others contributes to deficit thinking. The close association to medical models of service that understand and make determinations about people with different abilities as something to be fixed or healed also contributes to deficit-based thinking. People including Ed Roberts, Victor Peneda, Alice Wong, Judy Heumann, Frank Stephens, and Judith Snow have advocated for a shift in the way society responds to the needs of people who speak, think, move, and act with assistance from devices and support providers. Including all students in the team process as active participants is one way teams can lean against the deficit-based mindsets that many associate with identifying and supporting students with disabilities in schools.

Underlying Need to Shift Our Mindset to Support Compliance and Collaboration

In this book, we address the pervasive biases in education that understand *different* abilities as *dis*abilities. We want to encourage you and ourselves to embrace another way of thinking. We want to lean hard against a culture that tells us that people with different abilities are people with defects. So we use the word "disability" not to describe people, but to align our communication with current legal terminology, hoping that soon this word will not be used to refer to the rich tapestry of abilities and ways of learning and being that people bring to public schools.

In this book, we want to invite you to champion this shift of mindset. Here is one practice that we hope you'll consider adopting: When you approach eligibility, planning, and placement decisions, remember that the problem being addressed by student support teams, 504 teams, or IEP teams is not a student or a student's profile as a learner. *The problem that is being addressed is the fit between a child and the way schooling has been provided.*

We've learned a lot about this fit in recent years, especially when the impact of COVID-19 disrupted education. Now, we know that there are many ways that people can engage in teaching and learning. So please join us in leaning against thinking and talking in ways that identify students as problems, people with deficiencies, people who need to be fixed or healed. Instead, we hope you'll continually think, speak, act, and remind others about the focus of teams in schools, which is to find a better fit between the way schooling happens and the beautiful, unique, amazing way that an individual child learns.

A RESPONSIVE APPROACH TO TEAMING

One way we can support all members of the team to remain available for thinking, talking, and planning together is to embrace a responsive approach to the team process. Such an approach embraces all aspects of compliance and specific practices that promote effective, sustained, and responsive collaboration. Responsive teams come together during meetings to accomplish three tasks in repeating cycles of collaborative inquiry. These three tasks are as follows:

- *Identifying questions* that inform data review and group decisions. Questions often come from guidance documents or research about the team process. Questions also emerge from guidelines or points of reference that help us make sense of our data. In special education, guidelines or points of reference come from several places:

  - Laws and regulations (see "Summaries of Important Information" in the Appendix section of this book)
  - Research (e.g., evidence-based practice)
  - Curriculum learning strands and standards
  - Cultural norms, values, and the vision for the student's future

- *Looking at data together* to understand the fit between student and schooling in relation to the questions
- *Making decisions* driven by data using facilitation and a problem-solving approach

Figure 1.2 depicts these three tasks as a cycle that repeats over and over, creating a pattern or routine for conversations about eligibility, plan development, and placement determination.

Figure 1.2 • Responsive Teaming Cycle

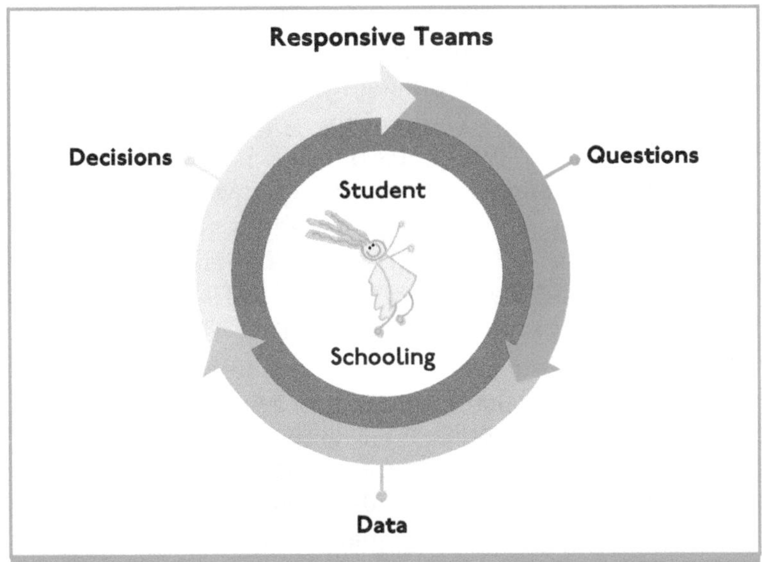

The benefits of a responsive team approach align strongly with what we know about successful team dynamics. A team is the group charged with developing an educational program or plan for an eligible student with a disability. Successful teams engage in specific activities that include creating a vision, building the capacity of people, using data to inform decisions, and engaging stakeholders in the process of making decisions and implementing plans (Leithwood et al., 2004). In order to accomplish these activities, team members must partner effectively because the task of responding to the fit between the student and schooling is given to the entire group, not just to one member or to the district. Team members bring their particular expertise regarding the student's strengths, needs, interests, preferences, and the interventions that have been tried. Responsive teams recognize and honor the authority of this expertise. Successful teams seek to build relationships with all team members and try to compose "living, breathing" plans that are "continually reviewed by the team working with the student" (Lesh, 2020).

COMPARING SECTION 504 AND SPECIAL EDUCATION REGULATIONS

When we refer to Section 504 of the Rehabilitation Act and special education regulations, we are referring to two different sets of federal laws. It is also important to remember that these two provisions are quite different in both the nature of the legal protections they offer and the populations of students who are protected. Section 504 of the Rehabilitation Act is a civil rights law that protects some students who are considered general education students with disabilities. IDEA 2004 is the current authorization of a federal law that is specific to special education and the rights of the group of students who are being evaluated and who are found eligible. IDEA 2004 is not a civil rights law; however, all children who are found eligible for special education under IDEA are also protected under Section 504. While this handbook is not a law book, we do believe that all team members need to have a working knowledge of some of the broad aspects of Section 504 and IDEA 2004 regulations. We have found that there are many confusions and misconceptions about the protections afforded under both acts for students with disabilities.

In each chapter, we will offer a summary table to address key elements of each provision. We'll focus on elements that are important for team members to know and understand and on elements that may be connected to misunderstandings.

Table 1.1 introduces overarching differences between Section 504 and IDEA 2004.

TABLE 1.1 Differences Between Section 504 and IDEA 2004

KEY ELEMENT	SECTION 504	IDEA 2004
Name of law and related regulations	Section 504 of the Rehabilitation Act of 1973 (Section 504)	Individuals with Disabilities Education Act of 2004 (IDEA)
Statute (legal citation)	29 U.S.C. § 794 et seq.	20 U.S.C. § 1400 et seq.
Regulations (legal citation)	34 C.F.R. § 104	34 C.F.R. § 300 et seq.
Type of law	Civil rights law that protects "the rights of individuals with disabilities in programs and activities that receive Federal financial assistance from the U.S. Department of Education" (Office for Civil Rights, 2020) The procedural provisions applicable to Title VI of the Civil Rights Act of 1964 apply to this part. These procedures are found in 100.6–100.10 and part 101 of this title. 34 C.F.R. 104.61.	Law that makes a free appropriate public education (FAPE) available to eligible children with disabilities (IDEA, n.d.).
Agency that monitors compliance	U.S. Department of Education Office for Civil Rights (OCR)	U.S. Department of Education Office of Special Education and Rehabilitation Services (OSERS) and Office of Special Education Programs (OSEP)

OUR INTENTION IN THIS BOOK

In this book, we propose a responsive team approach for any team partnering to make decisions on behalf of a student. Basically, this is a "how-to" manual that offers a consistent, clear, and responsive approach to decision-making.

In each chapter, we will explain the specific criteria that are identified in IDEA 2004 and in Section 504 of the Rehabilitation Act. These criteria are the tools that all team members need to understand and use to make decisions that comply with federal and state regulations. *Questions* about these criteria will lead team members to a deeper understanding of these regulations and also to a more complete understanding of a particular student. Additional questions related to learning strands and standards, the cultural norms and values of team members, and the vision for the student will also be important in guiding teams to use data and make decisions in order to improve the fit between the learner and schooling. We will discuss these criteria broadly; however, these criteria will vary from team to team, based on the needs and circumstances of a particular child. We will also describe strategies that teams can use *before, during,* and *after* team meetings to gather and review *data* together, rather than designating one person as the "expert" who presents data to the group and tells the group what it means. Finally, we will give you practical tools to connect the questions with individual data points from multiple sources to support the claims that team members make about how to interpret and make *decisions*.

The benefits of a responsive team approach are that all members will be informed, all members will have a voice, and all members will become fluent with the routines of making decisions that are compliant and collaborative.

WHAT TO EXPECT AS YOU CONTINUE READING

Here's a summary of what to expect in the chapters ahead.

Chapter 2 explains what we mean by *responsive teams*. We share a bit of the research that supports this approach to teaming. We also share some of the reasons why you and others should adopt this approach to strengthen collaboration and compliance to optimize academic and social-emotional outcomes for students.

Chapters 3 through 9 are organized into four sections. Each of Chapters 3 through 8 compares the IEP (from IDEA 2004) and 504 (Section 504 of the Rehabilitation Act) processes. Each of these chapters also concretely compares the "frequent approach" and the "responsive approach" advocated in this handbook. The term "frequent approach" refers to practices that we have experienced as familiar or happening in many of the schools in which we have worked and consulted. The term "responsive approach" refers to a contrasting way that you and others may want to consider so that you can act as a supportive team that prioritizes shared understanding and collaborative practices. For details about the focus of each chapter, see the table of contents.

We've organized this book to address these elements:

- Chapter 3 and Chapter 4 consider initial referral and eligibility determination.
- Chapter 5 and Chapter 6 describe the development of individualized plans and determination of educational placement.
- Chapter 7 and Chapter 8 invite readers to consider responsive teaming over time with attention to independent evaluations, manifestation determinations, and reviews and reevaluations of IEP and 504 plans.
- Chapter 9 concludes with a summary of key ideas and practices related to responsive teaming, as well as QR codes linking to resources and tools for implementation.

You can also expect a variety of tools:

- Checklists
- Graphic organizers
- Strategies
- Stories

These are designed to help you understand and apply the ideas discussed in each chapter and to measure the changes that result as you apply these ideas to support children with disabilities and the members of their teams.

WHO IS THIS BOOK FOR?

In writing this book, we have thought about and consulted with people in several different roles.

Special education teachers, related service providers, paraeducators and educational team leaders: This book is for special education service providers in a range of roles and positions who want to make the most of the team process. We are especially mindful of your need for specific strategies to facilitate teams effectively, to partner with other team members (including parents, guardians, students, and your colleagues, as well as community providers), and the way time works in schools. In thinking about you, we want to give you these items:

- Tools for keeping teams talking and making decisions together
- Strategies for documenting decisions and organizing information
- Ideas for facilitating courageous conversations and helping all team members reach consensus
- Information to demystify compliance for all members of the team

Parents/guardians and advocates: This book is for parents, guardians, advocates, and other adults who speak on behalf of children with disabilities. We are grateful for all that students, parents, and guardians have done to bring equity and access to our field of education. In thinking about you, we offer these particulars:

- Tools for getting the information you need to be full and equal members of the team
- Strategies for understanding and interpreting data in partnership with other team members
- Ideas to strengthen your advocacy on behalf of the children you support
- Information about how you can engage with other members of the IEP team effectively, even if you disagree

General education teachers: This book is for general education teachers across the PreK–12+ span who work diligently to know, understand, and teach children of all abilities. You bring knowledge about the curriculum and information about teaching and learning in the classroom that all members of the team need and value. In thinking about you, we believe you will benefit from these elements:

- Tools for understanding what information you already have at hand that the team needs to know
- Strategies for talking with other team members in a way that honors your expertise and their expertise and leads the entire team to a place of confidence about teaching and learning and what can be possible for this child in the general education setting
- Ideas for organizing and sharing information so everyone can understand your expertise
- Information about the importance of your role and the ways we can plan to support both the child and the work you're doing in the classroom with all students

Principals and school-based leaders: This book is for principals, assistant principals, deans, and heads of guidance departments who support educators and families to partner well on behalf of students. You understand how trends and patterns in data offer information about teaching and learning. You also understand and encourage a network of good-faith relationships, and you help people remain connected when differences arise. In thinking of you, we are providing this support:

- Tools to assist with the implementation of consistent protocols for teams supporting children with disabilities
- Strategies to support a facilitated approach to teaming
- Ideas for documenting decisions in relation to data gathered by the team
- Information that will allow you to evaluate the impact of using these tools, strategies, and ideas in your building

Special education administrators, evaluators, and central office leaders: This book is for special education administrators and district-level leaders who are responsible for compliance with IDEA 2004 and Section 504 of the Rehabilitation Act. You know the law and regulations, and you also know the people inside and outside of the district who are working to improve academic and social-emotional outcomes for students with and without disabilities. You understand norm-referenced data and the connections between scores and the profiles of individual students. In thinking of you, we offer this assistance:

- Tools to support consistent, data-based decision-making across all teams serving students with disabilities

- Strategies to resolve disputes and arrive at agreements at the planning team level
- Ideas for sharing information and clarifying the connections among regulatory criteria that guide decisions, data collected by teams, and the decisions made by teams about eligibility, service delivery, and placement
- Information to support in-district professional learning to strengthen collaboration and compliance

Professional development providers/higher-education faculty/state department of education staff: This book is for those who are training educators and educational leaders and who are looking for ways to inspire and equip people who give their lives to teaching and learning. You bring new ideas, fresh perspectives, and a growth mindset to the people you are coaching and mentoring. In thinking of you, we would like to share this information:

- Tools that can be used to strengthen adults' understanding and ability to support the team process
- Strategies to build the capacity of adult learners to consider multiple claims and ideas while insisting that these claims and ideas connect to data *before* proceeding with decision-making
- Ideas that are based in evidence and connected to current research in education
- Information that adult learners can use in districts, in schools, and in families to strengthen collaboration and compliance when planning for students with disabilities

For people in all roles: The process of determining eligibility, developing plans, and deciding upon educational placements requires team members to make claims and support them with available data. In this book, we will describe a responsive approach that invites team members to use data to construct a student profile to summarize strengths and areas of need before making decisions. A responsive team process connects questions and criteria for making decisions to qualitative and quantitative data before decisions are made.

Another important point we want to emphasize is that our work has been primarily in the northeastern United States.

As you read this book, we hope you will discover tools and thoughts that prompt your thinking about how you can strengthen responsive teaming in your school and in your state. It is likely that we will occasionally suggest or reference practices that are common in the Northeast but may not be required in your jurisdiction. Remember, always check the local and state guidance where you are practicing before making any changes in your practice. Responsive teaming is not a "lone ranger" approach, but one that we hope you'll enjoy in dialogue and collaboration with others. We believe our ideas will inspire some new thinking and our tools will offer new ways to implement responsive practices, and we invite you to make changes and adjust whatever you discover in this book to fit with the requirements in your area. We'll also welcome any feedback about how we can make changes to this book and the professional services we provide so that we avoid, as much as possible, contradicting compliant approaches in your area. Please reach out to let us know how we can improve our work!

Most of all, in writing this book, we thought of all of the students who are supported by teams of adults and whose strengths, interests, preferences, and individual learning profiles are at the heart of what we do in school. You have learned in the past, you are learning now, and you will continue to learn and grow in the future. In thinking of you, we bring faith in your unique and amazing capacities for learning; hope in your potential to discover the wonder of yourselves and to contribute to the wellness and joy of others; and love for you, exactly the way you are.

SUMMARY: OUR WISHES FOR YOU AS YOU READ THIS BOOK

As you read this book, what we wish most is that you will be inspired in the work you're doing as part of a team that supports children with different learning profiles. The word "disability" is important as well as stigmatizing. It leads children to services and supports; it leads children to struggle and shame. Our wish for you and for every child whom you are serving is that the convening of the team would be a time for confident partnership, a time of celebration of accomplishments, a time when the learning profile of the child becomes ever more clear.

We wish for you a team process that energizes every member of the team. We hope that every time the team communicates or comes together around the table, there is a sense of anticipation that successes will be named, noticed, and celebrated and that needs will be named, noticed, and addressed. We hope that every time a team member has a great idea or a compelling concern, the rest of the team will listen and that team member will feel and know that they've been understood and taken seriously.

We wish for you many new ideas and understandings about what it means to work together, to collaborate and comply with regulations. We hope you will discover ways of working that are not afraid of looking at data and discussing what it really shows about the fit between an individual student and the way schooling is happening. We invite you to connect every claim about what should or could or might be done to what the data has told you about what works at school for this uniquely capable child.

We wish for you a journey that leads to a new place—a place in which your teams are stronger, safer, and always growing in trust and goodwill. May the team meeting table be a place of community and hospitality as much as it is a place of successful planning.

With confidence in your tremendous gifts and abilities as members of the team,

Albert and Laurel

CHAPTER TWO

Why Do We Need Responsive Teams?

> *"When I think about the most important piece of an IEP meeting, it's the concept that families are equal decision-makers. There are so many instances where a parent or family member isn't equal to the team because they don't have the same information, cultural context, or formal education. The most important aspect to the IEP process is for IEP team leads/chairs to create an environment where collaboration is the standard."*
>
> —O. Sophia Johansson, Massachusetts Families Organizing for Change

GUIDING QUESTIONS FOR THIS CHAPTER

- What are some of the hidden factors that impact team dynamics?
- What is the primary problem being addressed by 504 and IEP teams?
- How does a responsive teaming approach address this problem?

When we gather at the table to consider a referral and to plan for a student identified as having a disability, we come as people with diverse backgrounds. Yes, everyone involved cares about the child, yet the care that is expressed comes from different insights regarding the child, as well as different beliefs, values, and hopes for the child. Responsive teaming means that people listen actively, with a sense of curiosity and respect, to one another's perspectives and priorities. The purpose of listening is to understand and empathize in order to identify questions, look at data that responds to these questions, and then make decisions together that respond to the data. When teaming is responsive, all voices are heard, team members feel understood, and the decisions made reflect available data and a robust vision of the child as a learner and a unique person, in and out of school. See Chapter 9 for QR codes linking to our **Responsive Teaming Survey** to measure these outcomes with your team. This tool is also available on our companion website.

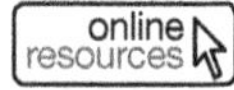

COMPLIANCE AND RESPONSIVE TEAMING

As we join together at the planning table, federal regulations require that we think, talk, and make decisions as a team. The regulations for Section 504 of the Rehabilitation Act require that elementary and secondary schools ensure that a team of people who have knowledge of the child and evaluation tools make decisions about eligibility and placement (34 C.F.R. 104.35(c)(3); OCR, 2020). Similarly, the Individuals with Disabilities Education Act (IDEA) 2004 regulations require an IEP team that consists of the following people:

- The child's parents/guardians
- At least one of the child's general education teachers
- At least one of the child's special education teachers
- A representative of the district
- People who are qualified to interpret evaluation results, including related therapists
- "Whenever appropriate, the child with a disability" (34 C.F.R. § 300.321)

Guidance about the team process emphasizes the need for this team to consider the needs of the child together, to pool their expertise and knowledge, and to partner to "design an educational program that will help the student be involved in, and progress in, the general curriculum" (OSERS, 2019). Whether groups are gathering to consider eligibility, program planning, and placement of children with disabilities under Section 504 of the Rehabilitation Act or under IDEA 2004, decisions must be made by teams of people who know the child.

COLLABORATION AND RESPONSIVE TEAMING

This all sounds great; however, as most of us know, the work of collaborating, particularly when the cultures, feelings, mindsets, roles, and responsibilities of team members are diverse, has implications that extend far beyond a compliant process. While the regulations tell us what to do—to partner as a team—there is no guidance in the regulations that will help us understand how we can collaborate effectively. And as many of us who have experience with teamwork understand, the "how" of teaming is where an effective partnership happens.

This is why we need responsive teams. We need to know not only who is on the team, and what their relationship to the child is, but also how to connect with one another. We need to know how to engage in a process that builds a *team* rather than a mere collection of people who hold a child in common. We need to remember that team members have a significant investment in the child and also have significant investments in their roles as parents/guardians, educators, and community service providers. We need a process that promotes mutual respect, that inspires people to wrestle honestly with problems and barriers, that compels team members to join together to find and strengthen the fit between the child and schooling, thereby helping to design and implement an effective educational program. We need a process in which the people who are sitting at the team meeting table have a shared understanding about the decisions that the team is required by law to make; a shared understanding about the data that will be used to inform decisions; and a shared understanding of all of the people who are coming together to educate and care for the child. Our teams need to be responsive to the legal requirements of the 504 or IEP process and, more importantly, to each other as people. We must collaborate as we comply because compliance and collaboration are intertwined.

CASE STUDY: ALBERT'S TEAM

We will use our names whenever we present case studies throughout this book. The specifics of the cases come from our experiences in the field. We are committed to protecting the confidentiality of all team members, so using our names and the names of family members seemed like the easiest way to ensure that even our unconscious biases don't influence the selection of pseudonyms. We know you understand, and we thank you! Now, let's dive into our first case study:

> Imagine Albert, a student who is in ninth grade. It's March 1, and Albert moved into his current school district two years ago. Before this time, he was educated in Germany; however, he is multilingual and his family speaks fluent German, Russian, and English in the home, depending on the extended family who live with them. His father is from Germany, and his mother has lived in the United States and abroad throughout her life. She was educated outside the United States until entering college. Albert's parents have had consistent concerns about him since moving into the district, particularly about his reading.
>
> Albert's high school teachers are also concerned about him. The problem is Albert's behavior in class, particularly in English and world history. Teachers report that Albert is disrespectful and disruptive when he is in the room. He often interrupts teacher lectures. He will not take notes and instead turns to neighboring students and wants to talk with them while the teacher is speaking.
>
> During small-group work, Albert listens actively to peers and seems to enjoy debating and discussing his ideas; however, he won't take on assigned roles in the groups and will not read or write if given the responsibility to do these activities. Instead, he excuses himself and requests a pass to the guidance office.
>
> When asked to remain in the room, Albert raises his voice, joins other groups, or sometimes simply puts his head down and refuses to participate. These behaviors happen at least once a week in English and history—sometimes more frequently.
>
> In January, Albert began taking health class, and his health teacher has just reported similar concerns to guidance. Albert's math, science, world language, and physical education teachers report no concerns and find Albert a joy to have in class.

After receiving a call from the guidance counselor in mid-February, Albert's parents have requested a "comprehensive evaluation to determine whether Albert is eligible for special education."

WHY DO WE NEED RESPONSIVE TEAMS?

If you're reading this book, you know Albert's story, or one that is similar. It's clear that Albert, his parents, and his teachers (and likely his guidance counselor and maybe even the principal) are all striving and struggling with the fit between Albert's profile as a learner and schooling. Maybe this is not how you thought about Albert's case. That's OK. Usually, when hearing a story like Albert's, people tend to identify with one or more of those in the story. Maybe you are the parent of a child with a disability and you connect with Albert's parents. Maybe you are (or were) a student who found ninth grade less than compelling and you connect with Albert. Maybe you are a high school teacher and you connect with the English, history, and health teachers mentioned in the story. Maybe you're a guidance counselor or the principal or assistant principal (AP) in a school and you can relate to these people.

One reason we need responsive teams is because of the intersection between legal requirements and personal relationships that happens every time a referral for evaluation is made. We'll come back to Albert's story later in this chapter after offering some thoughts on this intersectionality.

In this book, we offer an approach to teaming in which compliance and collaboration are equally important. We propose that teams can respond to the law and to the people involved in designing and implementing educational programs for students with disabilities. Based on our work in the New England region of the United States, we know that it's possible to engage teams to create an experience of partnership.

Our proposal is that all teams should focus on these three tasks (see Figure 2.1), which recur throughout the processes of determining eligibility, designing educational programs, and determining placement:

- *Identifying questions* that inform the group's collection and review of data and the group's decisions

Figure 2.1 • Responsive Teaming Cycle

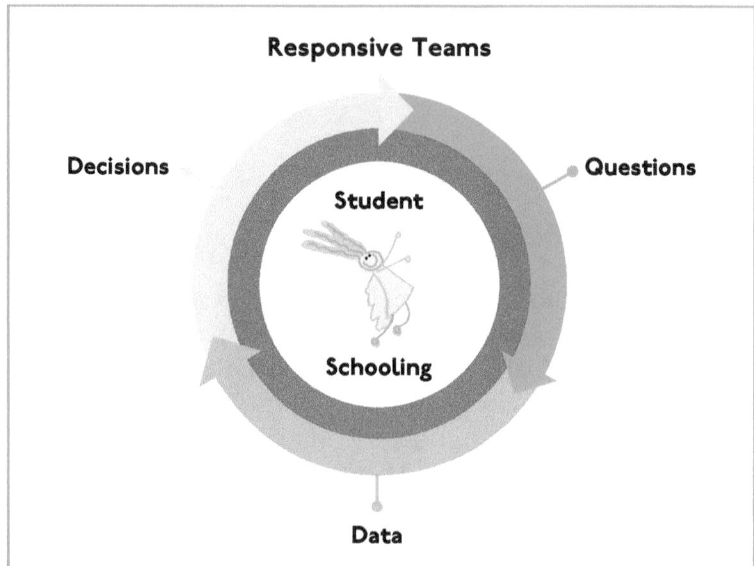

- *Looking at data together* to understand the fit between the student and schooling in relation to the questions
- *Making decisions* anchored in the data using facilitation and a problem-solving approach

We propose that teams engage in these three tasks together, rather than completing activities related to each task individually or independently of other team members. Here's a bit more about how these three tasks can be accomplished in a way that establishes and supports the growth of responsive teams.

IDENTIFYING QUESTIONS THAT INFORM TEAM DATA COLLECTION AND DECISIONS

We propose a process in which teams begin their work by clearly identifying and discussing the questions that will guide compliant IEP and 504 team processes. As noted earlier, some questions will arise from IDEA and Section 504 criteria. For the purpose of this book, we will focus only on federal criteria because free and appropriate public education (FAPE) and least restrictive environment (LRE) are enforced in all 50 states, the District of Columbia, and U.S. territories. We urge you to follow a similar process to identify any jurisdiction-specific questions with your teams as well so that there is a shared understanding from the point at which a team forms about the "rules" that must be followed.

In the remaining chapters of this book, we will discuss specific questions that correspond to processes related to initial referral and eligibility determination, planning or program design, placement decisions and progress monitoring, and responsive teaming over time with attention to manifestation determinations, reviews, and reevaluations.

Teams identify questions in response to specific criteria. A criterion is a specific requirement or piece of guidance that comes from federal regulations or from specific guidance documents issued by the U.S. Department of Education Office of Special Education and Rehabilitation Services (OSERS) or by the U.S. Office for Civil Rights (OCR). One example of a group of criteria that all team members should understand and discuss are the federal definitions associated with eligible students with disabilities. These definitions are available in the regulations; however, we often find that members of teams charged with identifying eligible students do not have shared awareness of these terms and their regulatory definitions.

Understandably, acting on a team that is charged with determining eligibility without knowledge of the terms that define eligibility can be confusing and stressful. As you read Chapter 3 and Chapter 4, you'll learn more about these criteria and the ways that you can make them available and understandable for all members of the teams in which you participate.

RESEARCH TO CONSIDER

IDEA and Section 504 criteria will likely provoke questions. Why is it important to ensure that team members pose questions to build shared understanding of these federal criteria? There are several answers to this question. One is that it can be difficult for team members to understand the difference between what is legally required and what is being recommended (Zirkel, 2020). Another is that research shows that school-based team members often have limited fluency with

(Continued)

(Continued)

the requirements of regulations and tend to rely on other people rather than primary sources to understand the requirements for teams serving children with disabilities (Militello et al., 2009; O'Connor et al., 2016; Schimmel & Militello, 2008). A third reason is that teachers, parents, and administrators often feel frustrated and unclear about how to navigate the required process (Chaisson & Olson, 2007). We know from brain science that when people lack knowledge, feel confused, or experience frustration, their availability for decision-making and self-regulation decreases. This may explain why people sometimes experience the team process as difficult, cumbersome, and ineffective.

The good news is that any team member can do something to change this. In preparing for Section 504 and IEP team meetings, it is important that all team members have access to key criteria and that they have an opportunity to pose questions and build understanding about how these criteria will be used by the team to collect and interpret data and make decisions. This means that access to the criteria and discussion of their meaning, related recommendations, and how the team will use key criteria to respond to the child's needs must consider each team member's multiple identities. For example, individuals' educational experience, personal beliefs, and potential anxieties related to these criteria must be uncovered and welcomed in the conversation.

Further, an understanding of how key concepts, such as *disability, disorder, eligibility*, and *delay* or *impairment*, are conveyed in team members' heritage language(s) will help the team anticipate and "short circuit" misunderstandings and apprehension. Taking the time to build a shared understanding about key criteria, as well as a shared understanding of what these criteria mean *emotionally* to all team members, is important to equip team members with the information they need to analyze data and resolve differences in perspectives and values before making decisions on behalf of the child. We'll share more about how to use questions as the foundation of establishing a responsive team in the chapters ahead.

STRATEGIES TO CONSIDER

- Discuss, print, and share key criteria with team members at the very start of the team process. Have these available for reference during team meetings as they are defined and discussed. Use these reference sheets during conversations about data and when making decisions.

- Create short information briefs (2–5 sentences) with visuals to allow team members to quickly reference and recall important criteria. Be sure to translate these into the heritage language(s) of all team members.
- When a team is considering difficult questions or experiencing "big" feelings, take a break, use questions carefully and intentionally to build trust, and approach problems with a sense of curiosity rather than solutions or opinions about what should happen. Invite team members to articulate their feelings with phrases such as, "I worry that . . ." or "I'm afraid that . . ." and hold space for team members to be heard and understood.

In Albert's Case . . .

Suppose that when the district representative (maybe the special education director, maybe the principal, maybe a team leader, school psychologist, 504 coordinator, or guidance counselor) reaches out to Albert's parents about their request for a "comprehensive evaluation" the conversation goes something like this:

District representative: Hello, Mr. & Mrs. J-M. This is Sharon calling from Albert's school. How are you today?

[*Sharon listens to Albert's parents and inquires about any specifics before continuing the conversation.*]

District representative: I'm interested in learning more about your request for a comprehensive evaluation. Can you tell me what's happening and how you want the school to help?

Albert's parents: We are so worried about Albert. Since we came to the United States two years ago, he's really hated school. He loved school in Germany—it was so easy for him and he had so many friends. Soccer was his life, and he was such a happy child. Now, we've been here two years and he's ready to drop out. We think it's because he's struggling with reading and he's ashamed. We hate to have him evaluated, but something is really wrong, and we have to get him help!

District representative: Wow! I had no idea that things had been so difficult. I'm so sorry to hear about how hard school has been for Albert, and I'm really glad that we're talking about this now. Is there anything else you think I should know about what's happened so I can understand the fit between Albert's learning and what's happening at school?

Albert's parents: Well, we've previously shared our concerns about Albert with his guidance counselor. Also, we just got a call from the guidance counselor saying that Albert's teachers feel as if he's disruptive and disrespectful in class. What?! Albert?! We have raised him to respect adults, and now you're telling us he's disruptive? We're telling you he can't read! Why isn't anyone helping him?

[*Warning: Here's where responsive teaming kicks into high gear!*]

District representative: Whoa! I am so sorry that you've gotten this message about Albert. I met him last week, and I have to say that I found him to be a very articulate and respectful young man. What I heard you say is that you're concerned about reading and that your concern has lasted for several years. Is that right?

Albert's parents: Yes! Thank goodness someone from school is finally listening!

District representative: Did you know that there is a whole team of people who are listening at our school? I can tell it might not have felt like it before, but I want to fill you in about the team and how we will be working with Albert and your family to get some answers to your questions about reading. Can you tell me what you know about the "comprehensive evaluation" process?

Albert's parents: Well, we know that kids get evaluated and then get special help—extra tutoring and services. Is that right?

District representative: I'm glad you are aware of your right to request an evaluation. I can see why you did this. There are actually laws and

> regulations that surround two different approaches that we might take to this evaluation. No matter where we begin, it's important that you understand that not all students get evaluated to determine eligibility for special education before getting help. At our school, we can offer some help to any student, and I can share some of the extra help that's available right now to assist Albert with reading and schoolwork. Only students who are suspected of having a disability are entitled to a "comprehensive evaluation." So if you want to proceed, we will need to talk about the definitions of different disabilities and the characteristics that Albert might be demonstrating as a learner. I have some material to show you, and I want to be sure you understand some of the basic rights that protect Albert and you before we decide whether to get your written consent for an evaluation. Can we meet to look at some information together so we can decide how to proceed?

We hope you can see how Albert's parents and the district representative are already engaged in building shared understanding about the regulations and aspects of a compliant process while building a collaborative relationship. This is why we need responsive teaming—so that we give equal weight and priority to compliant and collaborative approaches to team decision-making.

We also hope that you can see that responsive teaming involves cultivating a thoughtful approach to communicating. There are some important guiding questions to keep in mind, particularly during the early stages of becoming a team. While Albert's parents may or may not have in-depth knowledge about their rights, the district representative is typically familiar with the rights of parents and the steps in a compliant response to a parent referral for evaluation. What matters most at this point in the process is keeping the conversation headed in a direction that builds the team by cultivating relationships. Here are the questions to keep in mind at this stage:

- Is there a shared understanding between the person referring and the district about "suspected areas of disability" and the learner characteristics that may be associated with these disabilities? If not, what is the best way to introduce and build a shared understanding?

- Is there a shared understanding about the evaluation and eligibility determination process? If not, what is the best way to introduce and build this shared understanding?
- What are the needs of the student being identified in this conversation? How can these be clarified so that they can be clearly communicated when they are shared?
- What are the needs of other team members being identified in this conversation? How can these be named, acknowledged, and supported to strengthen the relationships among team members?

While it's not possible to script all of the details and nuances of a responsive approach to teaming, we hope that these guiding questions and the case study in this chapter give you a sense of the opportunities for strengthening collaboration within a compliant process from the very first conversations about the fit between the student and schooling.

LOOKING AT DATA TOGETHER TO UNDERSTAND THE FIT BETWEEN THE STUDENT AND SCHOOLING

Just as teams need support to build a shared understanding of, and fluency with, key questions or criteria, it is critical that all members of the team have equitable access to the data that is used to inform decisions. This involves a shift from having individual team members hold on to data as their area of expertise toward identifying, gathering, and sharing meaningful data that can be understood by all team members before the group gathers to make decisions.

A responsive team approach does not necessarily mean that we will change the way we evaluate students. It may be that a teacher is gathering information about a student in the classroom when other team members are not present. An evaluator may be working directly with a student in a one-to-one testing setting. Certainly, parents/guardians may be at home talking with their child about school when other team members are not there. All of this is important and should be expected; however, it is also important that after a critical observation, a norm-referenced testing session, or a key conversation at home, team members have the opportunity to gather and share this data with all other team members in a way that leads to a complete and shared understanding about what happened and what it tells us about the child's profile as a learner. Responsive collaboration means that all data is treated as equally important because it enriches team members' understanding of the child's learning profile. No piece of data is privileged above others because of its type (e.g., testing result, observation record, significant anecdotal note) or because of the identities or roles of the collectors/reporters.

A responsive team approach does mean that we will certainly change the way we share the results of evaluations. While formal evaluation reports will likely continue to be produced due to professional recommendations and the needs of students and schools, these reports may be linked or referenced in summaries of evaluation results that are offered in language that is accessible to all members of the team. In addition, it is critical that the results of evaluations are explained and interpreted with a focus on understanding the student's profile as a learner—meaning assets, challenges, learning preferences, and the fit between the child and the interventions that have been provided at school.

It is interesting to note how a child's performance compares to other children of the same age or grade level; however, care must be taken when describing scores and tasks, particularly on norm-referenced tests, so that all team members understand how the scores explain what a child can or cannot do when learning in a classroom. Any piece of data should be available and *accessible*, meaning useful and understandable, to each member of the team to support a shared understanding of the fit between the child's unique learning profile and schooling. This means that any piece of data that is presented to the team should be useful and understood by all members of the team. Data that is not useful and understandable to all team members is likely not to be helpful in supporting team-based decision-making. These considerations of equity in availability and accessibility of data are crucial to responsive collaboration.

RESEARCH TO CONSIDER

Why is it important to consider the ways we gather and share the data that we use to support team decisions? One reason is that in order to be effective with data-based decision-making, teams must be able to use data to understand and solve new problems (Bolhuis et al., 2016). A second reason is that there is a great deal of debate about whether tests associated with processing and cognition provide data that is associated with improved outcomes for students (Powers & Mandal, 2011). One more reason is that parents, students, and general educators are required to participate as part of the group that makes decisions based on data, yet they are often unable to participate fully due to lack of advance access to evaluation data or lack of understanding about what the data means in terms of the student's learning profile or classroom instruction (Lo, 2012; Nagro & Stein, 2015; O'Connor et al., 2016). A responsive team approach might mean that we gather different types of data. This approach might also mean that we present data in a way that more easily allows members of the team to use it to understand the profile of the student and to support claims about eligibility, instructional planning, and placement.

STRATEGIES TO CONSIDER

- Activity for personal reflection: Review several evaluation reports for a child and highlight the specific data points that you understand in green. Next, highlight the data points that you definitely don't understand in pink. What do you notice? Could this data be made more useful for you? How?
- Reorganizing data activity: Use the **Summary of Evaluation Data Template** to reorganize information for your next team meeting. If you're not sure how to sort a particular data point, write down a question for the evaluator or team to consider. This tool is linked in Chapter 9 and is available on our companion website. online resources
- Needs assessment activity: Interview or survey members of your teams either in person or via Google forms. If you use a survey, let people know that they will complete it anonymously and ask them for honest feedback. Ask team members questions such as these: Do you understand the data in our IEP or 504 evaluations? Does it help you to have them read at a meeting? What would help you to understand the data better? What would help you to use the data to

make decisions about eligibility, supports and services, and placement? Be sure to include general educators, principals, special educators, parents/caregivers, students, and community provider agency representatives in your interviews or surveys. Let people know that your goal is to understand their perspective and think about how to make data more accessible for everyone on the team.

In Albert's Case . . .

Fast forward to the meeting with Albert's parents regarding their referral for evaluation. Here is the conversation as it might unfold, with a particular focus on the identification of criteria and data that could be included on an evaluation consent form.

District representative: Thanks for taking the time to meet with me so that we can plan well for the next steps for Albert. I'm hoping we can talk a bit about the options we have for responding to your request for a comprehensive evaluation and also, if needed, identify areas of suspected disability in a way that we're required to. Finally, I'm hoping to share some written information about your rights in this process. Is there anything you're hoping to accomplish today? I'll make a list of what we want to get done on newsprint so we can stay on track if that's OK.

Albert's parents: Yes, it's fine to keep a list of what we want to do. That will help. Also, I just want to understand this disability thing. Do you think Albert is disabled?

District representative: No, I don't think Albert is disabled because I don't have any information to suggest that he is. That word, "disabled," is an important word for us to talk about. As I mentioned when we talked on the phone, by regulations, schools are required to do comprehensive evaluations only for students who are suspected of having a disability. It's a legal term, not a term that suggests anything about Albert's potential as a person. Are you comfortable talking more about this? Is there anything I can do to explain it better?

Albert's parents: So for us to get a comprehensive evaluation, we have to say Albert is disabled?

District representative: Not really. What we need to do is figure out whether we think Albert might have a disability. We also need to figure out whether we think Albert needs access or needs services to make progress in school. It's about the fit between Albert's profile as a learner and how school works for him. Maybe we could start by looking at some definitions from two different regulations that schools have to follow. Once we get into these definitions, we might be clearer about how to move forward. Is that OK with you? I'm open to other ideas.

Albert's parents: Sure. Let's have a look.

District representative: [*Shows the definition of "disability" from Section 504 on a laminated page or projected on a screen*] Let's start with this definition from Section 504. Section 504 is a civil rights law that protects children who might have a disability and ensures that they have equal access to school.

Here's the definition: "Section 504 protects qualified individuals with disabilities. Under this law, individuals with disabilities are defined as persons with a physical or mental impairment which substantially limits one or more major life activities. People who have a history of, or who are regarded as having a physical or mental impairment that substantially limits one or more major life activities, are also covered. Major life activities include caring for one's self, walking, seeing, hearing, speaking, breathing, working, performing manual tasks, and learning."

When you and I talked, you mentioned that you have been concerned for several years about Albert's reading. If you believe that Albert's reading is substantially limiting his ability to learn at school, that means that you suspect that Albert may qualify for protection under Section 504. We don't know this for sure yet. The reason we have to evaluate Albert is to collect data so we can decide as a team whether Albert does have a qualifying disability. Does this make sense?

Albert's parents: So if we believe that reading is the problem, we should evaluate to find out?

District representative: That's right. And we want to evaluate and find out not just whether Albert has disabilities; if he does have disabilities, we evaluate to find out about how to get a better fit between Albert's profile as a learner and the way we help him in school.

Albert's parents: You keep saying "Albert's profile as a learner." What does that mean?

District representative: [*Shows the parents a* ***Student Profile Template****, linked in Chapter 9*] Here's a tool that we'll use when we meet together after the evaluations are complete. We use the information from evaluations as well as any information that you and other team members bring so that we can get a good picture about Albert's strengths and needs, your family's culture and Albert's vision for the future, and steps we've already taken to support Albert at school. This information is what we'll use to decide whether Albert has qualifying disabilities and, if he does, to start planning next steps.

Albert's parents: This is great. We'll have a lot of information when we're done. When do we start?

District representative: Well, first we need to think about whether we are evaluating to figure out if Albert is eligible under Section 504 or whether he has disabilities that could result in the need for special education and related services. The definitions of "disability" are more specific under special education regulations than they are under Section 504. Let's get a look at these definitions before we decide what to do next.

[The district representative shares definitions from IDEA 2004 for specific learning disabilities affecting reading, other health impairment, and communication. After discussion of the definitions, the parents report that Albert was always considered a slow reader in Germany, but they partnered him with another student in his classes who read aloud to him and would scribe answers if needed. Albert's parents thought this happened for children who needed it in all schools.]

You've just shared some important data with me. The story about Albert's school in Germany and how he was supported is qualitative data—just the kind of thing the team needs to know about in order to understand Albert's strengths, needs, and what's worked for him in school in the past. We will need to gather additional information using qualitative and quantitative methods so that we get a comprehensive understanding of Albert's strengths and areas of need.

The information you've shared tells me a lot about the fit between Albert and schooling. I know the team will want to hear more from you as we move through the evaluation process. We will also use tools that compare Albert to children who are his age. We'll look at his speed of reading, how smoothly he reads, and whether he understands what he has read after reading aloud and silently. We'll also do some testing of his writing, and we'll look at samples of his responses to chapter questions, reading prompts on statewide tests, and other classwork from English, history, and health classes. Depending on what evaluators notice during testing sessions and what we discover today, we may also look at Albert's abilities related to attention, executive functioning, and understanding and use of language. Are there other areas that you think might be important so that we can understand the fit between Albert and school? We want to be sure to address all areas of suspected disability and complete a comprehensive evaluation for Albert.

Albert's parents: Well, it's all pretty overwhelming, but we'll think about it and let you know.

District representative: It's OK. We'll be testing Albert for several weeks, and we'll be talking to you and to him and to his teachers to get more information. We just need you to sign a consent form before we start testing. I'll put it together for you right now, and you can

> take it home to read it more closely. Please get it back to me as soon as you're ready so we can begin testing. You can accept the consent as I write it. You can also reject it if you don't agree or if you change your mind. You can also accept parts of the evaluation and reject other parts. Here's a brochure that explains your rights, and I'm happy to sit with you to answer any questions or talk about changes to the consent form if you'd like to do that.

You get the idea. This meeting doesn't have to be long—maybe 30 minutes. It could be done remotely or in person, as long as it's possible to share documents and information. We don't recommend doing it by phone because there could be difficulty communicating and getting shared understanding about the definitions and decisions. No matter what happens, the outcome of this meeting is a decision—after the relevant criteria and data have been discussed—about whether an evaluation consent will be offered by the district and signed by the parent.

If parents come in with more knowledge than Albert's parents had, a meeting like this one could be an opportunity for an extended talk about the data that will be collected, to identify tools and expectations about the process, and to build a shared understanding about what's involved in the review of evaluations and participation in the eligibility determination meeting. Ultimately, the parents and the district have built a shared understanding about why the child is being evaluated, the area(s) of suspected disability, and the next steps in the process. Hopefully, there is also a feeling of partnership and mutual support as well. When this happens, the team is poised for responsive practice!

MAKING DECISIONS USING FACILITATION AND A PROBLEM-SOLVING APPROACH

Often, when the time to meet as a team arrives, members come with specific claims or ideas in mind. This happens because team members have invested a great deal of time and thought in understanding the child. Several members of the team have spent time in formal observation or testing. Other team members have reviewed schoolwide data and have gathered work samples for the team to consider. Several team members have spoken with the child, observed the child informally, or have ideas about how to help the child based on their own experience and expertise. While a compliant process avoids decisions made outside of the team process, it is simply not reasonable to expect team members, all of whom are invested in the child's success and overall well-being, to come without specific opinions or ideas about what could happen next.

Team members' claims, opinions, or ideas about next steps on behalf of the child can reflect their explicit and implicit assumptions about everything related to the team's process. These assumptions likely connect to each member's multiple identities. For example, a parent or caregiver who is an immigrant to the United States might come with notions of shame and dishonor attached to a confirmation of a disability or a placement outside the general education classroom. An upper elementary, middle, or high school student might bring a similar fear of being ostracized because of placement outside the "regular" class. It is also possible that a parent/caregiver or student might welcome a placement outside the general education classroom if it appears to provide a better opportunity for success. Responsive practice invites team members to ask and listen for *personal meaning*: "What does this process mean to you?" "What does [a given term, idea, or possibility] mean to you?" Members of a responsive team are always aware that a particular determination, a specific element in a plan, and a particular placement can carry different meanings for different stakeholders. And members of a responsive team are always asking about and listening for this meaning.

A responsive team approach takes advantage of this situation by encouraging each member of the team to come prepared with ideas based on the data. Before the team convenes around the table, responsive teams have gathered, organized, and shared a great deal of data. This may happen formally, or it may happen as pieces of data merit the attention of one or more members of the team. A key commitment of responsive teaming is ensuring that every member of the team has access to all of the information that they need, in a format and language that they understand, with enough time to think and consider how the data connects to the questions or criteria and the decisions that the team is required to make. By the date on which the team convenes, every team member should know and understand the criteria that will guide a compliant process, the data that the team will be looking at and analyzing together, and the decisions that will need to be made together by the end of the meeting.

If this sounds like a lot of before-the-meeting work, it is. The payoff for this pre-meeting effort is this: By ensuring that each member of every team comes to the table well prepared, we are ensuring a process that builds trust, strengthens partnership, and ultimately improves outcomes for students (Cadieux et al., 2019). Based on feedback from all team members, our work in New England suggests that as teams engage in increased preparation before team meetings, one added benefit is that meetings are shorter, more efficient, more effective, and more satisfying for all team members.

During the meeting, we can use specific facilitation tools and strategies that support open participation by all members of the team. We can also support one another as team members to share impressions and recommendations only after we have engaged actively in looking together at data and using it to map out the fit between the child as a learner and the way schooling has happened. Responsive teams follow a problem-solving approach that carefully reviews data as a group in order to construct the child's profile as a learner. The team's collaborative decisions about the child's program and placement respond directly to this learning profile. Using facilitation techniques and mapping out the learning profile of the child first, as a team, are keys to effective team decision-making.

RESEARCH TO CONSIDER

Why is it important for the team to join together using facilitation techniques and a problem-solving approach to review data and map the learning profile of a child before making team decisions about eligibility, instructional planning, and placement? Facilitation techniques are recommended to ensure that all members of the planning team are able to participate actively and contribute equitably to decision-making (Beck & DeSutter, 2020). A number of studies suggests that school-based teams often struggle to use data effectively to understand and resolve problems, largely because there is not a coordinated approach "about how to use data and available research to craft, implement and evaluate evidence-based

(Continued)

(Continued)

solutions for the problems that they identify" (Algozzine et al., 2014). Finally, facilitation and problem-solving approaches are critical to the early identification and resolution of differences and areas of dispute. "Early dispute resolution strategies not only help stakeholders avoid conflicts arising from mistrust and miscommunication, but they also help resolve substantive disputes so that expensive and adversarial due process hearings or litigation can often be averted" (Feinberg et al., 2002).

STRATEGIES TO CONSIDER

- Create and share a detailed agenda for the 504 or IEP team meeting (see our **Sample Meeting Agendas**, linked in Chapter 9 and available on our companion website). online resources Include specific questions that the team will be required to answer. Include important criteria that the team will consider. Share this agenda well before the meeting occurs. You might even share it when the consent to evaluate is signed. Be sure to invite other team members to make changes, ask questions, or sort out any confusion about the agenda before the time to convene arrives. Be open to suggestions to improve the agenda for everyone.
- Use a Data Wise approach to reviewing data. This approach is modified based on the work of Kathryn Parker Boudett and her colleagues at the Harvard University Graduate School of Education. Basically, instead of reading reports or "presenting" information during a team meeting, the group around the table spends time looking at data together and identifying, together, the "high points" and "low points" that they see. The group begins by pointing out specific elements of the data and avoiding any analysis, opinions, or conclusions. This "round" of conversation allows all team members to look directly at results of evaluations, work samples, schoolwide data, or other information about a student. Identifying "high points" and "low points" together levels the playing field and ensures that all members of the team have looked at and understood the data before moving on to conversations about eligibility determination, planning, or placement. For more information about this approach, see https://www.gse.harvard.edu/ppe/data-wise-massive-open-online-course-mooc-offered.
- Create a Student Profile Data Wall. This approach is modified based on the work of Douglas Reeves at the Center for Performance Assessments. In this model, the room in which the team convenes becomes a gallery. The walls are lined with newsprint (Jamboard works in virtual meetings). Team members review data individually or in small groups and sort the data by placing single important data points on separate Post-its and then organizing each Post-it onto newsprint sheets (or Jamboard pages) with these labels:

- Student Superpowers
- Student Strengths
- Student's Solid Skills
- Student's Areas in Need of Support
- Student's Possible Disability-Related Needs
- Interventions That Work Well
- Interventions That We Tried That Aren't Working Well (Yet)

Once each team member or small group of team members has found all of the important data points, each data point is placed on a single Post-it and placed on the newsprint where the team member or group believes it belongs, and then the group does a gallery walk to see what others are thinking. Finally, the group sits together at the team table and creates the child's learning profile by agreeing about key strengths, areas of need, and best interventions. Only after this work is completed can the team begin to answer eligibility determination, planning, and placement questions.

In Albert's Case . . .

Let's go back to the initial meeting between Albert's parents and the district representative. So far, Albert is out of the loop and has not been brought into the process. The involvement of the student is another important aspect of responsive teaming—one that can provoke big feelings in different members of the team. We feel very strongly that the student should take an active role if a team is truly going to embrace a responsive approach. This does not mean that the student is present during every moment of the time that adults meet. What matters most is how the student is brought in and supported during the process. Different students will benefit from different approaches to involvement in the team. For many students, particularly those in secondary schools, being referred for evaluation is stigmatizing. Responsive teams acknowledge and lean hard against this so that students have a strong, positive understanding of the referral, evaluation, and eligibility process well before a team meeting is held.

Here's an example to show how the conversation among Albert's parents, the district representative, and Albert might go in order to set the stage for responsive teaming:

District representative: Now that we know we're referring Albert for an evaluation under IDEA as a student who might have a specific learning disability affecting reading, with possible concerns related to attention, executive functioning, and communication, I'm hoping that you'll agree to have me call him down to talk with us.

Albert's parents: What? Does Albert know we're here doing this? He is going to flip!

District representative: No, Albert doesn't know anything yet. That's why I want to bring him down. We are a team—the both of you, lots of other people here in the school, and Albert. We're all going to be in this process together. That's why I'm hoping you'll be OK with having Albert come down right now, before you have signed the consent or even gotten it from me. I don't want Albert to feel that this is something being done to him. I want him to understand and, hopefully, agree that what we've talked about is what he wants and needs. Are you OK with this? Do you have any questions, or is there anything I don't know that you want to tell me?

Albert's parents: So you're up for telling him about this now? You're going to help us tell him?

District representative: I'm offering to have us tell him about the process together. I also want to give him a chance to share how he feels and what he thinks before we do anything. This evaluation is going to involve a lot of time and cooperation from Albert. If we end up having a plan, or offering him help in any way, he's going to have to agree to take the help. That's really what I want to talk to him about. I also have some ideas about ways we might help him now, while the evaluation is going on. I want to know what he's open to and interested in. OK?

Albert's parents: OK. This is weird for us. We're used to dealing with Albert on our own, and it's not always easy. He's a great kid . . . it's just that school is not his favorite place these days.

District representative: I hear you. I want to hear Albert. Maybe, together with Albert, we can do something about that.

[*The district representative leaves the parents and goes to get Albert from class. For some students, there could be a need for advanced warning; in those cases, the district representative would have gotten permission from the parents during the original phone call, and Albert would know he was going to be coming to a short conversation about how to make school a better fit and that his parents would be there too. Either way, Albert arrives on the scene with the district representative.*]

Albert's parents: Hey, Albert. How are you?

[*Albert says nothing. He sits in a chair near the back of the room and folds his arms.*]

District representative: Albert, thanks for coming down with me. We have a problem we're hoping you can help us with. We're looking for your advice. Will you help us?

[*Albert looks up. Nods. Says nothing.*]

District representative: Thank you. I was hoping you'd agree because without your advice and help we're not going to be able to solve this problem. We need you.

Albert: What do you mean? Do you mean *I'm* the problem? Is that what you're trying to say?

District representative: Actually, no, you're not the problem. I hope you never feel like you're the problem, Albert. I'm sorry if anyone here has made you feel that way. Actually, the problem is school. All of us at school haven't figured out how to work with you well, and that's on us. So we need you to fill us in, give us information, and help us figure out how to make school different—better—for you as a learner. So I guess I'm wondering first about school. What are your thoughts?

[*There's a long silence—literally two minutes. Albert's parents start to talk, and the district representative asks them to wait. It's uncomfortable. It's awkward. It's long.*]

Albert: Seriously? You really want to know what I think? I'll bet my parents don't want to know.

District representative: [*Helping the parents to wait . . .*] I won't speak for them. But I will speak for me. You and I don't know each other very well, but I'm on your team and I can't be a good team member if I don't know what you think. So can you tell me anything about school?

Albert: It sucks. That's what I can tell you.

District representative: Really? All of it sucks? That's funny because I just saw Mr. Che, and he told me that you are the superhero of Algebra II. He's planning to recommend you for AP Trig next year if you're interested.

Albert: No . . . you're kidding, right?

District representative: Nope. Not kidding. You don't have to do it. You'll decide. So tell me what else is working at school for you. I'm not totally believing the "everything sucks" story.

[*Albert continues to share information about sports, friends, and even mentions a clip from a video in world history that led to a pretty cool discussion that he enjoyed.*]

District representative: Can I ask you another question? [*Albert nods.*] Do you have plans for what you're going to do after high school? [*Long pause . . . again*] You know—like, what would be *great* if it happens when you're done here?

Albert: Well, it will be great to have a diploma and be out of here!

District representative: So a diploma is something you want? [*Albert's parents smile. Albert nods.*] You'll walk across the stage . . . prom . . . graduation parties . . . and then . . .

Albert: Well, I'm thinking about engineering, but I don't know if I have four more years of school in me. I love the math and the idea of designing things. It's just the school . . .

District representative: What about the school? Math is great for you. Why not more school?

Albert: You know, all the reading and writing and all the time and work—it's too hard. People just want me to read, read, read all this crap. And even at a school for engineering I'm going to have to take a bunch of classes that I hate—like more English and history and stuff like that.

District representative: I hear you. It sounds like the reading and writing make school hard. And maybe it's harder when the work isn't interesting. Is that right? Did I hear you right?

Albert: Yeah. It's because I suck at reading. [*Silence*]

District representative: Can I say something? [*Albert nods.*] Do you want to get better at reading? [*Silence*]

I think you see how this unfolds. The parents join in eventually. The district representative suggests some technology that can be added to Albert's Chromebook right away and tells him that one of his team members (a reading specialist) will meet him in the library whenever they can set up a good time for both of them (e.g., before school, after school, during lunch, or during a class) to get a look at what the technology can do in terms of accessing text. They talk about headphones and when these could be helpful (or not) and what other kids will think. In the end, the district representative helps Albert to understand the specific learning disability (SLD) definition and how his job will be to give feedback about the technology that gets tried out, to share work samples with and without technology, and to do the evaluations with team members to the best of his ability. Albert agrees, albeit reluctantly. His parents are thrilled that they didn't have to convince him to participate. Already, the early stages of responsive teaming are a success.

OVERALL ROLES AND RESPONSIBILITIES OF SECTION 504 AND IEP TEAMS

As we mentioned in Chapter 1, it's difficult to understand some of the important differences between teaming for students with disabilities under Section 504, a civil rights law prohibiting discrimination, and teaming for students with disabilities under IDEA 2004, a law requiring the provision of special education to students with disabilities. In each chapter, we offer a summary chart that shares some of the important differences that impact members of 504 and IEP teams as they work together. Key differences in 504 and IEP team roles and responsibilities are shown in Table 2.1.

TABLE 2.1 Summary of Section 504 and IDEA 2004: Team Roles and Responsibilities

KEY ELEMENT	SECTION 504	IDEA 2004
What are the general provisions of each regulation?	Discrimination prohibited. (a) *General.* No qualified handicapped person shall, on the basis of handicap, be excluded from participation in, be denied the benefits of, or otherwise be subjected to discrimination under any program or activity which receives federal financial assistance. 34 C.F.R. 104.4(a)	The purposes of this part are as follows: (a) To ensure that all children with disabilities have available to them a free appropriate public education (FAPE) that emphasizes special education and related services designed to meet their unique needs and prepare them for further education, employment, and independent living; (b) To ensure that the rights of children with disabilities and their parents are protected. 34 C.F.R. 300.1
Who is protected?	*Handicapped persons* means any person who (i) has a physical or mental impairment which substantially limits one or more major life activities, (ii) has a record of such an impairment, or (iii) is regarded as having such an impairment. 34 C.F.R. 104.3(j)(1) *Physical or mental impairment* means (A) any physiological disorder or condition, cosmetic disfigurement, or anatomical loss affecting one or more of the following body systems: neurological; musculoskeletal; special sense organs; respiratory, including speech organs;	"Child with a disability" means a child evaluated in accordance with §§300.304 through 300.311 as having an intellectual disability, a hearing impairment (including deafness), a speech or language impairment, a visual impairment (including blindness), a serious emotional disturbance (referred to in this part as "emotional disturbance"), an orthopedic impairment, autism, traumatic brain injury, any other health impairment, a specific learning disability, deaf-blindness, or multiple disabilities, and who, by reason thereof, needs special education and related services.

KEY ELEMENT	SECTION 504	IDEA 2004
	cardiovascular; reproductive, digestive, genitourinary; hemic and lymphatic; skin; and endocrine; or (B) any mental or psychological disorder, such as mental retardation, organic brain syndrome, emotional or mental illness, and specific learning disabilities. (ii) *Major life activities* means functions such as caring for one's self; performing manual tasks; walking, seeing, hearing, speaking, breathing, learning, and working. 34 C.F.R. 104.3(i)	34 C.F.R. 300.8(a)(1)
Who is on the team?	The team includes a group of persons, including persons knowledgeable about the child, the meaning of the evaluation data, and the placement options. 34 C.F.R. 104.35(c)(3)	The IEP team for each child with a disability includes (1) The parents of the child; (2) Not less than one regular education teacher of the child (if the child is, or may be, participating in the regular education environment); (3) Not less than one special education teacher of the child, or where appropriate, not less than one special education provider of the child; (4) A representative of the public agency who— (i) Is qualified to provide, or supervise the provision of, specially designed instruction to meet the unique needs of children with disabilities; (ii) Is knowledgeable about the general education curriculum; and (iii) Is knowledgeable about the availability of resources of the public agency. (5) An individual who can interpret the instructional implications of evaluation results, who may be a member of the team described in paragraphs (a)(2) through (a)(6) of this section;

(Continued)

(Continued)

KEY ELEMENT	SECTION 504	IDEA 2004
		(6) At the discretion of the parent or the agency, other individuals who have knowledge or special expertise regarding the child, including related services personnel as appropriate; and (7) Whenever appropriate, the child with a disability. 34 C.F.R. 300.321(a)
What are the major responsibilities of the team?	Evaluation and Placement: (c) *Placement procedures.* In interpreting evaluation data and in making placement decisions, a recipient shall (1) draw upon information from a variety of sources, including aptitude and achievement tests, teacher recommendations, physical condition, social or cultural background, and adaptive behavior; (2) establish procedures to ensure that information obtained from all such sources is documented and carefully considered; (3) ensure that the placement decision is made by a group of persons, including persons knowledgeable about the child, the meaning of the evaluation data, and the placement options; and (4) ensure that the placement decision is made in conformity with 104.34. 34 C.F.R. 104.35	Individualized education program team or IEP team means a group of individuals described in §300.321 that is responsible for developing, reviewing, or revising an IEP for a child with a disability. 34 C.F.R. 300.23

This table does not address all requirements and provisions of Section 504 and IDEA 2004. It is meant to introduce you to some of the important aspects of these two laws. We strongly recommend that all team members refer directly to the regulations whenever questions arise. These tables are meant to assist you to find key elements and guide you to starting points for your review.

SUMMARY

Why do we need responsive teams? In addition to all of the ideas, research, and strategies we've shared in this chapter, we hope you understand that we need responsive teams, now more than ever, because our modes of educating students have changed. Recently, all schools across the country have reconfigured teaching and learning to provide in-person learning, hybrid learning, and remote learning options. We have also had the opportunity to consider remote and hybrid modes of evaluating and convening teams. We've accomplished much over the past few years, and we have many opportunities for growth and change, particularly as we consider what's best and what's possible for students with disabilities. We've also learned about the importance of parental support and input into the educational process for all students, and especially for those whose learning profiles challenge us.

If these recent years have taught us anything, it's that we need each other. We have to partner in order to effectively educate children. We have to know and respect one another, help one another, encourage one another, and support one another. We have to pull in the same direction. A responsive team approach is about learning how to do this, especially as members of educational teams serving children with disabilities. If you'd like to take a first step, you can begin by looking at the **Establishing a Responsive Team Checklist** (see Appendix). Whether you use this tool for personal reflection about your participation on teams or you use it as a way to assess needs with a group of other team members, we're sure it will provide some strong initial questions to help jump-start your journey toward a more responsive approach to teaming. We wish you well, and we're here to support you on your way!

CHAPTER THREE

Referring Students and Obtaining Parental Consent

"In reality, people who work serving all people never really get paid what they deserve, so I think, in the end, it's always somewhat a labor of love. It's good to see it that way . . . you have to understand first that you're dealing with a human being, just like you. And that is very important . . . try to just cross that bridge into the humanity of the other person."

—Alfredo Chapelliquen, Translator, Parent, Advocate

GUIDING QUESTIONS FOR THIS CHAPTER

- What are the before and during referral processes under Section 504 and IDEA?
- How can responsive teams navigate before and during referral activities in ways that strengthen collaboration and compliance?
- What are the specific actions responsive team members might embrace when they offer to evaluate or decline to evaluate a child?

The heart of responsive teaming is thinking about and opening our hearts to "the humanity of the other person." A student is referred because one or more adults who work with or care for this learner expect one thing as they think about the fit between the student and schooling, and they are seeing another. Perhaps the student's reading does not match expectations for complexity or quantity of text at the student's current grade level. Perhaps the student's behavior is signalling a fit that is currently not working. These differences between expectation and lived experience create two opportunities for responsive teams:

- *Think about the adults.* When the adult(s) who made the referral and the team members who receive it are worried and thinking about the student, these individuals may not be thinking deeply about the concerns of the adult(s) who made the referral.
  - What concerns might these adults have for the student?
  - What could the student's difficulty potentially mean to the adults?
- *See potentially different perspectives:* All of the adults who work with or care for this student may not see a difficulty. A particular behavior (e.g., reading short books without chapters) may not be understood as a problem by all of the adults who care about a third-grade reader. A middle schooler's oppositional behavior at home may not manifest in school.

  Both of these opportunities can help team members recognize the need to attend with care to the social-emotional needs of all of the adults who care about a student. This means that throughout the referral and consent process, members of a responsive team are asking their own questions and listening for one another's questions. Chapters 1 and 2 introduced the responsive teaming cycle (Figure 3.1), in which team members do three things:

- *Identify questions* about the student's experience of schooling that inform the group's collection and review of data and the group's decisions;
- *Look at data together* to understand the fit between the student and schooling in relation to the questions; and
- *Make decisions* anchored in the data using facilitation and a problem-solving approach.

In this chapter, we're inviting you to consider all three of these tasks as you think through the processes that happen before referral, referral, and response to referral. We also invite you to consider the feelings and perspectives of other team members, especially when they differ from your own. We believe this approach will have a significant impact on the decisions that teams make together.

Figure 3.1 • Responsive Teaming Cycle

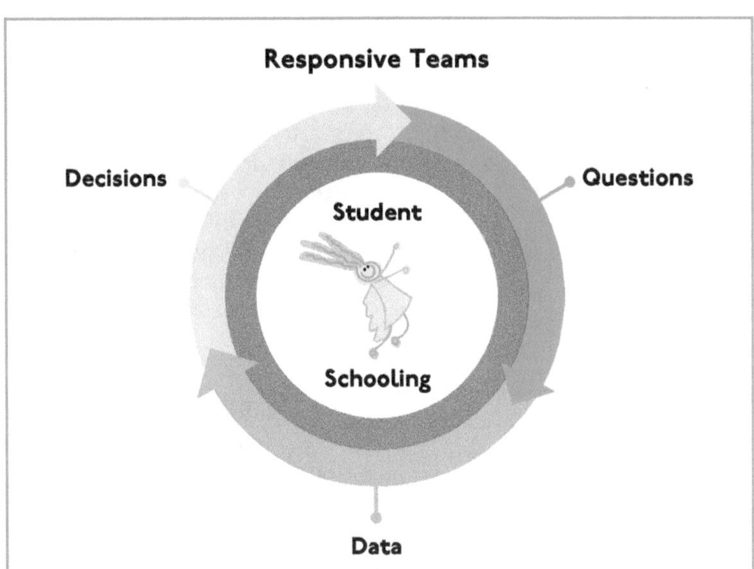

BEFORE REFERRAL

The before referral phase includes identifying and locating students who may be at risk for an IDEA- or Section 504–eligible disability, commonly known as "child find." It also includes strategies to respond to the "academic, social, emotional and behavioral" needs of all students within a multi-tiered system of supports (Center on Multi-Tiered Systems of Supports, 2021). Table 3.1 compares IDEA and Section 504 "child find" regulations.

The requirement to find children who are disabled is given to school districts. This is important for responsive teaming. When a parent refers a child for a 504 or special education evaluation, there may also be a need to rebuild broken trust. This statement in no way suggests that districts have "dropped the ball" if parents/caregivers refer a child before school staff do. We are simply pointing out one of the differences of

TABLE 3.1 Child Find: Section 504 and IDEA Guidance

QUESTION ABOUT COMPLIANCE	SECTION 504 REGULATIONS	IDEA 2004 REGULATIONS
What are the "child find" requirements?	A recipient that operates a public elementary or secondary education program or activity shall annually (a) Undertake to identify and locate every qualified handicapped person residing in the recipient's jurisdiction who is not receiving a public education; and (b) Take appropriate steps to notify handicapped persons and their parents or guardians of the recipient's duty under this subpart. 34 C.F.R. 104.32	(a)(1) The state must have in effect policies and procedures to ensure that (i) All children with disabilities residing in the state, including children with disabilities who are homeless children or are wards of the State, and children with disabilities attending private schools, regardless of the severity of their disability, and who are in need of special education and related services, are identified, located, and evaluated; and (ii) A practical method is developed and implemented to determine which children are currently receiving needed special education and related services. (c) ***Other children in child find***. Child find also must include (1) Children who are suspected of being a child with a disability under §300.8 and in need of special education, even though they are advancing from grade to grade; and (2) Highly mobile children, including migrant children. 34 C.F.R. 300.111(a) and (c)

perspective or feelings that can emerge early in the process of identifying students with disabilities. This matters because team members need to recognize not only the needs of children in the stages before referral but also the needs and feelings of adults. By thinking and talking openly about the child find requirement and trying to understand the different expectations that team members may have of one another, responsive teams can interrupt early experiences that can cause misunderstandings and distrust. We will look more closely at some of the differences between the frequent approach and a responsive approach to activities that happen before referral so that you can understand some of the opportunities that exist at this stage in the process for responsive teams.

When we use the word "frequent," we want to respect what commonly happens in schools. What we do frequently in schools represents what we understand to be doable and best at a particular time. It is often quite good. We contrast these "frequent" approaches with the new ways of thinking and acting that we are proposing. The term "responsive approach" describes some ideas that we have not often seen implemented in schools and that we believe could strengthen teaming. Frequent and responsive approaches to enacting the child find regulation are compared here.

- The **frequent approach** is that certain school staff members are aware of the child find regulation. Parents and caregivers are not typically informed of this requirement.
- Districts and schools pursuing a **responsive approach** strive to ensure that all staff members and all parents/caregivers are informed of and understand the child find obligation. Written (paper, electronic) and oral notices are posted prominently and repeated regularly for all staff members. Paper and electronic notices are made available in the 500 most commonly used words in English and in parents'/caregivers' heritage languages.

While only "child find" is encoded in IDEA and Section 504 regulations, we propose that the collaborative processes of the responsive teaming cycle (Figure 3.1) can strengthen a district's approach to both child find and its student support or child study teams. In the frequent approach to child find, all educators in a school community might not understand this obligation or seek out IDEA- or Section 504–eligible children as actively as the regulations require. A responsive approach to child find invites educators to seek all eligible children with systematic effort. Table 3.2 suggests questions, data, and decisions related to a district's child find process.

TABLE 3.2 Child Find: Questions-Data-Decisions

QUESTIONS	DATA	DECISIONS
How are we educating parents/guardians and the larger community about "child find"?	Review documented electronic and paper notices using the 500 most commonly used words in English and in parents'/caregivers' heritage languages. Review documented efforts to share information orally and in writing with human services agencies.	Initiate, maintain, or upgrade education and outreach efforts with parents/guardians. Initiate, maintain, or upgrade education and outreach with community human services agencies.
How are we looking for IDEA- and Section 504–eligible learners?	Review documented efforts to locate eligible students within private schools, migrant families, homeless, and homeschooling families, as well as students susceptible to trauma. Review documented efforts to contact human services agencies within the community.	Maintain or upgrade our system for seeking IDEA- and 504-eligible students to routinely "scan" our vulnerable student populations.
How are we teaching district staff about child find?	Review documented participation of licensed and support staff, including office staff, lunchroom staff, and custodial staff, in child find trainings. Review child find notices currently available in staff handbooks, periodic newsletters, and staff web portals.	Maintain or widen the inclusion of staff roles in child find trainings. Maintain or increase the frequency of child find trainings. Maintain or upgrade notices in staff handbooks and periodic newsletters and in staff web portals.

Our proposal for responsive student support teaming (Figure 3.1) can strengthen a school's or district's student support or child study team processes. At the before-referral stage, the team needs to begin by identifying questions to investigate the current fit between the student and schooling. When an adult who works with or cares for a student expresses a concern about the student's progress, responsive team members will pose two essential questions:

- Has the student had an "*adequate* opportunity" to learn the particular skills or behaviors in question? (Klingner & Edwards, 2006, p. 109, italics added)

- Does the team suspect that the student may have an IDEA- or Section 504–eligible disability?

An "adequate opportunity" to learn matters a great deal. Klingner and Edwards (2006) write,

> This concept of adequate opportunity to learn is a fundamental aspect of the definition of learning disabilities as part of its exclusionary clause: *When children have not had sufficient opportunity to learn, the determination cannot be made that they have a learning disability*. (p. 109, italics added; Office of Special Education Programs, n.d.)

When team members ask questions about the student's "adequate opportunity" to learn, they are asking about access to tiered interventions that directly respond to the identified learning challenge(s). Multi-tiered Response to Intervention (RTI) models aspire to "high-quality schoolwide academic, social, emotional and behavioral programming and supports designed to meet the needs of all students" in the Tier 1 core program (Center on Multi-Tiered Systems of Supports [MTSS Center], 2021). Tier 2 provides additional "small group, standardized academic interventions or targeted behavioral or mental health supports using validated intervention programs" to support students who are not making satisfactory progress in the Tier 1 program alone (MTSS Center, 2021). In Tier 3, schools provide "intensive intervention for students not responding to Tier 2 through instruction and supports that are intensified and individualized based on student need" (MTSS Center, 2021). At all tiers, approaches and supports should reflect "evidence-based practices and fidelity of implementation, with consideration for cultural and linguistic responsiveness and recognition of student strengths" (MTSS Center, 2021).

We should note that the tiers in a multi-tiered system of supports refer to specific evidence-based interventions, not to students themselves. When educators and parents/caregivers provide a Tier 1, Tier 2, or Tier 3 intervention, they are responding to a student's *present* need on a particular day in a particular discipline or in a particular learning or life task. Students have shifting needs that may require shifts in the intensity of intervention to meet the given learning scenario. It is possible that, at a particular moment in time, a student needs a Tier 1 behavioral support, a Tier 2 reading intervention, and Tier 3 intensive instruction in math.

The frequent approach to student support teams may not document a student's "adequate opportunity to learn" (Klingner & Edwards, 2006, p. 109) within a tiered system of supports in a way that informs the general education program or illuminates the efforts of an IEP or 504 team, if one is convened, to develop a learning profile for this student. Table 3.3 suggests questions, data, and decisions related to a district's provision of "adequate opportunity to learn" in the general education program.

TABLE 3.3 Adequate Opportunity to Learn in the General Education Program: Questions-Data-Decisions

QUESTIONS	DATA	DECISIONS
Which Tier I, Tier 2, and Tier 3 supports have been tried with this student? Consider: • Frequency, duration, and period of implementation • Fidelity of implementation • Documented results (i.e., improved fit between learning needs and schooling)	Evidence of key elements of research- and evidence-based Tier I instruction (e.g., systematic academic language instruction, explicit reading instruction, systematic SEL instruction, standards-aligned instruction) Documented Tier I, Tier 2, and Tier 3 supports relative to implementation (frequency, duration, period of implementation, fidelity) and results (qualitative and/or quantitative measures)	Convene or upgrade the level of support provided by a mixed-stakeholder student support team to define the problem(s) and identify possible solution(s). Review Tier I, Tier 2, and Tier 3 programs and practices in which the student is currently enrolled for their research or evidence base. Investigate research- and evidence-based interventions.
Which Tier I, Tier 2, or Tier 3 supports might improve the fit between this student's needs and the schooling experience?	The perspectives of multiple roles (parents/guardians, educators, the student) to define the problem(s) and identify possible solutions The research or evidence base for supports that have been provided	

Adequate opportunity to learn refers to access to a learning opportunity provided with fidelity. This means that the student has had access to the research- and evidence-based elements of the approach, practice, or strategy that make it effective (e.g., technique, frequency, duration, longevity). If the student support team determines that the student has not experienced adequate opportunity to learn, team members may suggest one or more Tier 1, Tier 2, or Tier 3 interventions in the general education setting. Resources to identify appropriate research- and evidence-based interventions include these:

- What Works Clearinghouse (WWC)
- Best Evidence Encyclopedia (BEE; Johns Hopkins University's Center for Data-Driven Reform in Education)
- Evidence-Based Intervention Network (EBI Network; University of Missouri)
- IRIS Center (Vanderbilt University and Claremont Graduate University)
- The Meadows Center for Preventing Educational Risk (The University of Texas at Austin)
- Center on Positive Behavioral Interventions and Supports (U.S. Department of Education Office of Special Education Programs [OSEP] and Office of Elementary and Secondary Education [OESE])
- National Center on Intensive Intervention (American Institutes for Research)
- Institute of Education Sciences (U.S. Department of Education)

Note that there are many similarities among these resources; people might find certain resources easier than others to search and interpret.

If it appears to team members that the student has had access to adequate opportunity to learn, this impression could lead the team to suspect that the student might be living with an IDEA- or Section 504–eligible disability. The team will pose a question, consider data, and arrive at a decision, as described here:

- **Question:** Which suspected area(s) of disability might be relevant to the student's current fit with schooling?
- **Data:** The team will likely review (1) qualitative and quantitative data, (2) data related to the student's academic, social, emotional, and behavioral wellness, (3) data related to the immediate concern(s) and other indicators of the student's current fit with schooling, and (4) regulatory definitions of Section 504– and IDEA-eligible disabilities.

- **Decision:** The team will identify one or more suspected areas of disability and refer the student for an evaluation.

The key question for an IEP or 504 team upon receiving a referral is this: Does this difficulty in the fit between the student's profile and their experience of schooling relate to a disability as defined by Section 504 or IDEA? If the answer is "yes," the team will collaborate to identify one or more possible disability categories to guide the evaluation process. If the answer is "no," the team must decline to evaluate. Later in this chapter, we will consider the actions that a responsive team can take when it must decline the evaluation.

CASE STUDY: LAUREL'S TEAM

Laurel is a fourth grader who lives with her parents and extended family. Her father did not graduate from high school, though her mother did. Most of the family has lived in town for generations. Laurel's grandmother lives in Peru and visits on occasion. Other extended family members live with Laurel and her parents on occasion. Laurel's father is a mechanic. Her mother works in the local bank as a teller. Laurel has one younger sister.

Recently, Laurel has begun acting out at school. She got into a scuffle on the playground and tried to throw a boy over the fence, ripping his shirt. When asked about the fight, Laurel replied, "I just don't like him." No further information was offered. Last week, Laurel and a friend were found to have placed a variety of wet food items in a number of the heating vents in classrooms. This was discovered because a student who sat near one of the vents reported a strange smell. It turns out that foods such as bread, cheese, oranges, and chocolate were found lying in bowls of water in the vents in several classrooms. When asked, Laurel shared that she was "conducting an experiment" and trying to grow penicillin. The custodian was very concerned and suggested to the principal that Laurel and her friend be expelled and sent to a school where they could be watched all the time, "like where disturbed kids go."

The principal has added Laurel to the Student Support Team agenda for next week.

We'll follow Laurel's story through this chapter, describing how a responsive team might be formed from this point on.

At this stage, the team needs to begin by identifying questions for talking about the fit between Laurel and schooling. In the stages before referral, this is one essential question that should be discussed: Does the team suspect that Laurel may be a student with a disability? After the questions are clear, the team needs to review and organize data from a variety of sources. The data must be used to answer questions or support claims that are made. Finally, the team needs to make decisions about next steps. These decisions can include a wide range of options, even if one of the options is to refer Laurel for an evaluation under Section 504 or IDEA. Here's how a responsive team might navigate the stages before referral for Laurel:

Student support team (SST) coordinator (assistant principal): Welcome, everyone. Let's go around and do introductions. For the next 15 minutes, we'll be discussing the fit between Laurel P. and schooling, particularly in relationship to her strengths as a learner and barriers to success at school. When you introduce yourself, please share your name, your role, and say one strength that you can see in Laurel when it comes to her life and work at school. Please write the strength on a Post-it and hang it on the whiteboard in the column labeled "Laurel's Strengths" after introductions are over.

[Team members include Laurel, her mother, the custodian, Laurel's homeroom teacher, and a school psychologist/behaviorist. The team identifies the following strengths, and team members put the Post-its on the whiteboard after introductions end: "Comes to school every day; loves reading; eats healthy lunches and snacks; very polite; helps out with classroom chores; excels at math problem-solving; excited about the science fair.]

We have already identified seven strengths that Laurel has. Can we talk about how we know Laurel is good at these things? For example, I said that Laurel comes to school regularly, and I know that because I have your attendance data here. Laurel, you've attended school for 53 of the last 55 days. Excellent! Now, let's hear from your mom about healthy eating, and then we'll come to you, Laurel, and then the rest of the team can chime in.

[The team explains how they identified these seven areas of strength. The team shares data, including attendance data, benchmark data about reading, menu of lunch/snack foods eaten this week, story

about adult interaction before school, story about volunteering to clean the classroom during recess, copy of work problem responses on three recent math tests, and pictures of science fair project in progress. The SST Coordinator takes notes in the ***Student Profile Template*** *(linked in Chapter 9 and available on our companion website) and links pictures of the work samples as well as brief summaries of other data aligned to Laurel's strengths.]*

online resources

We have a lot of information about your amazing strengths and superpowers, Laurel. Now, we're going to talk about some of the background experiences and fit with schooling that's happening for you, Laurel. Can you start by telling us one thing that you think might not be working so well at school?

Laurel: Well, I think we're here because of my penicillin experiment, right?

Laurel's mom: That's not all we're here about, and you know it, girlie.

SST coordinator: Let's try to hear what Laurel is telling us. Laurel, can you help us understand the stories of things that you think we might be here to talk about? Remember, you have lots of strengths and there's lots that's going well—and we also have to figure out how to make the fit between school and you a bit stronger. Tell us what's not working.

Laurel: Well, mostly, I'm bored. I mean, I love school, but I just have lots of ideas, and I get so sick of the same old worksheets and sitting around all day, especially when it's nice out. I just want to do things that are exciting. So you're probably thinking about me trying to throw Shane over the fence, and the foods in the vents, and maybe me getting out of my seat and going out of class a lot.

Laurel's mom: OK. That's better. I agree, that's why we're here.

General education (GE) teacher: Me too. That's really it. I'm concerned about some of the ways you show me that school isn't working, Laurel. To be honest, I think you've got a lot of thoughts and a lot of energy, and I wonder whether it's hard for you to sit and wait and do worksheets or tests or other things that you might think are too easy. I also wonder if it's hard for you to know what other kids need in order to work with you.

Laurel: I don't want to work with other kids. They're stupid. Whenever I work with them, my grades are lower. They just goof around. I'm doing my science project on my own, and it's *great*! Definitely don't want to work with other kids.

Laurel's mom: Wow! That's a problem. You need to work on that attitude, kid.

SST coordinator: Actually, we're wondering whether there's something really cool and unique about you, Laurel. We wonder whether you have ways of thinking and learning and deciding what to do with your body that we could understand better. [*Looking at Laurel's mom*] I want to ask something, and it's a bit of a hard question, but I'm wondering if you're familiar with the ways we support students who have a very individual learning profile and need different approaches to teaching.

Laurel's mom: You mean SPED? Are you saying Laurel's SPED?

SST coordinator: No—I actually can't say that. I know this is hard. Things aren't the same now as they were when we were in school. I guess the best way to explain it is that we wonder whether Laurel's profile might fit with one of these definitions. [*Shows the parent a laminated page with IDEA disability definitions on it and a sticky flag beside two of the definitions: Autism and Other Health Impairment*] Do you mind taking a minute to read these two definitions? I think other members of the team are familiar with them, but if not, I have extra copies, and I'd like to invite everyone to look at the definitions for Autism and for Other Health Impairment. Laurel, here's a card for you that explains some of the legal language in a way that might make what we're talking about clearer. [*Hands Laurel two summary cards explaining Autism and Other Health Impairment in the 500 most common words in English*]

[*Team reads the definitions.*]

Laurel: Wow, this is so weird. Are there people like this?

Laurel's mom: This is weird. I'm reading this autism thing, and I guess I never really knew what it meant.

Custodian: I've never seen this before either. I think that Laurel is really good at communicating. I'm just not sure about whether she always understands what other people are expecting, even though I think she wants to, based on the times I see her in the hallway and on the playground.

SST coordinator: Well, there are some different ways that autism gets defined, depending on where you look. At school, we use this definition because it comes from federal regulations that we have to follow. I'm going to ask the team to tell me whether you think that Laurel might be a child whose profile could fit with this definition. This is a yes or no question, but I'm going to ask you to tell me your answer and also offer one story or bit of data that makes you think that your answer could be appropriate. Are you ready? Laurel or Laurel's mom, do you want to go first?

Laurel: No. I mean, I don't want to go first. I'm going to just listen, and I'll say later what I think.

Laurel's mom: Yes. I'll go first. I'm not too concerned about communication, unless we're talking about in writing. But Laurel does have some unusual interests, and she's not always aware of what other people expect her to talk about. The social thing . . . that's really got me thinking.

Like throwing Shane over the fence. Why would she do that just because she doesn't like him? I don't know. It seems like an unusual solution to something that's not really a problem. She could just stay away from him, right? It seems like a big reaction to a small problem—and that kind of thing happens a lot.

School psychologist: It seems like we're seeing similar things at school. I think we can come up with some strategies to try right away. [*Looking at the GE teacher*] I'm wondering whether it would be helpful for me to come in and observe in your classroom, especially during times when Laurel's superpowers are in full force, and maybe at times when it's harder to see those superpowers. [*Turning to Laurel*] What do you think? Could I come in and then afterward meet with you and your teacher so we can come up with a plan for times that might be boring?

Laurel: OK. Do I get to say anything about the plan?

School psychologist: Absolutely. Without you, our plan is not going to be that great. With you, we can come up with a plan that will work for everyone.

GE teacher: Of course. This is a great way for us to start.

Custodian: What exactly are you going to do?

School psychologist: Oh, sorry! I've done this with other students in Laurel's classroom. Basically, it's a way to help Laurel and her teacher collaborate to identify and solve problems. It's called collaborative problem solving, and the process was developed by Dr. Ross Greene. After observing a few times and getting to know each other, Laurel, her teacher, and I will have a conversation to identify what happens when things are not working for Laurel and to come up with a plan that works for Laurel, her teacher, and others

	in the classroom to help address what's not working and make it work better.
Laurel's mom:	That sounds great!
Laurel:	I knew you'd like it. I know some other kids who have done it, and it's OK. Sometimes, it works pretty well.
SST coordinator:	Outstanding! I'd also like to talk with this team about some longer-term things we might want to consider. Let's talk a bit more about the criteria for autism and come up with a plan for next steps regarding that part of our conversation.

The conversation continues with all team members chiming in. Strategies that have been tried are identified, and Laurel and others who have directly observed her share data that show whether those strategies worked or didn't work to address social skill and communication needs. This is the point at which the team is suspecting that there could be a disability. It's important to note that this team is putting interventions into place right away while also planning for the referral. Responsive teams know the importance of engaging tiered supports and differentiating while also preparing for the longer process of referral and, if consent is given, evaluation. We've moved from the stages before a referral to referral together, in a way that includes the key people and has allowed all team members to have input. The questions that will guide decision-making have been established, and this team is already sharing and using data to inform decisions. As you might have guessed, the outcomes of this brief student support team meeting are the implementation of tiered interventions and a referral for special education evaluation.

REFERRAL

A responsive approach to the initial referral increases accessibility to the required procedures and seeks to connect the concern(s) prompting the referral to IDEA- or Section 504–eligible disabilities. Table 3.4 compares IDEA and Section 504 regulations regarding compliance elements of the referral process.

TABLE 3.4 Compliance in Referral: Section 504 and IDEA Guidance

QUESTIONS ABOUT COMPLIANCE	SECTION 504 REGULATIONS	IDEA 2004 REGULATIONS
When do protections under the regulations begin?	"To be protected under Section 504, a student must be determined to: (1) have a physical or mental impairment that substantially limits one or more major life activities; or (2) have a record of such an impairment; or (3) be regarded as having such an impairment." 34 C.F.R. 104.3(j) Procedural safeguards apply to "identification and location of students with disabilities, evaluation of such students, and due process" (OCR, 2020, Question 5).	IDEA protects eligible students from birth through age 21. "Infants and toddlers, birth through age 2, with disabilities and their families receive early intervention services under IDEA Part C. Children and youth ages 3 through 21 receive special education and related services under IDEA Part B" (IDEA, n.d.). Procedural safeguards are extensive, with some beginning with the identification and location of students with disabilities and extending through the eligibility determination and beyond, for eligible students. For details about regulations explaining procedural safeguards, see 34 C.F.R. Section 300.504. Details regarding when IEPs must be in effect are available at 34 C.F.R. 300.323.
What are the required procedural safeguards?	A recipient that operates a public elementary or secondary education program or activity shall establish and implement, with respect to actions regarding the identification, evaluation, or educational placement of persons who, because of handicap, need or are believed to need special instruction or related services, a system of procedural safeguards that includes notice, an opportunity for the parents or guardian of the person to examine relevant records,	(a) General. A copy of the procedural safeguards available to the parents of a child with a disability must be given to the parents only one time a school year, except that a copy also must be given to the parents— (1) Upon initial referral or parent request for evaluation; (2) Upon receipt of the first state complaint under §§300.151 through 300.153 and upon receipt of the first due process complaint under §300.507 in a school year;

(Continued)

(Continued)

QUESTIONS ABOUT COMPLIANCE	SECTION 504 REGULATIONS	IDEA 2004 REGULATIONS
	an impartial hearing with opportunity for participation by the person's parents or guardian and representation by counsel, and a review procedure. Compliance with the procedural safeguards of section 615 of the Education of the Handicapped Act is one means of meeting this requirement. 34 C.F.R. 104.36	(3) In accordance with the discipline procedures in §300.530(h); and (4) Upon request by a parent. See 34 C.F.R. 300.504 for additional details regarding procedural safeguards.

Legal protections afforded under Section 504 and IDEA, including procedural safeguards, are extensive. Note that a student who is protected under IDEA also has the civil rights protections of Section 504. A responsive team communicates with the student and parents/guardians to ensure that they understand these protections and to ensure that they are aware of the rights and protections available (see Table 3.5).

Table 3.5 compares frequent and responsive approaches to compliance elements of the referral process.

TABLE 3.5 Compliance in Referral: Frequent Versus Responsive Approaches

PRACTICE	FREQUENT APPROACH	RESPONSIVE APPROACH
Referral	A referral form is available in district and/or school offices and/or online.	A referral form in parents'/guardians' heritage languages using the 500 most common words in English is available in district and school offices and online. The referral form includes a statement of the concern, provides succinct definitions of eligible disabilities in the 500 most commonly used words in English and in parents'/guardians' heritage languages, and records a connection between the concern and an IDEA- or Section 504–eligible disability. All staff members and parents/guardians know that an oral statement (e.g., "I wonder if my child has a disability") made to any district staff member qualifies as a referral.

PRACTICE	FREQUENT APPROACH	RESPONSIVE APPROACH
		Educators are asked to document "child study or student support strategies." Educators consider "ways we've tried to improve the fit between the learner's needs and schooling."
Parent/guardian/ student rights	District issues the "Notice of Procedural Safeguards."	District representative (team chair) talks directly with the parent/guardian and student to review key protections using comprehensible input and with an interpreter, if needed, in the dominant heritage language. District offers a summary using the 500 most common words in English and translated if needed to the dominant heritage language to accompany the formal "Notice of Procedural Safeguards."
Communication, including written notifications	District issues prior written notice (offer/ decline to evaluate) and consent to evaluate to parents/ guardians. District awaits return of signed documents. Written notifications are generated using software and state-mandated forms.	Team members (including parents/guardians and students) communicate regularly (weekly/ biweekly), beginning when a referral is received while awaiting the parents'/guardians' response to the prior written notice that the district is offering or declining to evaluate. Methods for exchanging information are identified and clarified so that all team members can communicate easily and actively with one another and make information available to the rest of the team. Oral communication is initiated, with a translator if needed, to ensure parents'/ guardians' understanding of next steps if they accept or decline the offer to evaluate. State-mandated and software-generated notices, translated in the dominant heritage language if possible, are accompanied by personal notes (on Post-its) and short summaries using the 500 most common words in English and are accompanied by oral communication with an interpreter if needed (optimizing accessibility and maintaining timeliness) in the dominant heritage language.

The responsive approach to the referral process builds relationships. Regular communication through personal interactions builds confidence in the process and trust in the team. When team members strive to make communication easy and comprehensible for everyone on the team, people can feel seen, respected, and connected. This climate is the foundation of responsive teaming.

RESEARCH TO CONSIDER

Research suggests several key considerations that should inform a school's referral process.

- The referral of English learners (ELs) is complicated by the challenges inherent in distinguishing between typical language acquisition processes and learning disabilities (Klingner & Harry, 2006). One challenge is that we do not yet have an assessment of language proficiency that reliably indicates when an English learner can be tested in English. Students who are ELs can appear to be proficient in English because they have attained a level of basic interpersonal communication skills (BICS) that is well below their cognitive academic language proficiency (CALP; Cummins, 1984). Another challenge is that educators often misinterpret ELs' limited English proficiency as low intelligence or as a language or learning disability (Klingner & Harry, 2006). A third challenge is the prevalent misunderstanding that an EL who is found to have a disability cannot receive both language development and special education services (Hoover et al., 2019). English learners should continue to receive English language instruction (English as a second language [ESL] or English language development [ELD]) and bilingual education, if applicable, until they are determined to be fully English proficient.
- The referral of students with limited or interrupted formal education (SLIFE), including ELs, migrant, and homeless students, can misinterpret learning gaps, delays in academic language development, and behavioral difficulties as disabilities (World Class Instructional Design and Assessment [WIDA], 2015).
- When a student presents a level of achievement or pattern of behavior that contradicts the expectations for typically developing peers, the first question to ask is, "Has the child had an *adequate* opportunity to learn this skill or behavior?" (Klingner & Edwards, 2006, p. 109, italics added). Klingner and Harry (2006) emphasize the fundamental nature of "adequate opportunity to learn":

> This concept of adequate opportunity to learn is a fundamental aspect of the definition of learning disabilities as part of its exclusionary clause; *when a child has not had sufficient opportunity to learn, the determination cannot be made that she has a learning disability.* (p. 2249, italics added)

Thus, the adequacy of a school's Response to Intervention (RTI) model deserves attention, particularly "quality instruction and ongoing progress monitoring within the general education classroom" (Klingner & Harry, 2006, p. 2249). In a multi-tiered RTI model, "it is the core program, or Tier I, that provides the differentiated curriculum and instruction" that gives all learners equitable access to high-quality academic language development and grade-level content (Fisher et al., 2011, pp. 23–24).

This research, which primarily focuses on English learners suspected of having disabilities, informs the work of all teams because the identified considerations set the stage for team members to inquire together about the fit between the student's learning profile and the way schooling happens.

Let's return to our case study to follow Laurel's team members as they consider the needs suggested by Laurel's learning profile.

CASE STUDY: LAUREL'S REFERRAL

In Laurel's case, the SST decided to offer immediate interventions in the general education setting and also discussed the possibility that Laurel may be a student with a disability who requires specialized instruction. Let's see how this part of the process might unfold in a responsive way as we consider a phone call among Laurel's mom, the SST coordinator (assistant principal), and the IEP team chairperson (school psychologist/behaviorist).

SST coordinator: Hello, Ms. Peltier. I'm here with our school psychologist, whom you met at our student support team meeting about Laurel. How are you today?

Laurel's mom: I'm OK. It seems like Laurel is doing a little better, but I'm still pretty worried about her, especially since we talked about the autism thing.

School psychologist: I can tell you that Laurel has really taken hold of some of the planning we've been doing with her teacher. She really likes the structure of talking about a problem, brainstorming solutions, choosing one, and trying it out. She's a champion when things are organized and predictable for her.

Laurel's mom: Yes—and when they aren't . . . well, that can be hard, even here at home where things are usually pretty routine.

SST coordinator: I hear you! And that's why we wanted to follow up. This is about that Autism definition and also the Other Health

Impairment definition we looked at together when we met. Because several people on the team have some questions, the school is required to do some more work to look into this if you give us written permission. The requirement comes from two different sets of regulations: Section 504 of the Rehabilitation Act and the Individuals with Disabilities Education Act of 2004. It's called "child find," and basically, it says that schools have to reach out to offer an evaluation to students if they suspect that those students might have a disability.

Laurel's mom: I'm just not comfortable with that. I don't think of Laurel as a kid who is disabled.

School psychologist: Neither do I. I guess "disability" in the regulations means something different than it means in society. Basically, a student who learns in a way that fits closely with one or more of the definitions we shared at the meeting might be disabled according to the regulations. That doesn't tell us anything about what's possible for a child. In fact, it's the school's responsibility to be sure that kids whose learning profile is like one or more of the definitions gets an education that allows them to make progress. In some ways, getting a closer look at the fit between school and the way Laurel learns, and making the fit better, is a good opportunity for Laurel and for us. To start looking more closely, we do some evaluations, and we gather information from Laurel, from you, from teachers, and from evaluators. We need your signature on a consent form before we can do any of this. Nothing happens unless you agree to it first, and we have to keep you informed and consider your input along the way.

Laurel's mom: OK. That makes me feel a little better. So what happens next?

SST coordinator: Well, as we mentioned in our meeting, the school will send you a letter and a form to sign. In legal terms, the letter is called "Prior Written Notice," or PWN. You're going to learn a ton of acronyms as we move forward. [*Everyone laughs*] In fact, if I use terms that you don't understand, please stop me. I know this is all pretty new for you, and I really want to be sure you understand everything that's happening before you decide whether to agree or not. You can do that with anyone from the school. We all want to be sure you understand this as well as you need to so that we can work together to figure out what's next.

Laurel's mom: OK. Thanks. So I'll get a letter and a form.

School psychologist: Yes. You'll also get a packet of information that tells you about Laurel's rights and your rights. This evaluation process is a formal thing, and figuring out whether Laurel has a qualifying disability like Autism or Other Health Impairment is a process that has to be done in a way that complies with regulations. Please read the information and let me know if you have any questions about your rights. If you want us to help you find an advocate or other legal support, please let us know. We can help with that. Usually, we are able to find a way to navigate this well as a team with you. I just want you to know that you have the right to involve other people if you want to. You'll see that when you review the material. I can also meet with you to go over it if you'd like.

Laurel's mom: No, it's OK. I have a friend who went through this with her kid. She can help me if I have questions, at least for now.

SST coordinator: That's great! She can come to meetings with you if you invite her and you think it would be helpful.

Laurel's mom: Really? Wow! That's awesome. Maybe I'll ask her. When I get the letter and the form, what do I do? Where do I send them, and what happens next?

School psychologist: I'm the team chair. I'll take over from the SST coordinator. You'll be working with me and a whole team of people, including Laurel, her teacher, a special education teacher, and some others who will do evaluations. What drives all this is this question: Does Laurel have autism or a health impairment as defined in the federal regulations? We'll also ask this question: If Laurel has one of these profiles, does her learning profile affect her ability to make progress in school? Finally, if we say that her profile does affect her progress, we'll talk together about a third question: Does Laurel require specially designed instruction and related services in order to make effective progress in school? I know this is a lot to take in. You'll see all of this information in the materials that we send you. We basically want to get information that will help us decide together whether Laurel's strengths and needs seem to fit with one of the disability definitions, and then, if they do, how can we support Laurel to be sure school is a good fit for her. Does this make sense?

Laurel's mom: Yes and no. I'm sure I'll figure it out along the way. I can certainly ask you and my friend if I have questions. Will Laurel know what happens?

School psychologist: Yes. She's going to do some testing with me. She'll do some testing with a speech and language pathologist. A special education teacher will also test her. All of us will observe her. We'll also call you to get information from home. We're going to ask you, Laurel, and her general education teacher to share some stories and information with us. We'll put all of this into a summary of evaluation results. Your job is to help us out by providing information to people as they reach out to you and also to share your ideas and input about who Laurel is as a student and what might help us to make schooling a better fit for her.

Our goal, if Laurel is eligible, is to offer Laurel a free appropriate public education (FAPE) in the least restrictive environment (LRE). Those are legal terms, and you'll see definitions for these terms in the paperwork we send. These terms are really important because if Laurel is eligible for special education, they are two of her primary rights at school. We'll use these terms when we meet. By the time all this is over, you'll be an expert about the disability definitions and these two terms, I promise you!

Laurel's mom: Well, it's not what I was expecting when Laurel was born. I'm feeling a bit overwhelmed. Can you just remind me what's next?

SST coordinator: Sure. No worries. We'll help you through this. We're going to send you some information. Read it. Take notes and write down questions. Call us if you need any more information. And please sign and return the form telling us whether you're going to give us permission to evaluate Laurel, or if you'd rather not do that. Either answer is fine. We hope you'll let us do the evaluation, and if you don't let us do it, we'll still help you and Laurel.

School psychologist: Yes! Please call me any time. I'm happy to help you out with this and to talk about ideas you have for Laurel and school. Really. You have my direct number. I'll call you with any questions from the school part of the team too.

Laurel's mom: OK. Well, thanks for your time today. This is pretty scary—and a little bit exciting too. I'm hoping we can figure things out before Laurel gets really frustrated. Thanks so much for explaining all this to me. I'll get the form back to you as soon as I can.

You can see how this phone call, lasting about 15 minutes, helps to highlight the important information that will be shared in writing with Laurel's mother. Making a call like this one is foundational to responsive teaming. For a parent or guardian, receiving a referral packet in the mail with no explanation—or just participating in a series of conversations about what's wrong with their child—is an awful experience. The content of the packet is not the problem. The way it is frequently introduced and delivered is the problem. By spending just 30 minutes with a parent at the early stages of referral, responsive teams can build trust and shared understanding about the fit between the student and schooling, as well as the process for making the fit better. For many teams with whom we've worked, these 30 minutes have changed the trajectory for a child.

Let's apply our "question–data–decision" model of responsive teaming to key elements of practice in the referral process, beginning with the referral process itself in Table 3.6.

TABLE 3.6 The Referral Process: Questions-Data-Decisions

QUESTION	DATA	DECISION
How are we educating parents/ guardians and educators about the district's referral process?	Documented electronic and paper notices using the 500 most commonly used words in English and in parents'/caregivers' heritage languages Documented efforts to share information orally and in writing with parents/guardians and educators Content of educator training to include communications that qualify as a referral (e.g., "I wonder if my child has a disability")	Maintain, revise, or translate the current notices. Initiate, maintain, or upgrade education and outreach efforts with parents/guardians. Initiate, maintain, or upgrade professional development for educators; couple with "child find" education.
How easily accessible is our referral form?	Degree to which the form is currently written in the 500 most commonly used words in English and parents'/caregivers' heritage languages Availability online and in district and school offices	Maintain, revise, or translate the current referral form. Maintain or expand current availability.

QUESTION	DATA	DECISION
How comprehensive is the referral form?	The clarity with which the form solicits these items: A statement describing the concern(s) with as much contextual information as possible Information regarding adequate opportunity to learn, including Tier I, Tier 2, and Tier 3 interventions, if attempted	Maintain or revise the form.
How does our referral form help the adult(s) who made the referral connect the concern(s) they are experiencing to IDEA- or Section 504–eligible disabilities?	The clarity with which the form achieves these outcomes: Provides succinct definitions of IDEA- and Section 504–eligible disabilities in the 500 most commonly used words in English and in parents'/guardians' heritage languages Elicits a connection between the concern(s) and an IDEA- or Section 504–eligible disability	Maintain or revise the form.

When teams pause to consider these four questions about the referral process and the referral form itself, they are engaging the possibility of making the process and the form more usable and more satisfying for educators and parents/guardians alike. If you're looking for a place to start, providing written material in the 500 most commonly used words in English and in families' heritage languages can go far to increase accessibility. We also propose alerting the adults who make a referral to the federally defined disability categories. Equipped with this information, they can begin to consider whether or not the difficulty they are noticing in the student's schooling experience connects to one or more IDEA- or Section 504–eligible disabilities.

A key element of the referral process involves communication regarding parent/guardian and student rights. Team members can pose a question, consider data, and make a decision regarding the accessibility of the Notice of Procedural Safeguards.

- **Question:** How easily accessible to parents/guardians and students are the protections afforded by IDEA and Section 504?

- **Data:** Team members will review the district's documented process for providing the Notice of Procedural Safeguards relative to (1) a conversation among the team chair, parents/guardians, and the student to review key protections using comprehensible input and with an interpreter, if needed, in the dominant heritage language; (2) a summary using the 500 most common words in English and translated if needed to the parents'/guardians' and student's dominant heritage language; and (3) electronic and paper availability in district and school offices of the official document, the summary in English, and translations to the district's most common heritage languages.
- **Decision:** Maintain or upgrade current accessibility.

Providing to parents/guardians and students the mandated Notice of Procedural Safeguards fulfills the law. Reaching out to a student and their parents/guardians for a personal conversation in language they can understand will support understanding and reduce anxiety about a potentially scary process. And these gestures of support and concern will build connection and trust.

As we saw earlier in the case study of Laurel's referral, an indispensable commitment of responsive teaming is personal communication with parents/guardians and the student. This includes oral and written communication that is regular and as frequent as new information and team members' needs warrant. Team members can pose a question, consider data, and make a decision regarding norms for communication throughout the referral process.

- **Question:** What norms guide communication throughout the referral process?
- **Data:** The district's documented norms for oral and written communication regarding (1) the frequency of information exchange beginning when a referral is received while awaiting the parents'/guardians' response to the prior written notice that the district is offering or declining to evaluate; (2) methods for exchanging information so that all team members can communicate easily and actively with one another and make information available to the rest of the team; and (3) oral communication initiated, with a translator if needed, to ensure parents'/guardians' understanding of next steps if they accept or decline the offer to evaluate.
- **Decision:** Maintain or upgrade current norms for oral and written communication.

Team members can also pose a question, consider data, and make a decision regarding the accessibility to all team members of written notices.

- **Question:** How easily accessible to all team members are written notices (i.e., prior written notice, consent form, team meeting invitations)?
- **Data:** The district's documented process for providing written notifications relative to (1) translations of state-mandated notices in the dominant heritage language; (2) a summary of notices using the 500 most common words in English and translated if needed to the parents'/guardians' and student's dominant heritage language; (3) personal notes (on Post-its) to accompany notices; and (4) oral communication with an interpreter in the dominant heritage language, if needed.
- **Decision:** Maintain or upgrade current accessibility.

You are seeing a theme of responsive teaming: communication. We have found in our work with IEP and 504 teams that when legal documents are accompanied by personal oral and/or written communication in comprehensible language, students and parents/guardians feel supported, cared about, and connected to the team, helping the whole team work together in more satisfying ways.

As the case study of Laurel's referral illustrates, parents/guardians and the student are integral contributors in the process of understanding the fit between the student's learning profile and the current schooling experience. As the student and their parents/guardians consider the possibility of a disability, questions and feelings will arise. The volume of information and regulations related to the referral process can overwhelm. Teams committed to responsive practice are poised to accompany students and their families in their questions, feelings, and overwhelmingness. Personal communication, empathy, and step-by-step support are foundational practices during the referral process and in the team's response to referral.

RESPONSE TO REFERRAL

A responsive approach to the initial referral strengthens collaboration among team members and builds relationships with parents/guardians and students. In the sections that follow, we consider responsive actions of a team that declines to evaluate and a team that offers to evaluate.

If the Team Declines to Evaluate

If a parent/guardian referred the child whom the team has declined to evaluate, they may worry that their concern about their child's progress or well-being will not be addressed. If the team declines to evaluate a student referred by teachers, they may worry about the student and also feel frustrated if they perceive that they will not receive help in meeting an urgent concern. Because of the potential impact of a declined request, team members must respond with care and support. This response distinguishes responsive practice from frequent practice, as described here:

- In the **frequent approach,** the district representative (team chair) responds in writing to the parent/guardian or district staff member to decline to evaluate and explain why.
- In the **responsive approach**, the district representative confers with the team members regarding the referral before a written notice is sent. Prior written notice that the district is declining to evaluate is provided to parents/guardians in English or in the parents'/guardians' dominant heritage language accompanied by a summary in the 500 most commonly used words in English. The team chair initiates oral communication with the adult(s) who made the referral—with an interpreter if needed—to explain the team's decision, answer questions, and suggest next steps to respond to the identified concern(s).

From the very beginning of the team process, collaboration and personal communication are the habits of responsive teaming. The team chair will confer with the team about the decision to decline to evaluate, and the written notice to the parents/guardians is provided in language they can understand and accompanied by a conversation. If adults other than the parents/guardians made the referral, the team chair initiates a conversation with them. This personal communication is an important way to care for the educators who are seeking help in their work with this student.

Table 3.7 suggests questions, data, and decisions when a team declines to evaluate.

TABLE 3.7 When a Team Declines to Evaluate: Questions-Data-Decisions

QUESTION	DATA	DECISION
How can team members communicate to care for one another while awaiting the parents'/guardians' response to the prior written notice that the district has declined to evaluate?	Team members' preferred communication platforms (email, phone, other virtual platform, paper) Team members' preferred frequency of communication	Select one or more platforms for team communication. Determine how often communication will occur.
When a team declines to evaluate, how can the team support the student and the adults who work with and care for the student?	Identified concern(s) related to the fit between the student and their current schooling experience The degree to which the student has had "an adequate opportunity to learn" the relevant academic skills or behaviors (Klingner & Edwards, 2006, p. 109) in light of the student's prior and current access to "high-quality . . . academic, social, emotional and behavioral programming and supports" (MTSS Center, 2021)	Convene a student support team, including the IEP or 504 team members, as appropriate, to recommend resources, interventions, and next steps to respond to the identified concern(s). Review the district's or school's multi-tiered system of supports to recommend Tier I, Tier 2, and Tier 3 supports to respond to the identified concern(s).

The team will decline to evaluate when it appears that the mismatch between the student's profile and the schooling experience bears no connection to an IDEA- or Section 504–eligible disability. "No" can be hard to hear when you're asking for help. Feelings such as frustration, fear, and hopelessness might surface. This is the point at which the responsive team holds all stakeholders in care and support by initiating personal communication and helping the adult(s) who made the referral to identify next steps, including the convening of a student support team.

If the Team Offers to Evaluate

If the team offers to evaluate, responsive practice asks team members to plan to communicate for optimal collaboration. By regulation, the district must offer a comprehensive evaluation. A responsive team ensures that the consent offers an evaluation that all team members understand and agree is comprehensive. This means that the evaluation must gather data related to all areas of suspected disability. If the team has not discussed what the suspected areas of disability are and has not looked together at the definitions of each suspected area of disability together to decide which characteristics may align with barriers to student success at school, it could be unclear to some team members whether a comprehensive evaluation is being offered. Responsive teams avoid this problem by engaging in explicit communication and identification of the suspected area(s) of disability before offering a consent to evaluate.

Additionally, responsive teams ensure that all communications regarding processes and meetings are understood and easily accessible to all members of the team. Time is invested in discussing why a referral is being made and in explaining the language of disability to the student and the family.

Two key practices distinguish responsive teaming from frequent practice: collaborating to identify suspected areas of disability and ensuring a shared understanding of the eligibility determination process among all team members.

Table 3.8 compares IDEA and Section 504 regulations regarding parental consent.

TABLE 3.8 Obtaining Parental Consent: Section 504 and IDEA Guidance

QUESTIONS ABOUT COMPLIANCE	SECTION 504 REGULATIONS	IDEA 2004 REGULATIONS
What are the requirements for obtaining parental consent?	The regulations at 34 C.F.R. §104.36 do not include a requirement for getting parental consent for an evaluation to determine the existence of a disability under Section 504. The Office for Civil Rights (OCR) has repeatedly interpreted Section 504 as requiring parental consent prior to initial evaluation (OCR, 1997). See also Question 42 in OCR's "FAQ: Protecting Students With Disabilities" (last updated 1/10/2020).	The regulations at 34 C.F.R. 300.300 require parental consent before any of the following activities can take place: • Initial evaluations • Services • Reevaluations See 34 C.F.R. 300.300 for further details.

QUESTIONS ABOUT COMPLIANCE	SECTION 504 REGULATIONS	IDEA 2004 REGULATIONS
What is required if parents/guardians refuse consent?	"If a parent refuses consent for an initial evaluation and a recipient school district suspects a student has a disability, the IDEA and Section 504 provide that school districts may use due process hearing procedures to seek to override the parents' denial of consent" (OCR, 2020, Question 26).	(3) A public agency may not use a parent's refusal to consent to one service or activity under paragraphs (a), (b), (c), or (d)(2) of this section to deny the parent or child any other service, benefit, or activity of the public agency, except as required by this part. (4)(i) If a parent of a child who is homeschooled or placed in a private school by the parents at their own expense does not provide consent for the initial evaluation or the reevaluation, or the parent fails to respond to a request to provide consent, the public agency may not use the consent override procedures (described in paragraphs (a)(3) and (c)(1) of this section); and (4)(ii) The public agency is not required to consider the child as eligible for services under §§300.132 through 300.144. (5) To meet the reasonable efforts requirement in paragraphs (a)(1)(iii), (a)(2)(i), (b)(2), and (c)(2)(i) of this section, the public agency must document its attempts to obtain parental consent using the procedures in §300.322(d). 34 C.F.R. 300.300(d)(3)–(5)

Section 504 regulations do not specify a requirement for parental consent to evaluate a student for the existence of a disability. However, the Office for Civil Rights has repeatedly interpreted Section 504 to require parental consent prior to an initial evaluation (U.S. Department of Education OCR, 2020, Question 26). If consent is withheld, the school may request a due process hearing to seek a court-ordered evaluation.

IDEA regulations require consent before an IEP team may begin an evaluation. If a parent/guardian does not provide consent, school districts may consider initiating a due process resolution. A continuum of due process includes these options:

- **Mediation:** If both parties agree, this option leads to a nonbinding written agreement.
- **Advisory opinion:** This option, available in some states, provides informal input from a hearing officer about the decision that would most likely be rendered were the parties to pursue a formal hearing.
- **Due process hearing:** This option provides a formal hearing in which the hearing officer renders a binding decision.

Districts may hesitate to pursue due process because it costs money, takes time, and may be perceived as a "power play" that the district "forces" on the parents/guardians. The truth is that due process is a problem-solving resource if it becomes necessary. We encourage educators to pursue due process if they believe that there could be a violation of the "child find" regulation or a denial of free appropriate public education (FAPE) because the evaluation cannot be completed. When consent is withheld after personal communications have attempted to answer questions and resolve concerns or objections, there is an impasse. Failure to resolve the problem at this stage can lead to barriers for the student and difficulties in the home–school relationship in the future. If it appears to the team that the student has a qualifying disability, and initial efforts to resolve the problem that is preventing parental consent have been unsuccessful, it is best to pursue a due process solution. We hope that teams will understand that there is no shame in pursuing due process given that this third-party intervention will provide a solution that the invested parties could not obtain on their own. To the contrary, engaging due process means that both parties are committed to a path forward on behalf of the student.

Once consent is obtained, the team may initiate the evaluation. Frequent and responsive approaches to an evaluation are described here:

- In the **frequent approach**, the district representative (team chair) responds in writing to the parent/guardian or district staff member to offer to evaluate and explain why.
- The **responsive approach** could involve the following actions:

    1. The district representative confers with team members regarding the referral before a written notice is sent.
    2. Prior written notice that the district is offering to evaluate and the consent to evaluate are provided to parents/guardians in English or in the parents'/guardians' dominant heritage language accompanied by a summary in the 500 most commonly used words in English.
    3. The team chair initiates oral communication with the adult(s) who made the referral, with an interpreter if needed, to explain the team's decision, answer questions, and describe next steps (i.e., if the parents/guardians accept or decline the offer to evaluate).
    4. If the parents/guardians decline the offer to evaluate, the team chair initiates oral communication with the parents/guardians to understand their decision and to respond to any questions or concerns they might have about an evaluation.

From the beginning of the team process, collaboration and personal communication are the habits of responsive teaming. The team chair will confer with the team about the decision to offer to evaluate. The written notice to the parents/guardians is provided in language they can understand and accompanied by a conversation to help them understand their options and next steps if they accept or decline the offer to evaluate. We have seen in our work with IEP teams that, in many cases, this conversation increased parents'/guardians' comfort in accepting the offer to evaluate. If the parents/guardians decline an evaluation, the follow-up conversation initiated by the team chair often changed the "no" to a "yes" after questions were answered and concerns were addressed.

Table 3.9 suggests questions, data, and decisions when a team offers to evaluate.

TABLE 3.9 When a Team Offers to Evaluate: Questions-Data-Decisions

QUESTION	DATA	DECISION
How can team members communicate for optimal collaboration while awaiting the parents'/guardians' response to the prior written notice that the district is offering to evaluate, including the signed consent?	Team members' preferred communication platforms (email, phone, other virtual platform, paper) Team members' preferred frequency of communication	Select one or more platforms for team communication. Determine how often communication will occur.
How easily accessible are the consent to evaluate and communications regarding team meetings?	Parents'/guardians' and student's dominant heritage languages Language(s) in which consent form and communications regarding team meetings are currently available Parents'/guardians' and student's preferred platforms for personalized communication	Determine the need for an interpreter when the team chair talks with the parents/guardians and student to review the consent form and communications regarding team meetings. Determine the need to provide the consent form and communications regarding team meetings in a language other than English, accompanied by a summary in the 500 most commonly used words in English.

When a responsive team offers to evaluate, team members are immediately concerned with two things. First, the team wants to set up a system of ongoing communication that is workable for all team members (i.e., platform(s) for communication and desired frequency). This communication is important to build a sense of connection while the team awaits the parents'/guardians' response. Without this communication, the waiting period could be a silent period, and the silence could make people wonder what is happening with the referral. Second, the team wants to ensure that all written communications are easily accessible to all team members and that parents/guardians are welcomed into a relationship with the team. When the team chair reaches out to parents/guardians in a personal way, questions can be asked, understanding can be strengthened, concerns can be allayed, and trust can begin to grow.

As noted already, two key practices that distinguish responsive teaming from frequent practice are collaborating to identify suspected areas of disability and ensuring a shared understanding of the eligibility determination process among all team members. Frequent and responsive approaches in each of these practices are described here.

When Teams Collaborate to Identify Suspected Areas of Disability

- The **frequent approach** is that suspected areas of disability are determined by the district after referral information is gathered from team members (including the parent/guardian and student).
- The **responsive approach** means that (1) special education disability definitions are shared with all members of the team and used as a tool to identify questions that the team will discuss when reviewing evaluation results together, and (2) summaries of each disability definition are written in the 500 most common words in English and translated, if needed, to the dominant heritage language to accompany the regulatory definitions of each disability type.

When Teams Ensure a Shared Understanding of the Eligibility Determination Process Among All Team Members

- The **frequent approach** is that the eligibility determination process is explained at the team meeting.
- The **responsive approach** means that (1) the eligibility process is described using videos, infographics, and follow-up conversations with the parent/guardian/student; (2) interpretation in the dominant heritage language is available if needed; (3) all team members have access to this information before the evaluation process begins; and (4) all team members know the suspected area(s) of disability, the criteria that will be used to determine whether the student has one or more disabilities, and the additional questions for determining whether a student is eligible.

Responsive teams are committed to relationships grounded in collaboration and trust. Because team members come to the table with varying levels of prior knowledge about special education and IEP/504 teams, team members want to help one another build the knowledge they need to participate in a satisfying way in the work of the team. At the outset, the team's essential work involves identifying suspected areas of disability and determining the student's eligibility for services under IDEA or Section 504. When teams invest in building shared knowledge and understanding related to these two processes, all team members can be equipped to collaborate in this work. And the ability to collaborate in the team's work in satisfying ways builds trust in the team and in each individual's value to the team.

Table 3.10 suggests questions, data, and decisions regarding the identification of suspected areas of disability and explanation of the eligibility determination process.

TABLE 3.10 Identifying Suspected Areas of Disability and Ensuring a Shared Understanding of the Eligibility Determination Process: Questions-Data-Decisions

QUESTION	DATA	DECISION
How can team members collaborate in identifying suspected areas of disability?	Clear and specific descriptions of concern regarding the student's academic and social-emotional achievement and well-being Regulatory definitions of IDEA- and Section 504–eligible disabilities accompanied by succinct definitions in the 500 most commonly used words in English and translations in parents'/guardians' dominant heritage languages, if needed Stories about the student's behavior and learning that align with the disability definitions	Determine if illustrations of eligible disabilities in the student's academic or social-emotional achievement and well-being lead the team to suspect one or more disabilities.

QUESTION	DATA	DECISION
How can team members build a shared understanding of the eligibility determination process?	Multimedia descriptions of the eligibility process (e.g., video, infographics) in English and in parents'/guardians' and the student's dominant heritage languages Verifiable access to these materials before the evaluation process begins Formative assessment of team members' knowledge of the suspected area(s) of disability, the questions that will be used to determine if the student has one or more disabilities, and the additional questions for determining if the student is eligible	Determine the need to review the eligibility determination process at length, or merely to answer questions, at the initial team meeting.

We suggested earlier that responsive teams equip all team members to collaborate in the essential work of identifying suspected areas of disability and determining the student's IDEA or Section 504 eligibility. We have learned that equipping team members in this way builds trust from the beginning of a team's life. The "data" in this table suggests specific resources and actions to support all team members in this collaboration.

SUMMARY

A student is referred to an IEP or 504 team when the fit between the student and schooling is not creating the expected experience of success. A responsive teaming approach considers what the referral and the response to the referral could mean to the student and the adults who care for and work with this young person. This chapter proposed responsive practices in three phases of the referral process: before referral, referral, and response to referral. Within each phase, we compared compliance elements as prescribed in Section 504 and IDEA 2004 regulations, and we identified key practices and compared frequent versus responsive approaches. Chapters 1 and 2 introduced the responsive teaming cycle of questions, data, and decisions; in this chapter, we proposed foundational questions, the data team members would need to respond to these questions, and the decisions that would emerge from the questions and data to respond to a particular student and their team. We will apply the responsive teaming cycle of questions, data, and decisions in Chapter 4 through Chapter 8.

We introduced a case study that followed Laurel's referral and her team's responsive process. Table 3.11 illustrates how Laurel's team engaged the responsive teaming cycle to respond to Laurel's needs and team members' particular needs. Note that the responsive teaming approach does *not* require a team to pose all possible questions or review all possible data points. Rather, the responsive teaming approach invites a team to pose the particular questions and review the particular pieces of data that pertain to the fit between the student and their current experience of schooling. For this reason, Table 3.11 illustrates a subset of the questions, data, and decisions provided in the **Responsive Teaming Questions–Data–Decisions Tool,** linked in Chapter 9.

TABLE 3.11 Laurel's Case Study: Questions-Data-Decisions Summary

REFERRAL STAGE	QUESTION	DATA	DECISION
Before referral	Has Laurel had *adequate opportunity* to learn certain self-regulation (e.g., what to do when bored) and social (e.g., collaboration, responding to kids she doesn't like) skills?	Reports from Laurel and her teachers about her response to boredom Data regarding the efficacy of communication and social skill strategies that Laurel has tried to use	Plan for the school psychologist to facilitate collaborative problem solving with Laurel and her teacher (tiered intervention)
	Does the team suspect that Laurel may be a student with a disability?	Team members' responses to "What are Laurel's strengths as a learner?" and "What is not going so well in the current fit between Laurel and schooling?" substantiated by	Referral for special education evaluation

REFERRAL STAGE	QUESTION	DATA	DECISION
		qualitative (e.g., science project in progress, anecdotes) and quantitative (e.g., attendance, reading assessments) data IDEA disability definitions of Autism and Other Health Impairment	
Referral	Is Laurel living with Autism or Other Health Impairment according to the IDEA disability definitions?	Comprehensive evaluation for special education	"Yes" or "no" pending the comprehensive evaluation for special education
	If Laurel's learning profile matches one of these disability definitions, does her learning profile affect her ability to make progress in school?		
	If Laurel's profile affects her ability to make progress in school, does Laurel require specially designed instruction and related services in order to make effective progress in school?		
Response to referral	What kind of support does Laurel's mom need to respond to the offer to evaluate Laurel?	Laurel's mom's responses to offers of assistance in a phone conversation among the SST coordinator, school psychologist, and Laurel's mom	Determination that Laurel's mom is equipped with assistance or the readiness to request it

You can see how Laurel's student support team and her IEP team posed key questions, considered relevant data, and arrived at decisions anchored in the questions and the data. You can see that the questions, data, and decisions reflect both compliance with regulations and responsive practice. Both of these are the concerns of a responsive team.

CHAPTER FOUR

Evaluating Students and Determining Initial Eligibility

"What I love about special education is that it's a team. No one has to control what happens. We all do that together."

—Carol Caldwell Kelly, Special Education Teacher

GUIDING QUESTIONS FOR THIS CHAPTER

- How can teams approach eligibility determination with a mindset of inquiry and openness?
- Why is it important to frame eligibility determination as a search for the fit between the student's profile as a learner and schooling?
- What actions can responsive teams embrace to develop a shared understanding of the eligibility process and to act in ways that support all team members in their participation?

Now that your team has a signed consent to evaluate, you have entered a new phase of your work together. In this phase, there are many opportunities to connect and respond to one another as a team—and many chances to miss these opportunities. In Chapter 2, we considered why responsive teaming is important and looked at some of the research and strategies that support this approach. In Chapter 3, we considered activities before referral and the many ways that schools intervene when any child needs support for a stronger fit between their learning profile and the way schooling happens. In this chapter, we will consider how responsive teams approach this question: Does this child have a disability?

One helpful way of thinking about the evaluation and eligibility determination process is to approach this process as an investigation. Be curious! Whatever role you are playing, the work in this stage is to approach the child's learning and the way education is working for that child as something you are trying to understand, something that hasn't yet been fully figured out. People who are part of the team are "on alert" and looking for information that can help to explain what's working for the child and what's not working.

Another helpful aspect of evaluation and eligibility is for all team members to have a clear, shared understanding about the requirements of the process. There are several resources that have recently been offered by the U.S. Department of Education Office for Civil Rights (OCR) that provide some clarity about the eligibility determination process for 504 and IEP teams. We want to begin by sharing these documents and pointing out a few places that responsive team members might go to ensure that everyone has a shared understanding about what eligibility entails:

- Long COVID under Section 504 and the IDEA (July 26, 2021): On pages 2 through 5, there is a brief summary that compares "protections and services under IDEA and Section 504 for Children and Students with Long COVID." This section offers a concise summary of the differences between eligibility under Section 504 and under IDEA. There is also a summary of the evaluation procedures and implementation procedures under each of these provisions.
- Return to School Roadmap (August 24, 2021): This document issued by the U.S. Department of Education Office of Special Education and Rehabilitation Services (OSERS) references several question-and-answer resources about IDEA 2004 and other documents that clarify the requirements under IDEA. Excerpts from these documents may be used by teams as a reference when planning together for eligible students.

WHAT'S DIFFERENT ABOUT RESPONSIVE TEAMING?

How is a responsive team process different from the way we frequently approach evaluation and eligibility determination? For starters, there is much about the evaluation and eligibility determination process that is based on routine practices rather than thoughtful, team-strengthening actions. In their book, *Street Data*, Shane Safir and Jamila Dugan (2021) cite research by Maina and Haines that distinguishes between "default" and "intentional" practices (p. 156). Default practices are things we do automatically because that's how we've always done them. Intentional practices are those that focus on aligning our values with our actions and offer choices, approaching problems with a spirit of discovery and a search for new ways of working better together (Safir & Dugan, 2021).

The evaluation and eligibility determination process has many default practices that we simply need to abandon, especially if we want to collaborate and embrace a student-/teacher-/parent-centered approach. All too often, team members are working independently. Each team member is gathering information, often using formal assessment tools as the primary tools for evaluation. Often, observations are conducted without clearly identified questions or criteria, so each person is looking at what matters most to them, rather than trying to gather data based on a shared set of indicators. And remember, as we've already noted, everyone on the team is watching the child closely during the evaluation stage, including parents/guardians, the student, and the general education teachers. When people are on high alert, they are watching and closely noting what they see, often with a much clearer view of what's wrong than what's right.

Another important element of the investigation process has to involve thinking about school and what's been tried already with this student. In our default mode, team members hesitate to dig deeply into the way education impacts the child, what's been tried by teachers, and the way we are doing schooling for all students. A responsive team is willing to do the hard work of considering the impact of schooling as it exists on the child, and it is willing to make changes to the way schooling happens if there is evidence to show that the individual student needs such changes in order to access or make effective progress in school. A team that responds to the student also embraces the opportunity to learn about the student's unique culture. Responsive teams explore the values and priorities of the student in the context of their family and the opportunities for adjusting schooling to support students to grow in a direction that not only builds skills but embraces the student's culture and identity.

There are some real differences between the frequent approach to the evaluation and eligibility determination processes and a responsive approach that complies with regulations and builds strong relationships among team members. Table 4.1 illustrates some additional "procedural" differences between the frequent approach to evaluating students with disabilities in public schools and a responsive team approach.

TABLE 4.1 Frequent Versus Responsive Approaches

PRACTICE	FREQUENT APPROACH	RESPONSIVE APPROACH
Conducting evaluations	Evaluators schedule sessions with the student/family to conduct assessments or collect data. Evaluation procedures are known and determined by each evaluator.	Before assessments are conducted, all team members know which assessment tools will be used. The connection between disability definitions, the questions answered when determining eligibility, and the data that will be collected from assessments and other activities are clear to everyone on the team before evaluations begin.
Contributing evaluators	School- or district-assigned evaluators complete evaluation activities and submit reports within the state or federal timelines.	All team members (including parents/guardians and students) contribute information as well as qualitative and quantitative data to be considered at the initial eligibility meeting.
Evaluation reports	Evaluation reports are issued per the timeline in state or federal regulations. Language in evaluation reports is formal and includes quantitative and qualitative data that evaluators understand and interpret at the initial meeting.	Evaluation reports are issued to all team members at least seven days prior to the team meeting at which they will be discussed. A summary of evaluation results that describes the profile of the child (strengths/areas of need) and the criteria that the team will use to determine eligibility is drafted and shared with all team members

PRACTICE	FREQUENT APPROACH	RESPONSIVE APPROACH
		at least seven days prior to the team meeting at which eligibility will be determined. Summaries of evaluation reports are written using the 500 most common words in English. All materials (formal reports and summaries) are translated in the dominant heritage language, if needed, prior to the eligibility determination meeting.
Presentation of reports at the eligibility determination meeting	Evaluators take turns orally summarizing reports. Team members who did not conduct evaluations share observations or concerns and ask questions.	Because reports are made available prior to the meeting and written summaries are provided, no evaluators read or orally summarize reports at the eligibility determination meeting. Team members who did not conduct evaluations are invited to ask questions about the reports and summaries. Instead, team members create a learning profile of the child together by identifying the child's strengths and needs using data from the evaluations and team member reports.
Eligibility determination	Evaluators determine whether a child has a particular disability. Team members determine whether the child is eligible for services under Section 504 or under IDEA or state special education regulations.	Team members discuss the criteria associated with definition(s) of suspected area(s) of disability and work together to construct a profile of the child as a learner, including strengths, areas of challenge, and areas that might be associated with the suspected area(s) of disability. Data from evaluations are used by all team members to support claims about whether the child has a particular disability; whether the disability affects progress or access; and whether the child requires accommodations, modifications, related services, or specialized instruction.

(Continued)

(Continued)

PRACTICE	FREQUENT APPROACH	RESPONSIVE APPROACH
Documentation, signatures, and next steps	District issues prior written notice and, if the child is eligible, works with the team to complete required plans/placement determination and other documentation. If signatures are required, the district awaits return of signed documents or documents are signed at the meeting. Next steps and options are discussed and clearly documented.	Team reviews all decisions and next steps. Parents/guardians and students are given time to review plans and decisions, informed of options for any response, and encouraged to ask questions and reflect on the team process before signing documents. Notices, reminders, and next steps are accompanied by personal notes, expressions of gratitude and partnership, and encouragement to ask questions and communicate with team members. Preferred contact information for all team members is shared and stored in a shared location where all team members (including the parents/guardians and students) can access it.

RESEARCH TO CONSIDER

Research suggests that there are several frequent practices that may have an impact on the ability of team members to come together as equal, contributing participants in eligibility decisions. Some of the findings cited in recent research about the eligibility process include the following:

- The evaluation process for English learners does not gather sufficient information about "relevant cultural, experiential, and family background information to best frame diverse strengths and needs in the IEP" (Hoover et al., 2019, p. 19).
- School psychologists clearly have "the most authority and decision-making power" in the eligibility determination process (Klingner & Harry, 2006).
- "Because of time constraints, psychologists often perform their assessments independently and do not communicate the results or recommendations with the administrator, the special education teacher, and the other team members until the IEP meeting. This can contribute to inconsistencies and

misunderstandings between the IEP team members" (Madigan & Scroth-Cavataio, 2011, p. 27).

- When reviewing the results of assessments, effective collaborative planning relies on clear guidelines for decision-making; however, "it is clear that no such guidelines exist" (Scott et al., 2004, p. 392).
- Educational diagnosticians can meet with parents before meetings to offer a less stressful, less intimidating setting for discussing evaluation results. This can increase parent participation and reduce the tendency for evaluators to exclusively lead eligibility determination decisions (Collier et al., 2020).
- Barriers to child identification and eligibility include differences in the way programs identify and determine eligibility for children (Malone & Gallagher, 2009).

Clearly, there is growing recognition in the literature about the need for shifts in practice surrounding evaluation and eligibility determination. At first glance, the responsive team approach might seem like it would take much more time and effort. We want to assure you that this is not the case. In fact, by investing time in organizing and sharing information regularly with team members as evaluation data are gathered, the process uses the time of team members more effectively. It also allows all members of the team to share the responsibility of reviewing, understanding, and contributing to decisions about eligibility. Once the responsive team approach becomes a habit for all team members, the result is a more efficient and effective evaluation and eligibility determination process.

BEFORE CONDUCTING EVALUATIONS

Before beginning an evaluation, it is essential that all members of the team have a strong understanding of the eligibility process. Specifically, all members of the team should know that evaluations are conducted to determine whether a child has a qualifying disability. It may sound strange, but we have found that there are times when team members approach the eligibility meeting in a way that is similar to a parent–teacher conference. They know there is a child who may be striving and struggling in school, but they do not understand that when 504 or IEP teams are gathered the child is suspected of being disabled, not just suspected of having a difficult time in school or with learning. We have also seen situations in which some team members are not aware of the areas of suspected disability, even though they are gathering data or evaluating a child in order to figure this out. Sometimes, a few members of the team have this information, while other team members do not. Sometimes, people who participate on both 504 and IEP teams are not clear about the differences between eligibility for one or the other process.

Regulations to Consider

While no one member of the team can know everything there is to know about all of the processes and requirements for Section 504 and IDEA eligibility determination, there are certain key provisions of federal regulations that all team members must know before an evaluation begins. It is important that team members share information and respond to one another with openness. When team members combine their knowledge and understanding, the result is a fuller, shared understanding of what is required of the team. Table 4.2 shows some of the key regulations that 504 and IEP team members need to understand.

TABLE 4.2 Section 504 and IDEA Guidance

QUESTION THE TEAM MUST ANSWER	SECTION 504 REGULATIONS	IDEA 2004 REGULATIONS
Does the child have a qualifying disability?	If a child "(i) has a physical or mental impairment which substantially limits one or more major life activities, (ii) has a record of such an impairment, or (iii) is regarded as having such an impairment," that child has a qualifying disability. 34 C.F.R. 104.3(j)(1)	If the child has one of the following, that child has a qualifying disability: • Intellectual disability • Hearing impairment (including deafness) • Speech or language impairment • Visual impairment (including blindness) • Deaf-blindness (concomitant hearing and visual impairments) • Serious emotional disturbance (referred to in this part as "emotional disturbance") • Orthopedic impairment • Autism • Traumatic brain injury

QUESTION THE TEAM MUST ANSWER	SECTION 504 REGULATIONS	IDEA 2004 REGULATIONS
		• Other health impairment • Specific learning disability • Multiple disabilities • Children aged 3–9 experiencing developmental delays 34 C.F.R. 300.8(a)(1), (b), and (c) *Note:* Each of these disabilities is defined in the IDEA 2004 regulations at 34 C.F.R. 300.8.
How can the team determine if the disability is affecting the child to the point that they are eligible for services?	If the child's disability impacts major life activities that occur at school, including "caring for one's self, performing manual tasks, walking, seeing, hearing, speaking, breathing, learning, and working," that child is eligible for protection under Section 504 of the Rehabilitation Act. 34 C.F.R. 104.3(i)	If the child is found to have one of the disabilities listed previously and the child needs special education and related services [34 C.F.R. 300.8(a)(1)] in order "to address the unique needs of the child that result from the child's disability and to ensure access of the child to the general curriculum, so that the child can meet the educational standards within the jurisdiction of the public agency that apply to all children," that child is eligible. 34 C.F.R. 300.39

In order to make decisions about the questions indicated in Table 4.2, team members need to understand and organize the information that they gather during the evaluation process. From the time that consent to evaluate is received and team members know an evaluation is happening, each team member should understand the questions, data, and decisions that the team is addressing during the evaluation process. Table 4.3 summarizes these.

Often, certain team members hold expertise or pieces of knowledge related to these elements of eligibility determination. This is not a responsive approach. In order for a decision to be made by the team in partnership, all members of the team must know what the team is trying to do and understand the data that will be used by the team to make decisions.

TABLE 4.3 Responsive Teaming Before Beginning Evaluations

QUESTIONS	DATA	DECISIONS
What are the suspected areas of disability?	Prior written notice	What data is necessary to determine whether the child's profile fits with the suspected areas of disability?
What characteristics of the disability definition(s) impact schooling for this child?	Data from the general education classroom and whole school data collected about all students	What additional information is needed to confirm whether these characteristics fit with the definitions of the suspected area(s) of disability?
What are the characteristics and/or expectations of all students at this age or grade level in areas that may be impacted by the area(s) of suspected disability?	Curriculum standards associated with areas of impact Norm-referenced scores PBIS or diagnostic criteria for social-emotional-behavioral development Exemplars/work samples	How do we understand and use the data and additional information gathered to know whether this child is impacted to an extent that adjustments to schooling are needed to support access or progress?
What are the background experiences, cultural factors, and values related to the fit between the child and schooling that should be considered as data is gathered?	Interviews with the student focused on understanding student strengths, interests, preferences, and vision for schooling Interviews with parents or caregivers to understand family strengths, interests, preferences, and vision for schooling Interviews with educators to understand the student's strengths, interests, preferences, and successes related to the fit between the child and schooling Interviews with community providers or interpreters to understand cultural strengths, interests, preferences, and values associated with schooling	How do we adjust evaluation practices to ensure that qualitative data about the student's strengths, interests, preferences, vision, and culture inform decisions made by the team?

STRATEGIES TO CONSIDER

There are several strategies to consider before beginning evaluations.

- Create a Student Learning Profile (see the **Student Profile Template)**. Share the profile using a shared drive so that multiple people can add to it and review it. Ask evaluators, parents, the student, and others to check this template every Friday and add new information to it, based on what they are observing or gathering. This tool is linked in Chapter 9 and available on our companion website. online resources
- Create a short **IEP Team Video** introducing the evaluation process to team members. You can invite team members to watch it together at the school or, with permission, you can share it via email with team members. The student can view the video at school with a trusted adult. This tool is linked in Chapter 9 and available on our companion website. online resources
- Develop a paraphrased description of the suspected areas of disability and send it to all team members (see the **Autism Definition Summary** tool). Be sure to include references to primary source information from the regulations; however, the purpose of this tool is to remind everyone about the focus of the evaluation and the areas that the team will discuss together when the evaluation is complete. This tool is linked in Chapter 9 and available on our companion website. online resources

  One important thing to remember when identifying the areas of suspected disability: IDEA 2004 states in 34 C.F.R. 300.304(c)(6), "In evaluating each child with a disability under §§300.304 through 300.306, the evaluation is sufficiently comprehensive to identify all of the child's special education and related services needs, whether or not commonly linked to the disability category in which the child has been classified." When a team identifies the areas of suspected disability, the team should review the definitions and answer the following questions together using data from the whole school or classroom:

- What are the characteristics of this student that we suspect fit with the definition of disability under Section 504 or with one or more of the definitions of disabilities under IDEA?
- What are the types of disabilities the team suspects may be impacting this child in accessing or making progress with schooling?
- What are the assessment tools that will allow us to understand whether the child has one or more qualifying disabilities?

  There is nothing in the regulations that prevents the team from identifying suspected areas of disability during this stage of evaluation planning; however, teams must be careful not to use the process of identifying suspected areas of disability as a way of limiting the scope of the evaluation. All of the child's

(Continued)

(Continued)

special education and related services needs must be explored and considered in a comprehensive way, which means that all of the suspected areas of disability associated with the needs identified in the child's learning profile must also be considered.

- Interview the student, parent/guardian, and other team members in order to create a comprehensive picture of the current and historic fit between the child and schooling. We recommend an approach that embraces student and family culture, such as the one described by Dennis and Giangreco (1996).

When interviewing people about the fit between the child and schooling, Dennis and Giangreco (1996) recommend that interviewers seek help from cultural interpreters, consider the language and literacy status of team members, involve team members in planning interviews, preview interviews, be flexible and responsive during interviews, adapt the time frame of interviews to meet team member needs, and be aware of the nature and intent of questions you ask.

WHILE EVALUATIONS ARE HAPPENING

Teams can gather, organize, and share information throughout the evaluation process in a way that helps team members. When the evaluation process happens in a way that encourages team communication and organization of information, all team members are able to be part of the investigation of the child's learning profile.

RESEARCH TO CONSIDER

Sharing and organizing information while evaluations are happening also gives team members time to review and think about information before coming together to make decisions (Collier et al., 2020). This goes a long way toward addressing the potential anxieties of team members that we described in the introduction to this book.

Another advantage of this approach is that small chunks of information can be translated or interpreted over time, allowing increased access and eliminating the information overload that can happen when the language of evaluations is difficult for one or more members of the team to understand. When information is shared gradually, there are opportunities for asking questions, helping each other understand what's being discovered. This approach also offers an opportunity to gather detailed information about the culture, background, and experiences of the student that may inform the best options for intervention (Hoover et al., 2019). The chances to partner and strengthen relationships are much greater when teams move through the evaluation process in a way that is responsive to one another.

When organizing information, it can be helpful to provide a structure that aligns the questions that the team will consider, the data that will be used to answer each question, and the decision(s) that the team will make. Table 4.4 offers a structure that may be modified, depending on the specifics of a child's profile and the data that the team decides to collect during the evaluation process.

TABLE 4.4 Responsive Teaming During the Evaluation Process

QUESTIONS	DATA	DECISIONS
What information does each team member need to answer the question, "Does the child have a qualifying disability?"	Scores in specific domains from norm-referenced assessments Observations with specific focus on learning characteristics associated with the suspected area of disability Work samples	Does the child have one or more of the suspected disability/disabilities? Which specific data points support each team member's answer to this question?
	Stories and specific interactions Scores on criterion-referenced assessments (e.g., benchmark assessments, statewide assessments, etc.) Checklists and other informal data	

(Continued)

(Continued)

QUESTIONS	DATA	DECISIONS
If the child has a qualifying disability, is the disability impacting the child's access to the general curriculum so that the child cannot meet local educational standards?	Work samples of the child compared with grade-level exemplars PBIS data, incident reports, and attendance records compared with schoolwide expectations from student–parent handbook Stories and specific interactions compared with cultural norms and grade- or age-level expectations Informal assessment data	Is the disability impacting the fit between the child and schooling? Which specific data points support each team member's answer to this question?
If the disability is affecting progress or access, does the child require adaptations in order to make progress in school?	Intervention data Classroom observations focused on successful student schooling experiences Student reports focused on successful student schooling experiences Educator or school staff reports focused on successful student schooling experiences Parent reports focused on successful student schooling experiences	Does the child require supplemental aids and services in order to access schooling or make effective progress in areas impacted by the disability? What are the specific data points that support each team member's answer to this question?

It could be helpful to replace more general terms (e.g., disability, intervention, assessment) with more specific terms (e.g., autism, discrete trial teaching, discrete trial data sheets) so that team members are clear about the specific considerations relevant to a particular child. The more the team is able to come to agreement and shared understandings about the eligibility determination process during the time when evaluations are happening, the more efficient, targeted, and effective team decisions will be during the eligibility determination meeting.

STRATEGIES TO CONSIDER

How can teams do this well? In addition to sharing and reminding one another about the questions, data, and decisions that the team is exploring during the evaluation phase, the following strategies may also be helpful to strengthen responsive teaming while evaluations are happening:

- Use a **Multilanguage Translation Tool** such as the one created by Michelle Austin, ESL teacher from Worcester East Middle School (contact: mkaustinl@gmail.com) to share small chunks of information related to the student's learning profile with the team. This can be shared with permission from the parent or guardian, so be sure to get a signed release before using this type of tool.
- Create an **Annotated IEP Eligibility Meeting Agenda** and send it out to the team midway through the evaluation process. Include information on the agenda that will remind team members about the questions, data, and decisions that will be discussed at the upcoming team meeting.
- Use an **Abbreviated Eligibility Meeting Agenda** on the day of the meeting to keep the team on track and make the process visible for everyone.
- Create an **Evaluation Summary** that links work samples, formal and informal information, and assessment results with the questions used for identifying student strengths, areas of educational need, and areas of suspected disability-related need.
- Use an **Eligibility Infographic** to show considerations and next steps that happen for children who are eligible and for children who are not eligible. If your district offers Tier I, 2, and 3 interventions to students who are not disabled, be sure to identify these services and the questions associated with accessing them. This kind of information shows the team that services are available for all learners and that help is available for this child regardless of the outcome of the eligibility meeting.

These strategies will require shifts in practice from the way teams frequently approach evaluations. Of course, making these types of changes will require attention, explanation, and care for people. Please don't forget that as you change the way your 504 and IEP teams do their work, there will be questions and concerns. That's completely normal, and it's something you should expect. It doesn't suggest that these strategies won't work. It does suggest that people need help to make the kinds of changes we're proposing. These tools are linked in Chapter 9 and available on our companion website. online resources

BEFORE THE ELIGIBILITY DETERMINATION MEETING

As the eligibility team meeting approaches, members of the team have been involved in thinking about the student's needs in a focused way. Most people on the team who work in schools know that this has involved a great deal of time engaged with the student—observing, assessing, interviewing, and writing. For parents and caregivers, this time can be experienced as a time of waiting, a time of silence, a time of looking more closely at concerns associated with the student's learning. The closer people get to the eligibility determination meeting, the more concerns can grow, particularly if there is anxiety about what the outcome of the meeting might be.

It's important for team members to consider and even talk about the plan for addressing questions that can arise as the meeting date approaches. Table 4.5 describes the questions, data, and decisions that the team should consider during this time.

TABLE 4.5 Responsive Teaming Before the Eligibility Determination Meeting

QUESTIONS	DATA	DECISIONS
What can we do to support the fit between the child and schooling if the child is not eligible?	Intervention data Information about cultural values, norms, and priorities Detailed information about Tier I, 2, and 3 supports available or all learners aligned with specific barriers to child schooling success Information from community providers/ wraparound supports	What are the services and supports available to all learners that will strengthen the fit between this child and schooling?
What are the options for supplemental aids and services that we might consider if the child is eligible under Section 504 or IDEA?	Data from evaluations Information about cultural values, norms, and priorities	What are the supplemental supports and services that are available and proven to strengthen the fit between this child and schooling?

QUESTIONS	DATA	DECISIONS
	Descriptions of interventions and evidence that shows when, how, and where these interventions are effective What Works Clearinghouse, Center on PBIS briefs, or Vanderbilt University Evidence-Based Practice summaries to show the connections between available services and identified needs	
Whether the child is eligible or not, how will we know if the supports we recommend are working to improve the fit between the child and schooling?	General education, whole school, and referral data used to identify successes and barriers to the child schooling fit Specific data points from evaluations that are valid for ongoing progress monitoring and can be routinely and accurately collected and used for progress monitoring; this does *not* include norm-referenced data, grades, or data from statewide assessments	What are the specific data points we will monitor to understand whether the supports offered are strengthening the fit between the child and schooling and leading to success in identified areas of need?
How will we continue to partner well between home and school to support this child as a learner?	Reports of team members about successful teaming Perceptions of team members about the strengths of the team and aspects of the teaming process that feel supportive, reliable, and effective Perceptions of team members about areas of the teaming process that feel unsupportive, ineffective, or uncertain	What are the plans for ongoing communication and information and data sharing? What are the next steps for monitoring progress, revising supports, and celebrating successes?

Anticipating these questions is essential for all teams, especially those in which differences of opinion or values are identified early in the process. A familiar approach to teaming ignores the possibility that a child may or may not be found eligible. This is a gap in practice that can lead to significant misunderstandings and avoidable conflicts. It is critical that all team members discuss the possible outcomes and that they share information not only about the child but about potential interventions and expectations. When this happens, the team is ready to convene and engage in decision-making, even when there are differences of opinion.

RESEARCH TO CONSIDER

Research about the leadership of teams and about negotiation can help all team members understand what to do during this "before the meeting time" so that each team member is prepared and available to participate fully in the eligibility determination meeting when it happens. Here are some research-based practices that can inform what we choose to do to strengthen teams before the meeting:

- *Case conferencing.* Follow a facilitated approach to meetings, which includes a case conference between parents and either a chairperson (team leader or 504 coordinator) or a lead teacher. During the case conference, parents are given the opportunity to ask questions and identify areas of concern and suggestions for addressing identified needs. The chairperson can review the agenda and help parents to know what to expect. "Providing parents relevant information and the opportunity to voice concerns before the FIEP meeting was highlighted as a powerful strategy for diffusion of any preexisting conflict" (Mueller & Vick, 2019a). It is important to be clear that the case conference is not a team meeting; however, information can be shared and questions can be gathered and distributed so all members of the team have the important facts and priorities before the team gathers.
- *Intentional communication.* Prioritize opportunities to communicate and share information frequently and in ways that work for all members of the team. Parent and teacher "self-efficacy" (belief in one's abilities and skills related to a process or responsibility) can be lacking when it comes to the 504 or IEP team process (Beck & DeSutter, 2019; Lake & Billingsley, 2000). For this reason, it's important to remember the social and emotional needs of team members and prioritize communication, "getting-to-know-you" activities, and sharing information consistently before the team meets. This is especially true if there are language, social, educational, or cultural differences brought by different members of the team (Jones et al., 2020).
- *Address time-related issues.* Organization and scheduling are important aspects of planning for a face-to-face or virtual team meeting. Set up ways to organize and share information by using online asynchronous tools. Organizing

information so that it clearly lines up with the agenda for determining eligibility will help all members of the team to anticipate when and how this information will be used to make decisions. Discuss scheduling needs, including the best time and days for meeting with all team members before the eligibility meeting is set. Be sure the agenda includes time limits and is shared with all team members before the meeting. Ask team members what they need in order to participate for the entire meeting well in advance, and provide what assistance you can to help people be available (Menlove et al., 2001).

In focusing on these three research-based practices before the meeting occurs, teams establish a culture of support and partnership. This culture is critical if the team is going to make decisions together and trust both the people and the process involved in determining eligibility for Section 504 or special education.

If you are asking yourself, "How could I possibly prioritize these things in addition to all that I already do?" you're not alone. We hear this question often from parents, students, and educators. Please remember, these ideas might represent a major change of thinking and acting. Whenever people approach a big change, there are questions, concerns, and feelings of uncertainty. This doesn't mean that the change can't or shouldn't occur. It just means that the change has to happen after careful thought and after you find a place to start that is doable. We want to encourage and support you to try to implement what research tells us works. In the next section are a few tools and strategies that may help you move forward with changing practices in a way that fits with what research suggests.

STRATEGIES TO CONSIDER

Research makes it clear that, in the early stages of collaboration, teams need to invest time in communicating, building relationships, and understanding the processes by which shared decisions will be made (Jones & Peterson-Ahmad, 2017). Strategies that build trust and support effective teaming include these:

- Helping team members to identify choices and options
- Remaining flexible and considerate of others' points of view
- "Committing to work to find solutions when disagreements arise" and "demonstrating and modeling problem-solving skills"
- Respecting team members as equal partners in decision-making (ALLIANCE National Parent Technical Assistance Center at PACER, 2008)

(Continued)

(Continued)

The case-conferencing approach is one that embraces all of these strategies. Case conferencing involves talking with members of the team throughout the evaluation process. The purpose of the case conference is to help people get organized and have a shared understanding of the information and the process by which the team will make decisions. Case conferences are not 504 or IEP team meetings. They are not meetings in which any decisions about eligibility or planning are made. Case conferences are meetings in which team members get to know each other and prepare for shared decision-making.

Case conferences can happen in the context of one meeting with a larger group of team members or a series of smaller meetings with smaller groups of team members. These conferences can occur virtually or by phone. A case conference should last no more than 30 minutes and could be broken up into a series of shorter meetings of 10 to 15 minutes in duration. It's important to remind and encourage team members to hold each other accountable to the purpose of the meeting. No decisions are made about the child. Lots of information is shared about how information will be organized and used during the eligibility determination meeting. The group may generate questions, ideas, or concerns for the team to consider, but these are merely identified and not addressed at the case conference.

Here are some tools that you may find helpful as you consider the case-conferencing strategy:

- **Sample Case Conference Agenda (Slides)**
- **Tool for Identifying Questions for Eligibility Determination**
- **Visuals for Aligning Evaluation Data to Questions (Jamboard)**

These tools are designed to help teams organize information about the student's learning profile and about the interventions that have been attempted. They are also designed to help team members clarify the specific questions that will be used when making decisions together. Finally, these tools make connections between the specific types of data and data points and the questions for decision-making. These tools are linked in Chapter 9 and are available on our companion website. online resources

You may already be practicing some of what research suggests works to prepare teams well for the eligibility determination meeting. If you are, that's great! Don't stop doing this work. Perhaps you can use one or more of these tools to build on the practices you already have in place. Please feel free to apply the tools to any part of the process of working with decision-making teams. You can also modify the tools so that they fit more closely with your current practice.

If you're not using case conferencing or other strategies to support strong relationships and effective use of time, you may want to experiment with one or more of these tools. If you're not sure where to begin, choose one tool or strategy to try. In one sentence, write down the change that you hope happens using this tool. You can write something like this:

> *If I use the ____ tool before every team meeting, then I will see ____ change from ____ to ____.*

Once you've selected your tool and identified what will be different if the tool works, you're ready to commit to trying out the tool for a month or two. We would be thrilled to hear what happens as a result!

DURING THE INITIAL ELIGIBILITY DETERMINATION MEETING

By the time the eligibility meeting begins, team members should have previewed all of the information needed to complete the responsive teaming decision-making cycle. In particular, team members should have access to all reports as well as usable summaries at least a few days before they gather for eligibility determination.

As people gather, it's important to remember that any time spent greeting each other is time well spent. The team should take at least a few moments for informal check-ins and introductions. This type of start allows people to feel welcome and ready to partner. It establishes an atmosphere of trust and collaboration. Team members should give special attention to students, community members, advocates, parents, or caregivers. Because some members of the team spend more time together than others, it is critical to start the meeting with conversations that create an equal footing and show that, during this meeting, every person has equal power, influence, and voice. This will not happen automatically, and team members do need to give time, attention, and thought to creating an atmosphere that makes good-faith conversations and decision-making possible.

Responsive teaming is a practice that ensures the priority of collaboration and compliance. If a team has built a relationship and clarified the questions and data that guide decision-making so that all team members understand and can participate together, the day of the meeting becomes the main event. Team members are ready to talk and think together. They know what to expect, even though decisions have not yet been made or discussed. The group knows how this will happen and what information will be used. All of people's time and energy can be invested in looking at guiding questions, sorting data, and making decisions.

Table 4.6 shows the questions, data, and decisions that teams address during an eligibility determination.

TABLE 4.6 Responsive Teaming During Eligibility Determination

QUESTIONS	DATA	DECISIONS
Does this child have one or more of the suspected disabilities?	Specific data points from classrooms, referral, team input, and evaluations aligned to disability-related characteristics identified by the team prior to the meeting	Is this a child who has one or more of the previously identified disabilities? What specific data points support this claim?
If so, does the disability impact progress or access to schooling?	Specific data points from classroom observations, work samples, PBIS data, evaluations, parent input, reports of team members about the fit between the disability-related characteristics and schooling Consideration of cultural values and norms Consideration of access to evidence-based interventions	Is the disability affecting access or progress? What specific data points support this claim?
Does the child require supplemental aids and services in order to access schooling or make effective progress in school?	Pre-referral data, intervention data, classroom data Consideration of information about the fit between the child's profile and the interventions that have been successful	What supports will strengthen the fit between the child and schooling (regardless of eligibility)?

One important difference between a responsive team's process during eligibility determination and the more frequent approach is that no one reads their reports.

Really. No one.

The reading of reports in sequence, while a very common practice at 504 and IEP team meetings, is truly one of the uses of team time that works against collaboration and compliance. Each evaluator talks for 5 to 30 minutes in sequence. Much of what they say is understood by only part of the team. Unless people take detailed notes, they are not able to use the volume of information that is shared to make decisions. Even if they take detailed notes, the listening time goes on, often for the bulk of the meeting. The precious minutes that everyone has carved out of their schedules are spent sitting, listening, and looking at each other (or, admit it, looking at your phone under the table or your email if laptops are open). People are bored. People are confused. People are thinking about how they can leave early. Often, a parent or caregiver who has entered the meeting feeling anxious ends up feeling totally overwhelmed by the time team decision-making comes. We know we usually read reports at team meetings. We really need to stop doing it.

Instead, we propose a use of team time during the meeting that will help team members get excited about planning. A process in which back-and-forth conversation is what happens throughout the meeting. A time when there is dynamic engagement, a sense of unity and trust, and active team decision-making with the student at the center, being celebrated and supported.

CASE STUDY: ELIJAH'S TEAM

Here's how an eligibility meeting might play out:

- *Introductions:* "Good afternoon, everyone. So great to see you!" Rena, the team chair, has to shout above the chatter about last night's game and how well the student played. "Let's get started."

  Rena asks Oscar, the school psychologist, to open the **Learner Profile Jamboard** (see Chapter 9 and the companion website). This is the visual tool for capturing information as the team engages in conversation. Oscar uses Jamboard to allow all team members to see the questions and data points as they are identified. He could have chosen to do this using Google Slides or PowerPoint. Oscar is careful to be sure that everyone can see the profile.

Meanwhile, introductions begin, starting with the student and family. Each team member is asked to share the following information:

- Their name
- Their role
- One strength or characteristic of the student that is an asset to the school community

Rena and Oscar support each other by adding each strength to the Learner Profile Jamboard for the meeting. All members of the team can see the Learner Profile as notes appear.

- *Learner Strengths:* "Let's begin by adding more strengths to your profile."

Learner strengths are about the student's contributions to the school community and successes as a student. Rena invites members to share one strength or data point from an evaluation. Oscar adds each strength mentioned to the Learner Profile Jamboard. Rena reminds people to share only one strength at a time and makes sure Oscar gets the information down using the same words that the speaker uses. Both Rena and Oscar regularly ask team members these questions:

- "Did I get it right? Is this what you meant?"
- "Do you might repeating that? I want to make sure I got it all."
- "Thank you for saying that. Is this OK?"

Elijah's team members take turns identifying specific scores and data points that people have seen in the evaluation reports that were shared before the meeting. Strengths include observations that people have had of the student at school, at home, and in the community. Strengths include brief stories of events or interactions or awards that the student has received. Oscar includes the strength and notes the source of the information (e.g., specific score from a report, statement from a classroom observation, self-report of the student, etc.). Everyone in the room is speaking. No one is reading their report.

When this process is over, Rena thanks everyone and asks each person to look at all of the strengths and choose one that they feel is the most important for the team to remember when thinking about the fit between Elijah and schooling. Oscar highlights these by using a different color or changing the font so everyone can see the strengths that team members prioritized.

- *Barriers to Success at School:* Rena transitions the group by saying, "Now, let's move on to talking about some of the things that might be challenging—things that are barriers to academic or functional success at school. Remember, these things are not personal characteristics. These are problems of teaching and learning that we haven't figured out yet. Try to share any challenges or barriers using words that target a skill or an intervention."

Rena invites each person to share one challenge or barrier at a time. Using the Learner Profile Jamboard, Oscar uses the same note-taking process, documenting the needs using the words of the speaker and naming the source of the data that supports their statement.

A word about "barriers to success at school." It's important for team members to understand that the student is not the barrier. Also, a student's suspected disability is not the barrier. Kids aren't barriers. They aren't wrong or bad or broken. In education, we really need to get better at moving away from deficit-based thinking and talking about kids. This is Laurel writing, and I have to say that I'm not so good at this! It's really important for team members to keep in mind that, when kids strive and struggle to succeed in school, the problems usually happen because there is not a good fit between the system and what the system requires, and the needs of the child and family and what the child and family require. I always need a good team of people who help and remind me to stay away from language and thinking that "blames the child" or "blames the family." I try to stay open to this correction, and when I succeed, I learn and grow and change in ways that make me a better educator, a better parent, a better human being.

When this process is over, Rena thanks Elijah and his parents for being willing to listen and share information about what is challenging right now. Then, Rena invites Elijah to name one barrier that he wants to change. Elijah is not able to respond, even after Rena waits several minutes. Rena turns to Elijah's parents.

Elijah's mom says, "Well, I want to see Elijah doing things with other kids without having an adult right there all the time."

Rena checks in, looking for a more specific answer. She says, "Can you tell us what Elijah will do? What will it look like when he's really successful?"

Elijah's mom says, "Elijah will be able to be at a table. Another kid, or maybe two kids, will sit with him at the table. Elijah will do his part of the work. The other kids will do their part of the work. Elijah will ask for help from the kids if he needs it. The kids will do what they can to help him, or maybe, if they can't figure it out, then the whole group can get an adult to help. I'm just so tired of Elijah always sitting with an adult—he never gets the chance to just hang out and be one of the kids in class."

Oscar says, "Wow! That's a lot of information—and so important. Can you tell me what we'll see change in just a sentence so I can add it to our profile?"

Elijah says, "I can. Mom wants me to do the work in small groups with other kids and ask them for help. Right?"

Elijah's mom says, "YES!" and Oscar follows with, "That was great! Thanks, Elijah!"

Rena asks, "Elijah, is that something you want?"

After a few minutes of silence, looking down, Elijah whispers, "Yeah."

Rena asks the team, "How would we know if this is changing? What data would we use to be sure that this challenge is being addressed?"

Elijah's dad says, "Well, my wife would stop complaining about it!" Everyone chuckles.

Elijah's mom says, "Elijah could tell me who he worked with and what he did. Also, he would tell me that he did it without an adult. Elijah feels so ashamed about always sitting with an adult."

Russ, Elijah's teacher, says, "We usually do group work when we review for unit tests. I plan the groups ahead of time.

Elijah, you could let me know if there are specific kids you'd like to work with, and I could put you into a group with them."

Elijah asks, "When would I tell you? I don't want everyone to know."

Russ says, "I'll ask everyone in the class to tell me. I'll explain that I make the groups, but I'll let everyone share with me if they prefer working with certain people. I'll ask everyone to write names on Post-its and fold them up and put them in a box on my desk. OK?" Elijah nods. "If you don't tell me who you want to work with, I'll just put you with people who choose you or with people I notice are helpful. I can text your parents after class when we do this so they know the first names of kids you worked with, and I can just send a "+" if you did the work without an adult. OK?" Elijah nods.

Elijah's parents agree. Rena checks to be sure the cell numbers for Elijah's parents in the school database are accurate.

After Elijah shares, other team members share additional priorities for change, describing them in ways that are measurable and could be monitored for change over time with specific data.

- *Identifying Disability-Related Needs:* Rena transitions the group again, saying, "OK, everyone, now it's time for us to sort this data so we can use it to make eligibility decisions."

  Rena reviews the area(s) of suspected disability and points out keywords from the disability definition or questions that the team has previously generated about the disability characteristics. Oscar creates a page in the Learner Profile board for each keyword.

  After checking with team members to make sure that all of the important keywords are identified, Rena invites each person to look at the challenge page of the Learner Profile board and choose one challenge that might align with one of the key words. Oscar copies the appropriate "sticky" from the challenge page and pastes it into the page for the identified keyword. This continues until the team feels that all of the major challenges are sorted.

  There could be some challenges that don't fit with the key words from the disability definitions. That's OK. All people have needs—some needs are associated with disabilities, and some are not. Not all of a child's needs are associated with a disability. The team can make this determination together. One outcome of this process is that a team could discover that a child has many needs and that these needs are not primarily disability-related. It doesn't mean they aren't important or that interventions aren't necessary. It may suggest that supports and services other than those for disabled children are needed.

After the challenges are reorganized, Rena thanks the team for doing the hard work of partnering to sort the challenges well.

- *Reviewing Past Interventions and Supports:* Rena shifts the team, saying, "This is great—we're making progress. Now, let's talk about what we've already tried at school. We'll discuss things that have worked and things that might not have worked to help the student succeed in the past."

  Rena invites each person to share about one intervention or support that has been tried. Team input is recorded on the Learner Profile Jamboard. Before going around to ask for input from each team member, Oscar explains and records the following steps for sharing on chart paper so everyone can see them:

  - Name the support or intervention.
  - Name the barrier that you hoped would be addressed by this intervention (think about the Barriers to Success at School "stickies").
  - Tell whether you think it worked or didn't work.
  - Briefly share any evidence (from reports, observations, work samples, etc.) to show the team how you know that the support or intervention worked or didn't work.

  Oscar asks all team members to hold each other accountable for only sharing information using the posted structure. He explains, "We have to share in a way that captures exactly what we mean. In order for me to get it all down, we have to be brief and focused—otherwise, I might lose information. Also, because I want to hear everyone well, be sure just one person is talking at a time. If we need to figure out how to do this well, I have some strategies, but maybe we can just try to wait and listen to start out with. Oh, and one more thing: It's OK if you don't agree with what someone else is saying. Really. Good people sometimes disagree. Our job is to be sure to capture what everyone thinks and knows about Elijah. We can work out any places that need clarification after we're done sharing."

Rena helps people by calling on the next person who will speak. Oscar documents each past intervention mentioned on a separate page of the Learner Profile board.

At the end, Rena reviews the list of interventions and supports that have worked and those that haven't worked. She reminds people that this data will be useful when answering the eligibility determination questions about needed supports and services and when thinking about what supports might be helpful, no matter whether Elijah is found eligible today or not.

- *Eligibility Determination:* Again, Rena transitions the team to the next phase of the meeting, saying, "Excellent! We have a good sense about the strengths, barriers, disability-related needs, and supports and services that have been tried. Now, we're ready to answer questions together to determine eligibility. Remember, we need to answer these questions and connect our responses to the data we've just reviewed and sorted."

  Rena reads the appropriate eligibility questions (either Section 504 or IDEA, depending on eligibility; see Learner Profile Jamboard for examples). Rena invites each person to share their answer to each question without being interrupted by others. The eligibility questions are framed in a way that leads to a "yes" or "no" answer. In other words, everyone who answers the question is making a claim: either yes, the child has a qualifying disability, or no, they don't.

  Rena also reminds each team member to share at least one data point or piece of information from the Learner Profile Jamboard to support their answer. The reason for this is that all claims require support. It's important for the team to have a shared understanding about the different claims that can be made in response to the eligibility questions as well as the supporting evidence for each claim. Good decisions come when claims and evidence are clearly identified and thoughtfully considered. Again, Rena reminds the team that it's OK to disagree. She also reminds the team that it's essential to listen to what every person has to say without interrupting them. After everyone has shared their claim and supporting evidence, the team can ask clarifying and probing questions to get a better understanding about the different claims and reasons for supporting them. Rena assures everyone that the purpose of this part of the meeting is to be sure everyone shares their opinions and that everyone listens well to all members of the team.

A sentence stem that Rena or Oscar could post to help people answer eligibility questions could be as follows:

"I believe the answer to this question is _____ based on _____ data from the Learner Profile board."

This kind of prompt is most helpful if team members anticipate disagreement, which can make it hard for people to hear one another. When there is disagreement, keeping it brief, clear, and direct is actually the kindest and most helpful way to communicate.

Once each person has shared, the team chair should invite everyone to share "one good thing" by contributing statements about some of the following to the last page of the Learner Profile Jamboard:

- Share one positive thing about this student that's on your mind right now.
- Share one thing that you're feeling hopeful about.
- Share one thing that happened during the process or one person involved in this process that you're grateful for.

If a team member can't participate in this part, they can pass; however, it's really important to try to thank and encourage each other after the eligibility determination process has been completed.

By following this step-by-step process during the eligibility determination meeting, teams participate in a more interactive meeting, ensure that decisions about eligibility are truly the result of team consideration and input, and build stronger, more dynamic relationships with one another. The responsive team approach to 504 and IDEA eligibility determination meets all of the requirements for compliance. In fact, making decisions about the child's disability, how the disability affects the child in school, and whether the child requires accommodations, modifications, or supplemental supports and services to access the general curriculum or make effective progress more closely aligns with legal and regulatory language when each of these decisions is made with input from all members of the team. As we will discuss in the next section, this process also fits strongly with current research about family–school partnerships for all children.

AFTER INITIAL ELIGIBILITY IS DETERMINED

Regardless of the outcome of the eligibility determination, it is important for team members to recognize that students who are involved in 504 or IEP eligibility processes are students who have faced barriers to access or success at school. Responsive teams acknowledge this. What matters for any child in public school who is striving and struggling to succeed is that the adults involved are there to help the child and each other meet with success. In school, success means full access to all that the school community has to offer.

RESEARCH TO CONSIDER

So what does current research have to say about how to handle the "after-the-meeting" part of eligibility determination?

- Team members respond to the culture of the student and family in a way that affirms, supports, and empowers family–school collaboration.
- Team members demonstrate belief in the child's potential and abilities.
- Team members make commitments and honor them.
- Team members engage in family-oriented or person-centered planning.
- Team members communicate clearly about decisions and the reasons why decisions are made. (ALLIANCE, 2008; deFur, 2012; Dunlap & Fox, 2007)

All of these research-based approaches to supporting after-the-meeting collaboration can happen whether the child is found eligible or not. It's very important that once an eligibility determination is made there is a sense that the team continues as a group of people who are connected in their commitment to the success of the child and responsive to the concerns that team members have raised.

At this phase, the questions, data, and decisions that the team makes are different, depending on whether or not the child has been found eligible under Section 504 or IDEA. Table 4.7 offers a summary of the questions, data, and decisions teams may face at this time.

TABLE 4.7 Responsive Teaming After Eligibility Determination

QUESTIONS	DATA	DECISIONS
If the child is not eligible, what are the supports that will be offered to address identified barriers to the fit between the child and schooling?	Barriers identified in the learning profile Supports identified by the team as strengthening the fit between the student and schooling during the eligibility meeting	What will be done next to support a stronger fit between the child and schooling?
If the child is eligible, what are the supplemental supports and services needed to afford access or effective progress?	Evidence-based practices Student and family input and cultural considerations School-based considerations (e.g., course of study, curriculum frameworks, etc.)	What are the supplemental aids and services that will be offered?
How will we know that the supports are working to address identified barriers or disability-related needs?	Measurable outcomes identified by the team Specific data points identified by the team to measure each identified outcome	How will we know whether there is a positive change in the fit between the child and schooling when these supplemental aids and services are provided?
How will the team remain responsive during the next phase of partnership?	Team input about what worked during the eligibility process Team input about areas to be strengthened to support team partnership	How will team members share questions and data in the next phase of supporting the fit between the child and schooling? At what point will the team convene to monitor progress and make future decisions?

STRATEGIES TO CONSIDER

We often hear parents and educators express feelings of dissatisfaction about what happens after eligibility determination. Whether the outcome matches what was expected or not, people are often left feeling discouraged, unheard, or overwhelmed by what occurs when teams go through the eligibility determination process. Perhaps this has something to do with what happens after the eligibility determination is made.

Typically, an eligibility determination meeting ends with a finding of eligibility or of no eligibility. That's it. End of conversation. But there are many ways to conduct ourselves after a meeting that confirm that there is still a team, whether it's required by regulations or not. There is still a group of people who care about the child. This group is still invested in seeing the child grow, mature, and succeed. Strategies that matter after the team has determined eligibility are strategies that remind all members of the team about this. These include, but are certainly not limited to, the following:

- *Commitments of care.* No team should leave the eligibility determination without some clear commitments of care. These could be as simple as regular schoolwide commitments, such as upcoming parent-student-teacher conferences or open houses. Any schoolwide event provides opportunities for team members to commit to connecting and checking in. These could also include specific routines that individuals on the team have for providing care: guidance counseling appointments that happen every term or semester; homeroom or advisory periods at which students receive support and encouragement; lunch buddies or structured peer support that happens regularly at school; morning or afternoon check-ins with students (and families, if they provide transportation) to offer support and encouragement for overcoming barriers that the team has identified. There are any number of commitments that can be named and confirmed at the close of an eligibility meeting or in the days after the team has met.
- *Commitments of service and support.* For students who are found eligible, there are formal processes for making commitments of service and support in the form of 504 plans or IEPs. These plans are created so that individual commitments of service and support can be articulated, agreed upon, and monitored by members of the team. We'll talk more about this in Chapter 5.

  For students who are not eligible, we should still be making commitments of service and support. As mentioned previously, when a child's needs reach the point where that child is referred for evaluation and suspected of having a disability, there is something about the child's interface with the school system that is not working from the point of view of at least one member of the team. Therefore, it's critical that teams identify specific supports and services that are available to all children and that may offer assistance to make school a place of success for the child. So the commitments of service and support should be specific, documented, and followed up on, even if a child is not eligible for services under Section 504 or IDEA.
- *Commitments to the vision for the future.* Whether a child is eligible or ineligible, the team can commit to a positive future by engaging in structured activities to share the vision for the child. This can be a powerful way to end an eligibility determination meeting, regardless of the outcome. For students who are eligible, creating a vision is something teams often do, especially if the student is eligible for special education and over the age of 16. In some states, this happens for all students who have IEPs.

(Continued)

(Continued)

> We believe that ending an eligibility meeting with a brief conversation about the positive, possible vision for the student and connecting that vision to specific next steps can strengthen relationships among team members and improve outcomes for students. This idea is strongly connected to person- and family-centered planning models.

Most importantly, in order to help the team follow through on commitments, we believe that it's important to document the commitments that the team is making to the child either at the end of the meeting or shortly thereafter. This kind of visual representation can be used at the end of an eligibility determination meeting, either to segue into planning or as a way to help the team leave the meeting with a sense of closure and ongoing partnership.

The **Documenting Team Commitments Tool** shows one way to document team commitments for students, whether they are found eligible or not eligible. Using this tool or a similar type of documentation reminds team members that the eligibility determination is not the end of the team's concern for the child, nor is it the end of the team's support for each other in effectively educating the child. A responsive approach to eligibility determination always results in the identification of next steps to address identified needs, regardless of whether they are disability-related. A responsive team not only feels a commitment to the child and family, but it is willing to demonstrate that commitment by identifying options that will strengthen the child's success at school. The tool is linked in Chapter 9 and available on the companion website. online resources

SUMMARY

The process of evaluating students and determining eligibility is a time of uncertainty for everyone involved in the team process. This process involves significant commitments of time spent observing and assessing individual students. We believe it must also involve significant commitments of team members as they get to know and trust each other and as they prepare to make decisions together. Responsive teaming allows all members of 504 and IEP teams to communicate in ways that build understanding about the profile of the learner, the interventions and supports that have been tried, and the options for supporting student success in the future.

The guiding questions for making decisions and interpreting data are made clear repeatedly so that, by the time the team meets to determine eligibility, all team members know the data, know the questions to be answered, and know the process that will be used to answer these questions. The guiding questions for this phase of the process include these:

- What is the child's profile as a learner?
- What are the experiences the child has had in school?
- Which experiences represent a strong fit between the child and schooling?
- Which experiences do not represent a fit between the child and schooling?

Responsive teams acknowledge and embrace different perspectives, values, languages, and cultures as places of richness and opportunity. They lean intentionally toward student-teacher-parent-centered practices and away from default approaches. Perhaps this is because a responsive approach brings people together with a mindset of curiosity. Responsive teams approach evaluation and eligibility as an investigation. They also support one another by openly stating individual claims in response to eligibility questions. Team members connect each claim to specific qualitative and quantitative data points. The data used by the team comes from experiences shared by team members about the child schooling and from evaluations, work samples, and classroom data.

The decisions made by the team at this phase include answers to these questions:

- Is this child eligible for protection under Section 504 or under IDEA?
- What adaptations can we offer to support a better fit between the child and schooling whether the child is eligible or not?

Regardless of the final eligibility determination, success happens when the team discovers how to adjust the systems of the school to more effectively meet the needs of the learner. In the next chapter, we will shift our attention to responsive team practices when planning for students who are found eligible.

CHAPTER FIVE

Developing the Plan and Determining Placement

"I have this on my desk now.

- *'Did you mean it?'*
- *'Can you defend it?'*
- *'Did you say it with love?'*
- *What more can we really do?"*

—Patricia Neely Innes, Special Education Coordinator/Teacher, quoting Luvvie Ajayi Jones

GUIDING QUESTIONS FOR THIS CHAPTER

- Why is it important to align questions, data, and decisions when planning and determining placement under Section 504 or IDEA?
- What are the common practices that responsive 504 and IEP teams can embrace to maintain compliance and collaboration throughout the planning and placement process?

By now, you might be thinking that a lot of responsive teaming happens before the team meets. We hope that's your idea. When you have invested time in building relationships, organizing and sharing information, and communicating about needs, expectations, and priorities, the team is ready to come together to look at questions, review data, and make decisions. That's really what the agenda for a 504 or IEP team meeting is all about.

You may be wondering, if a child is eligible, what additional decisions the team must make using the evaluation data. Table 5.1 describes the questions that guide the planning and placement elements of 504 and IEP teams.

TABLE 5.1 Questions for Developing a Plan and Determining Placement

QUESTIONS	SECTION 504 TEAMS	IEP TEAMS
What are the required supports and services that must be included in a plan?	A written plan is not required under Section 504. This can be confusing because federal guidance often refers to a 504 plan (U.S. Department of Education, 2020). The 504 team is required to make and document "placement decisions" in conformance with the following regulations: (a) *Academic setting.* A recipient to which this subpart applies shall educate, or shall provide for the education of, each qualified handicapped person in its jurisdiction with persons who are not handicapped to the maximum extent appropriate to the needs of the handicapped person. A recipient shall place a handicapped person in the regular educational environment operated by the recipient unless it is demonstrated by the recipient that the education of the person in the regular environment with the use of supplementary aids and services cannot be achieved satisfactorily. Whenever	The IEP must include: (I) A statement of the child's present levels of academic achievement and functional performance, including— (i) How the child's disability affects the child's involvement and progress in the general education curriculum (i.e., the same curriculum as for nondisabled children); or (2)(i) A statement of measurable annual goals, including academic and functional goals designed to— (A) Meet the child's needs that result from the child's disability to enable the child to be involved in and make progress in the general education curriculum; and (B) Meet each of the child's other educational needs that result from the child's disability; (ii) For children with disabilities who take alternate assessments aligned to alternate academic achievement standards, a description of benchmarks or short-term objectives;

QUESTIONS	SECTION 504 TEAMS	IEP TEAMS
	a recipient places a person in a setting other than the regular educational environment pursuant to this paragraph, it shall take into account the proximity of the alternate setting to the person's home. (b) *Nonacademic settings.* In providing or arranging for the provision of nonacademic and extracurricular services and activities, including meals, recess periods, and the services and activities set forth in 104.37(a)(2), a recipient shall ensure that handicapped persons participate with nonhandicapped persons in such activities and services to the maximum extent appropriate to the needs of the handicapped person in question. (c) *Comparable facilities.* If a recipient, in compliance with paragraph (a) of this section, operates a facility that is identifiable as being for handicapped persons, the recipient shall ensure that the facility and the services and activities provided therein are comparable to the other facilities, services, and activities of the recipient. 34 C.F.R. 104.34	(3) A description of— (i) How the child's progress toward meeting the annual goals described in paragraph (2) of this section will be measured; and (ii) When periodic reports on the progress the child is making toward meeting the annual goals (such as through the use of quarterly or other periodic reports, concurrent with the issuance of report cards) will be provided; (4) A statement of the special education and related services and supplementary aids and services, based on peer-reviewed research to the extent practicable, to be provided to the child, or on behalf of the child, and a statement of the program modifications or supports for school personnel that will be provided to enable the child— (i) To advance appropriately toward attaining the annual goals; (6)(i) A statement of any individual appropriate accommodations that are necessary to measure the academic achievement and functional performance of the child on statewide and districtwide assessments consistent with section 612(a)(16) of the Act; and (ii) If the IEP team determines that the child must take an alternate assessment instead of a particular regular statewide or districtwide assessment of student achievement, a statement of why—

(Continued)

(Continued)

QUESTIONS	SECTION 504 TEAMS	IEP TEAMS
		(A) The child cannot participate in the regular assessment; and (B) The particular alternate assessment selected is appropriate for the child; and (7) The projected date for the beginning of the services and modifications described in paragraph (a)(4) of this section, and the anticipated frequency, location, and duration of those services and modifications. (b) Transition services: (1) Appropriate measurable postsecondary goals based upon age-appropriate transition assessments related to training, education, employment, and, where appropriate, independent living skills; and (2) The transition services (including courses of study) needed to assist the child in reaching those goals. (c) Transfer of rights at age of majority. 34 C.F.R. 300.320
What is the least restrictive environment (LRE) requirement for eligible students?	Children must be placed in the educational setting with nondisabled children to the maximum extent appropriate for the disabled child. Whenever a child with a disability is placed in a setting other than the regular education setting, the team must consider proximity to the child's home. 34 C.F.R. 104.34(a)	(2) Each public agency must ensure that— (i) To the maximum extent appropriate, children with disabilities, including children in public or private institutions or other care facilities, are educated with children who are nondisabled; and (ii) Special classes, separate schooling, or other removal of children with disabilities from the regular educational environment occurs only if the nature or severity of the disability is such that education in regular classes with the use of supplementary aids and

QUESTIONS	SECTION 504 TEAMS	IEP TEAMS
		services cannot be achieved satisfactorily. 34 C.F.R. 300.114
How do adaptations meet the free appropriate public education (FAPE) standard?	The team must determine the supports, services, and placement that are necessary to afford the child with a disability a free appropriate public education. 34 C.F.R. 104.34–104.37 Appropriate education under Section 504 means "regular or special education and related aids and services . . . designed to meet individual educational needs of handicapped persons as adequately as the needs of nonhandicapped persons are met." 34 C.F.R. 104.33	*Free appropriate public education* or *FAPE* means special education and related services that— (a) Are provided at public expense, under public supervision and direction, and without charge; (b) Meet the standards of the SEA, including the requirements of this part; (c) Include an appropriate preschool, elementary school, or secondary school education in the state involved; and (d) Are provided in conformity with an individualized education program (IEP) that meets the requirements of §§ 300.320 through 300.324 (34 C.F.R. 300.17). In 2016, the U.S. Supreme Court interpreted the FAPE standard in the *Endrew F. v. Douglas County School District* decision. "With the decision in *Endrew, F.*, the Court clarified that for all students, including those performing at grade level and those unable to perform at grade level, a school must offer an IEP that is 'reasonably calculated to enable a child to make progress appropriate in light of the child's circumstances'" (U.S. Department of Education, 2017).
What is the role of parents in planning and placement?	Parents must give consent for initial evaluations (U.S. Department of Education OCR, 2020, Question 26). Parents are assumed to be part of the "group of knowledgeable	Each public agency must take steps to ensure that one or both of the parents of a child with a disability are present at each IEP team meeting or are afforded the opportunity to participate, including—

(Continued)

(Continued)

QUESTIONS	SECTION 504 TEAMS	IEP TEAMS
	people" who participate in placement decisions (U.S. Department of Education OCR, 2020, Question 27). In addition, Section 504 regulations name parents as having the following rights: *Procedural safeguards:* A recipient that operates a public elementary or secondary education program or activity shall establish and implement, with respect to actions regarding the identification, evaluation, or educational placement of persons who, because of handicap, need or are believed to need special instruction or related services, a system of procedural safeguards that includes notice, an opportunity for the parents or guardian of the person to examine relevant records, an impartial hearing with opportunity for participation by the person's parents or guardian and representation by counsel, and a review procedure. 34 C.F.R. 104.36	(1) Notifying parents of the meeting early enough to ensure that they will have an opportunity to attend; and (2) Scheduling the meeting at a mutually agreed on time and place. (b) *Information provided to parents:* (1) The notice required under paragraph (a)(1) of this section must— (i) Indicate the purpose, time, and location of the meeting and who will be in attendance; and (ii) Inform the parents of the provisions in §300.321(a)(6) and (c) (relating to the participation of other individuals on the IEP team who have knowledge or special expertise about the child), and §300.321(f) (relating to the participation of the Part C service coordinator or other representatives of the Part C system at the initial IEP team meeting for a child previously served under Part C of the Act). (2) For a child with a disability beginning not later than the first IEP to be in effect when the child turns 16, or younger if determined appropriate by the IEP team, the notice also must— (i) Indicate— (A) That a purpose of the meeting will be the consideration of the postsecondary goals and transition services for the child, in accordance with §300.320(b); and (B) That the agency will invite the student; and (ii) Identify any other agency that will be invited to send a representative.

QUESTIONS	SECTION 504 TEAMS	IEP TEAMS
		(c) *Other methods to ensure parent participation:* If neither parent can attend an IEP team meeting, the public agency must use other methods to ensure parent participation, including individual or conference telephone calls, consistent with §300.328 (related to alternative means of meeting participation). (d) *Conducting an IEP team meeting without a parent in attendance*: A meeting may be conducted without a parent in attendance if the public agency is unable to convince the parents that they should attend. In this case, the public agency must keep a record of its attempts to arrange a mutually agreed on time and place, such as— (l) Detailed records of telephone calls made or attempted and the results of those calls; (2) Copies of correspondence sent to the parents and any responses received; and (3) Detailed records of visits made to the parent's home or place of employment and the results of those visits. (e) Use of interpreters or other action, as appropriate. The public agency must take whatever action is necessary to ensure that the parent understands the proceedings of the IEP team meeting, including arranging for an interpreter for parents with deafness or whose native language is other than English. (f) *Parent copy of child's IEP*: The public agency must give the parent a copy of the child's IEP at no cost to the parent. 34 C.F.R. 300.322

It's easy to see that the IDEA regulations are much more specific and detailed about the role and responsibilities for planning than are Section 504 regulations. There are additional, specific requirements outlined regarding the types of supports and services that must be considered for students under IDEA. One example is the requirement to consider assistive technology needs (Etscheidt, 2016).

A resource for understanding the requirements for planning under Section 504 (as well as other laws that protect students from discrimination) is the U.S. Department of Education Office for Civil Rights (OCR) "Back to School Binder" (2021). This was one of several publications issued by the OCR in fall 2021 at a time when many schools were resuming full in-person learning after disruptions caused by COVID-19. We recommend that teams use excerpts from pages 6 to 10 of this resource in order to create a common understanding about the requirements for 504 teams when planning and supporting a child who has been determined eligible.

Another resource that may be helpful to responsive teams in understanding the requirements for developing and implementing IEPs is the U.S. Department of Education's "Return to School Roadmap" which was issued on September 30, 2021. Section B of this document reviews some of the questions that have arisen about virtual and in-person convenings of the IEP team. Section C addresses consideration of special factors required by IEP teams. Sections D through H address additional roles, responsibilities, and requirements for IEP teams when planning and determining placement for eligible students. We recommend that responsive teams use documents such as the "Return to School Roadmap" to establish shared understandings about a compliant IEP process.

BEFORE THE PLANNING AND PLACEMENT TEAM MEETING

One aspect of responsive teaming is to identify the questions that will be essential for all team members to use before the team convenes to make decisions together. Table 5.2 identifies the important questions, data, and decisions that responsive teams consider before developing IEP and 504 plans together.

TABLE 5.2 Responsive Teaming Before Plan Development

QUESTIONS	DATA	DECISIONS
What are the measurable changes we will see? What data will show access, progress, or an improved fit between the child and schooling?	Team input Data used to identify needs (classroom data, schoolwide data) Data that show area(s) of strength or success in the fit between the child and schooling Data used to understand access, progress, and the fit between all children and schooling (e.g., curriculum standards, attendance rates, etc.)	How will we monitor success (access/progress)?
What are the areas in which disability-related needs exist?	Data from evaluations/ eligibility determination	What are the priority areas for supporting access or progress?

For students protected under Section 504, the priority areas identified for team decision-making are the categories under which accommodations, modifications, and services are organized, communicated, and delivered. The critical aspect of providing a free appropriate public education (FAPE) to students who are protected under Section 504 is clear alignment between disability-related needs and barriers to access, as well as documentation that shows the adaptations that the team identifies are consistently available to the student to provide access that is commensurate with the access that all other students have to schooling. Under Section 504, there is no requirement to have a written plan, nor are parents required to sign a plan before it is implemented. In addition, there is no requirement for monitoring progress other than by the methods used for all students (e.g., report cards, transcripts). That is why it is particularly important that teams who are planning for eligible students under Section 504 give particular attention to documentation and communication. Without support and a shared understanding about how the team will know whether the identified adaptations are effective in providing access to schooling, claims about violations of the student's right to a FAPE can be made.

For students who have IEPs, the priority areas for team decision-making are more extensive. Remember, all students who have IEPs are protected under Section 504. So the need to organize, communicate, and deliver accommodations, modifications, and services applies to these students as well. Because students who have IEPs are required to have a written plan, the mechanism for organizing and communicating about adaptations already exists. In fact, as Table 5.1 shows, an IEP must address many aspects of the student's educational program, all of which are determined as the result of team decisions. One notable aspect of team decision-making under IDEA is the need to develop measurable annual goals that are used to monitor individual progress. In the case of students who have IEPs, the development and measurement of goals by the team is a critical part of responsive teaming. Unless all team members understand and contribute to the development of goals, and also participate in identifying the data that will be used to monitor progress related to these goals, claims about whether the child is receiving a FAPE can arise.

Regardless of the type of team, the need for team members to ground their work with a focus on developing a plan that offers a FAPE is critical before starting the planning process. Let's revisit Albert's case (from Chapter 2) in order to set the stage for further exploration about how the planning and placement determination might unfold later in this chapter.

CASE STUDY: ALBERT'S TEAM

Later in this chapter, we'll join Albert's team after Albert is found ineligible under IDEA. What follows is a summary of the eligibility determination process for Albert:

> Albert was found to be a student with a specific learning disability affecting reading fluency and writing fluency based on classroom benchmark assessment data and norm-referenced intelligence and achievement testing. Classroom benchmark data show that Albert's reading fluency is 25 percent of the rate that is expected for ninth-grade students. His reading comprehension and fluency improve to 80 percent of the rate expected for ninth graders when he uses text-to-speech software. IQ and achievement data show that Albert's reading fluency,

reading comprehension, and writing fluency are two standard deviations below his verbal comprehension and abstract reasoning scores. Albert was tested in German as well as in English with similar results on norm-referenced IQ and achievement assessments. Clearly, Albert is a student whose profile fits the definition of Specific Learning Disability under IDEA.

The tiered supports that were put in place while his evaluation was happening supported him to reduce his reluctance to participate in reading and writing in the classroom. During the evaluation period, Albert's participation in group work in class improved. Data showed that during the first week of the evaluation period, Albert's teacher observed him participating for less than five minutes of a 50-minute group activity. The guidance office log and classroom sign-out log showed that Albert spent 40 minutes in guidance. By the sixth week of the evaluation period, Albert had attended five tutoring sessions and had used the new software on his Chromebook in class to support reading and writing. Some of his classmates had also requested access to the word prediction and text-to-speech software after seeing Albert use these during lectures and group work. Albert's participation data in Week 6 showed that he stayed in a 50-minute group for 45 minutes. Guidance logs and classroom sign-out logs showed that Albert had not been to guidance or signed out of the classroom in the past two weeks. Albert's writing samples were consistent from Week 1 to Week 6 of the evaluation period; however, Albert was no longer avoiding written assignments, and the length of output had increased by 36 percent when Albert used his Chromebook with word prediction software.

This data shows that the fit between Albert and schooling is improving with the addition of after-school tutoring and software. Albert has been identified as a student with a Specific Learning Disability that impacts his ability to read, write, and participate in group work. Because data shows that the fit between Albert and schooling has improved through the implementation of accommodations (software) and modifications (tutoring to support Albert to learn how to use the software), the team has concluded that Albert does not require specialized instruction in order to make effective progress or access schooling. Albert was found ineligible for services under IDEA; however, his parents were asked to sign a consent to evaluate Albert under Section 504 of the Rehabilitation Act.

At this point, the IDEA team is dismissed, and the 504 team is introduced. Within a week, the 504 evaluation is complete and the team convenes, finding that Albert is eligible for protection under Section 504 as a student with a Specific Learning Disability who requires supplemental support to access schooling.

Now, the 504 team must work together to determine placement; remember, Section 504 refers to supports and services as placement. We'll describe how the team uses tools and strategies near the end of this chapter.

Research and Regulations to Consider

Just as teams needed a shared understanding about the guiding questions, data, and decisions before engaging in eligibility meetings, all team members must have a strong working knowledge of these same elements for Section 504 and IEP planning. Figure 5.1 shows these four elements.

Figure 5.1 • Four Elements of a Compliant and Responsive Team Process

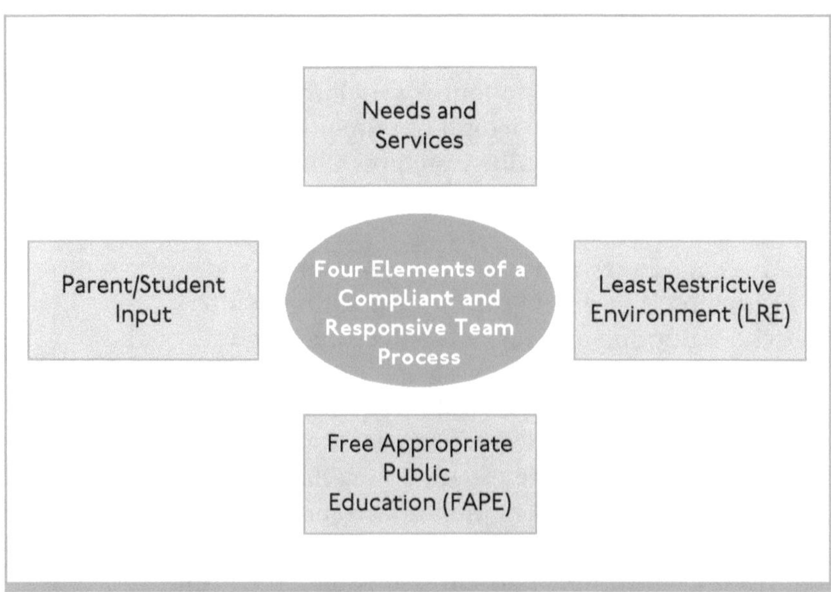

The four elements of a compliant and responsive team process for both IDEA and Section 504 that should be emphasized for all teams include the following:

1. *Determining needs and services:* Identifying the educational needs, appropriate supports, services, and placement by actively reviewing and connecting data to decisions.
2. *Prioritizing the least restrictive environment (LRE):* Considering the general education setting before considering any removal of the child from general education.
3. *Offering a free appropriate public education (FAPE) to students with disabilities:* This standard was most recently clarified by the United States Supreme Court in the *Endrew F. v. Douglas County School District* case (*Endrew F.*, 2017). The Supreme Court clarified that "to meet its substantive obligation under the IDEA, a school must offer an IEP reasonably calculated to enable a child to make appropriate progress in light of the child's circumstances" (p. 2). In addition, the Court states that the "educational program must be appropriately ambitious. . . . The goals may differ, but every child should have the chance to meet challenging objectives" (p. 13).
4. *Ensuring parent and student input:* Making sure that parents (including caregivers or guardians) and, in some cases, the student, are given the opportunity to participate in the decision-making process (Yell et al., 2020).

A responsive team process occurs when the key elements are defined and identified as questions for decision-making, data are reviewed and interpreted by the team in clear and explicit alignment with these questions, and decisions are articulated and documented, including input from all members of the team.

Determining Needs and Services

When determining the educational needs of the student and appropriate supports, it is important for all team members "to be knowledgeable about the student, the meaning of the student's current evaluation data, and placement options" (Moses et al., 2005, p. 51). In the previous chapter, we discussed strategies that teams can use to develop a learner profile together by sorting data from evaluations according to the questions for making eligibility decisions. A similar approach can be followed to identify student needs and required services, supports, and placement. We will discuss how to do this in the strategies section of this chapter; however, it's important to understand that current research emphasizes the need for teams to share a working knowledge of both the meaning of evaluation data and the options for services and supports before committing to a specific plan or placement.

Prioritizing the Least Restrictive Environment (LRE)

Because teams that convene to develop plans and determine placement are addressing the needs of students who have met with identified barriers to education, it is critical that all team members have a shared understanding about the requirement to consider all supports and services that could allow a child to continue to be educated, to the "maximum extent appropriate," with students who are nondisabled (34 C.F.R. 104.34). The legal requirement for identifying the placement for students under Section 504 and IDEA is commonly referred to as the "least restrictive environment," or LRE requirement. Removal of children from the general education setting, for any portion of the day, is not permitted under Section 504 or IDEA unless that child cannot be educated with supplemental aids and services in the general education setting (34 C.F.R. 104.34(a); 34 C.F.R. 300.114). Again, all team members should be reminded of this requirement before and during the meeting at which decisions about services, supports, and placement are made.

Offering FAPE

The term "free appropriate public education," or FAPE, has been defined differently under Section 504 of the Rehabilitation Act of 1973 than under the Individuals with Disabilities Education Act of 2004 (IDEA). In addition, the Supreme Court has offered two key decisions that impact how the FAPE standard has been applied in public schools for students who have IEPs (*Board of Education of the Hendrick Hudson Central School District v. Rowley*, 1982; *Endrew F. v. Douglas County School District*, 2017). In addition, the responsibility for implementing Section 504 requirements as well as the elements of IEPs falls on a wide range of educators, including general education teachers

(Shaw & Madaus, 2008; Yell et al., 2020). According to the U.S. Department of Education OCR (2010), essential elements of the FAPE standard under Section 504 include the following:

> An appropriate education may comprise education in regular classes, education in regular classes with the use of related aids and services, or special education and related services in separate classrooms for all or portions of the school day. Special education may include specially designed instruction in classrooms, at home, or in private or public institutions, and may be accompanied by related services such as speech therapy, occupational and physical therapy, psychological counseling, and medical diagnostic services necessary to the child's education.
>
> An appropriate education will include these items:
>
> - Education services designed to meet the individual education needs of students with disabilities as adequately as the needs of nondisabled students are met
> - Education of each student with a disability with nondisabled students, to the maximum extent appropriate to the needs of the student with a disability
> - Evaluation and placement procedures established to guard against misclassification or inappropriate placement of students and a periodic reevaluation of students who have been provided special education or related services
> - Establishment of due process procedures that enable parents and guardians to
> - Receive required notices
> - Review their child's records
> - Challenge identification, evaluation, and placement decisions
>
> Due process procedures must also provide for an impartial hearing with the opportunity for participation by parents and representation by counsel, and a review procedure. (para. 3)

The FAPE standard under IDEA as currently interpreted by the Supreme Court emphasizes the need for a student to receive "an IEP reasonably calculated to enable the child to make progress in light of the child's circumstances" (*Endrew F. v. Douglas County School District*, 2017). Children who are eligible under IDEA are also protected under Section 504, so the elements of the FAPE standard for Section 504 apply to all children who are found eligible under IDEA. All team members should be reminded about the elements of the FAPE standard(s) before and during team decision-making.

Ensuring Parent and Student Input

Finally, team members must cultivate habits that actively seek, encourage, and document the input of students and families throughout the team's decision-making process. Evidence that supports the need to prioritize parent and student involvement in the IEP and 504 team process abounds. First, there is the legal requirement for teams to consider input that is emphasized in regulations, case law, and legal guidance about the IEP and 504 process. Yell and his colleagues (2020) identify parental input as one of the two primary substantive aspects of compliance with IDEA. The regulations for IDEA 2004 explicitly require the district to make every effort to include the parent in the IEP team process (34 C.F.R. 300.322). The U.S. Department of Education OCR highlights many specific requirements for supporting parent involvement in the 504 process in their 2016 publication "Parent and Educator Resource Guide to Section 504 in Public Elementary and Secondary Schools." This publication includes specific scenarios describing the importance of obtaining parental consent for initial evaluations, informing parents of their rights, and avoiding any acts that could be considered retaliatory. Current research goes beyond the legal and regulatory provisions requiring parental input. Research shows that there is a need for schools and families to form intentional partnerships to maximize team effectiveness and to support improved outcomes for students with disabilities (Avendano & Cho, 2020; Lopez et al., 2019; Rispoli et al., 2019). From both a legal and educational perspective, the need to prioritize active and meaningful parent and student input into the development of educational plans is clear.

One additional and important element that research is showing us is that our deficit-frame approach to education is leaving many students behind (Safir & Dugan, 2021). In order to move away from practices that label students as lacking, or label educators as failing, or result in the identification of more students of color as disabled, or exclude students from their peers on the basis of their abilities, we must change the way we approach planning for individual students suspected of having disabilities. We must embrace a more equitable approach to our work. "Equity is an approach to ensuring equally high outcomes for all by removing the predictability of success or failure that currently correlates with any racial, social, economic, or cultural factor. . . . Equity isn't a destination, but an unwavering commitment to a journey" (Safir & Dugan, 2021, p. 29). Until we speak, plan, and act in a way that disrupts the stigma associated with a unique learning profile, we will continue to be divided in our approach to supporting learners who are striving to succeed at school. The role of the team is to "cultivate the unique gifts, talents and interests that every person possesses" (Safir & Dugan, 2021, p. 29).

In this book, we propose that the way to put this research into action is through responsive teaming. Scholars including Homa Tavangar and Will Richardson of The Big Questions Institute, facilitators including Luz Santana and Dan Rothstein of The Right Question Institute, and writer Luvvie Ajayi Jones, who authored the book *I'm Judging You: The Do-Better Manual*, seem to agree. We are building on the idea that in order to do better when planning for students with disabilities, people need to come together and engage in a process of discovery. They need to identify questions together, gather and share data together, and make decisions based on the data that was gathered, using the questions that guide the investigation. We believe that this process leads away from blaming students, parents, and teachers for barriers to learning success. We believe that this process leads toward a close examination of the fit and the possibilities for a better fit between a child and schooling. We believe that people who are committed to educating children successfully will be energized and empowered to partner by engaging in this process.

DURING THE PLANNING AND PLACEMENT TEAM MEETING

At the point of planning for an eligible student, responsive teams are engaged in a cycle of inquiry. Team members should have confidence and familiarity with responsive teaming and in understanding their work by aligning questions, data, and decisions. In Table 5.2, the team considered the student's profile and identified measurable changes that represent an improved fit between the child and schooling. The team also identified the data that could be collected and shared to show that improvements are happening. At the point of planning together, responsive teams continue their work by considering the questions, data, and decisions outlined in Table 5.3.

TABLE 5.3 Responsive Teaming During Planning

QUESTIONS	DATA	DECISIONS
What adaptations (supports and services) are most likely to be responsive to the child and work for improving access and progress in school (FAPE)?	Identified disability-related needs from the eligibility determination process Input from all team members, particularly the parent, student, and general education teacher Cultural and linguistic considerations	Who will oversee each adaptation to support progress toward each measurable outcome? How will adaptations be delivered? Who will collect data to measure the impact of adaptations?
How can these adaptations (supports and services) be provided in the least restrictive environment (LRE) that will support a fit between the child and schooling?	Data from implementation of previous interventions Student and general education teacher input Evidence-based practices	How can adaptations (supports and services) be delivered in the general education classroom if at all possible to support progress? When will adaptations involve removal from general education classrooms or typical school settings? What is the reason for removal? What is the criteria for a return to the general education classroom or typical school setting? What data will be collected to monitor progress toward this criteria?
How will we support one another to partner effectively as we implement supports and monitor changes during the period when this plan is in effect?	Data provided by all team members about preferred methods of communicating Team-generated schedule for sharing information, collaborative problem-solving, and celebrating successes	Who will share information with the entire team? On what schedule? What are the next steps for checking in to solve problems and celebrate successes?

In the next section, we will look at the specific strategies that can be used by all team members so that the time that is invested together around the table puts the recommendations from the law and current research into practice. Get ready to think about the time and resources available during team meetings in a whole new way!

STRATEGIES TO USE DURING MEETINGS

STRATEGIES TO CONSIDER

When the day of the meeting arrives, there are some very basic ways to ensure that the stage is set for adults to communicate and trust one another. This is where a responsive meeting begins. Fortunately, most of us know how to offer hospitality and welcome others; however, it can be difficult for us to remember how important these acts are when we are entering a "legal meeting."

Figure 5.2 summarizes the types of strategies that you might use during 504 and IEP team meetings to support responsive teaming.

Figure 5.2 • Strategies to Use During Meetings

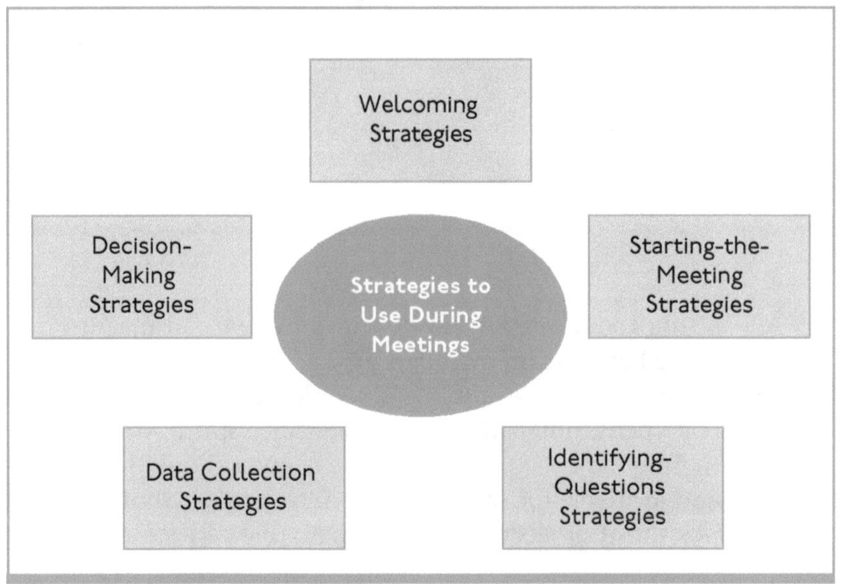

online resources

Here are a few ideas that we've collected from teams in the northeastern part of the United States to set the stage on the day of the meeting. Tools that you can use on the day of the meeting are linked in Chapter 9 and are available on our companion website. They include the following:

- **Abbreviated Section 504 and IEP Eligibility Determination Agenda**
- **Abbreviated IEP Planning and Placement Agenda**
- **Visible Note-Taking Tool (Example)**
- **How Responsive Was Our Team? (Survey)**

Welcoming Strategies

Figure 5.3 summarizes the strategies that you might use to welcome and ensure that team members are ready to partner together.

Figure 5.3 • Strategies for Welcoming Team Members

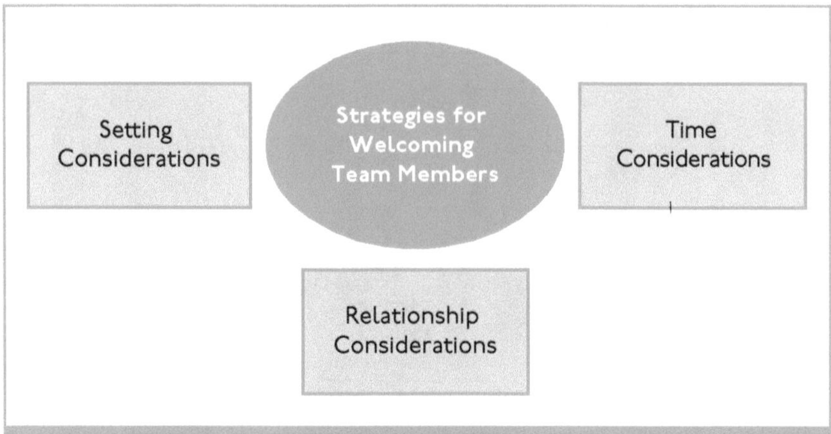

- *Setting considerations.* Set up the conference or meeting space before team members arrive. Be sure the room is clean, clutter-free, and tools people may need are available (e.g., pens, notepads, Post-it notes, newsprint, markers, highlighters, etc.). Copies of the agenda should be ready and available for each team member or posted on newsprint or electronically so everyone can see and use it during the meeting. Prepare newsprint, name tags/tents, whiteboards, or documents so that the room is ready for team members to see and sort data together.

- *Time considerations.* Any member of the team can reach out to other members to remind people about the meeting and encourage people to be on time and ready to talk. This message should be short, upbeat, and convey a sense of enthusiasm. For example, you might call, text, or email a message such as this one:

  "Good morning, team! This is a friendly reminder about Albert's (IEP/504) team meeting today at 9 a.m. Looking forward to seeing you at High School Conference Room #15 about five minutes before we begin. Thanks for bringing information and ideas so we can make decisions together! Please call me at 111-555-1111 if you have any questions or if I can support your participation in any way."

- *Relationship considerations.* Be sure that someone is available to greet team members when they arrive at the building. Parents/caregivers should be met at the door to the building and welcomed by a team member (not a secretary or monitor). Team members should enter the conference room at the same time rather than having some people enter and establish a place in the room before others. Students should arrive before the meeting starts if they are participating and should be given first choice of seating. If a student is not present, parents should be offered the first choice of seating, followed by others. Inquiries about the wellness and readiness of team members should be offered during entry so that people feel seen, heard, and cared for from the moment they arrive.

For more ideas about how to prepare the team and support positive relationships, see the **Strengthening the Team Checklist** (see Appendix).

Starting-the-Meeting Strategies

Figure 5.4 summarizes the strategies that you might use to start the meeting in a way that helps team members understand and use a responsive approach to teaming.

Figure 5.4 • Strategies for Starting a Responsive Team Meeting

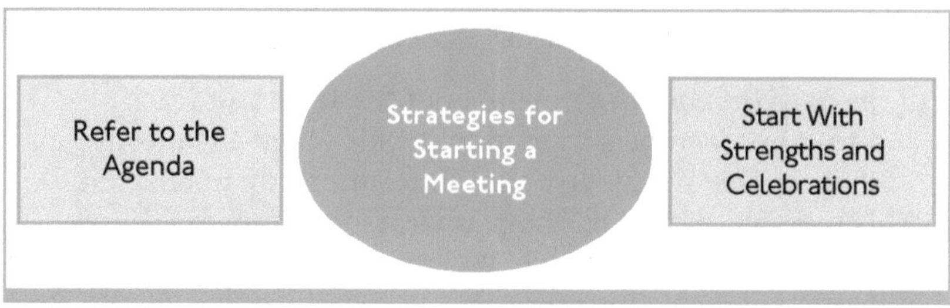

Once the team is gathered, it is important that all team members have a chance to introduce themselves. This time is critical and can make or break the ability of the team to respond well to one another. Strategies that can assist the team to start off with a positive tone include the following:

- *Refer to the agenda.* Whether you are in a 504 or special education team, the agenda for developing a plan and determining placement is very similar. The team must identify the profile of the learner (strengths/needs), identify questions to guide decisions, review the data that was collected and sort it according to the criteria, and then make decisions about the details of the plan and placement. The specific elements of the plan are different for 504 teams than for IEP teams; however, a responsive team process is the same for both types of meetings. Using the agenda as a tool to help the team stay focused, use time effectively, and support each other in the process is key. If each person has a copy of the agenda, you can invite team members to record names and roles of team members on the agenda so they know how to refer to one another. If there is a posted or projected "shared" agenda, the team chair can document this information during introductions for all members of the team.
- *Start with strengths and celebrations.* Team members can never overemphasize what is good, what's working, and what's worth celebrating when they gather together. Students who are evaluated under Section 504 or IDEA are students for whom the fit between their learning profiles

and their experience of schooling hasn't been found yet. It will be easy for team members to see what is wrong and harder for team members to feel confident and recall what is right and good; yet for every child, there is much that is right and good. If team members are struggling to find something good or to identify what's working at a particular time, they need support to do so. Often, having children participate in the meeting helps all adults to emphasize strengths and successes. This is why we recommend that students are present for the start of all meetings, even when they are very young. Whether the child attends or not is typically up to the parents, and this is a decision the team should respect; however, if the child is not present, showing a photo or short video (with prior permission from the parents) can help to ground the team in a way that keeps people focused on what is positive and possible for the child.

Identifying-Questions Strategies

A responsive team approach is inquiry-based. The team is faced with a problem. The problem is not the student. The problem is not the educator. The problem is the fit between the child's unique strengths, gifts, dreams, and abilities and what is happening at school. We're using the word "problem" intentionally here. When a student faces barriers to success at school, that's a problem. The team is the group of people who know the child and who care enough to invest time in gathering information to better understand the problem and to effectively resolve the problem.

This is a collaborative problem-solving approach that only curious people, open-minded people, and people who genuinely want to seek and find a sustainable solution can embrace. In order to do this work of inquiring and discovering possible solutions, teams need a shared understanding about the questions that apply to a particular situation—in this case, the problem of the fit between learner strengths, interests and abilities, and teaching. Teams cannot engage in shared decision-making using data unless they have a shared understanding about the questions that guide decisions. Figure 5.5 summarizes the strategies that you might use to help teams to identify the most important questions for a particular team meeting, given what's happening currently for the child at school.

Figure 5.5 • Strategies to Support Teams With Identifying Questions

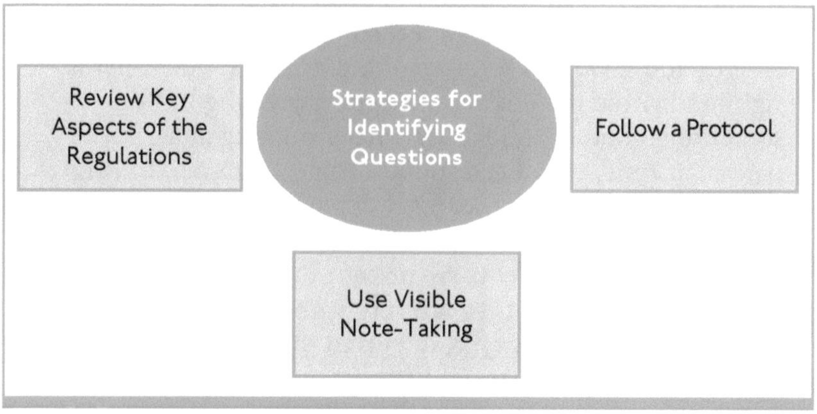

This is why we're urging you to shift your approach at review meetings to one in which the team identifies and refers to the questions to guide decision-making before talking about data. Some of the strategies that you can use to support teams with identifying these questions include the following:

- *Review key aspects of the regulations.* This can be done before, during, and after the team meets, but it is especially important during the team meeting. Key aspects include these:
  - *Disability definitions for suspected areas of disability.* Highlighting key words from these definitions helps team members to focus only on areas of disability-related need. IDEA regulations include specific definitions, and the eligibility process further identifies the disabilities that are suspected for an individual student. Section 504 identifies criteria for eligibility, and the team should have documented how the disability affects the child as part of the eligibility process. This is the place to find the disability definition for a child who is protected under Section 504.
  - *FAPE standard.* It is important to read the language from the regulations and remind the team about the standard for determining required levels of service. These definitions are available in the summary chart at the beginning of the chapter for 504 and IEP teams.
  - *LRE requirement.* Again, it is important to read the language from the regulations and remind the team

about the standard for determining how to deliver services without removing a child from their peers unless absolutely necessary. Children with disabilities must be educated to the maximum extent possible with their nondisabled peers.

- *Additional 504 or IEP specific requirements.* In the sample agendas linked in Chapter 9 and available on our companion website, you will see detailed lists of the key requirements for **504 Planning and Placement** and **IEP Planning and Placement.**

  - One note about 504 Planning and Placement: The review process for 504s is not set on a fixed schedule as it is with IEPs; however, 504 reevaluations are required periodically as well as at any time there is a significant change in the child's educational placement (U.S. Department of Education OCR, 2020). Therefore, our agenda for Section 504 includes eligibility determination, planning, and placement determination in one document, while the IEP agenda for planning and placement is separate from the sample agenda for special education eligibility determination. We do not recommend that you read the specific requirements to the team at the start of the meeting; however, we do recommend that you share these detailed agendas in advance or offer a summary before the meeting so that all team members are aware of the guiding questions for decision-making before they come to the meeting.

- *Procedural safeguards.* It is important for you and your team members to understand the procedural safeguards that apply to the team process and decisions. While all states and schools have specific notices of procedural safeguards for students on 504 plans and on IEPs and these notices must be distributed to parents regularly, we recommend having a highlighted copy of the safeguards document on hand during the meeting in case any questions arise. Highlighting key terms or noting frequently asked questions in the margins and having the appropriate notice available helps all team members to access the primary source of information if a team member has questions about the rights of students and families when planning together.

- *Follow a protocol.* Team members should experience the time during meetings as equitable, meaningful, and engaging. In order to accomplish this, team members benefit from structures that allow for equal air time and confirm that what one member has said has been heard by all. Protocols and visible note-taking accomplish these goals. The **Detailed 504 Planning Agenda** and **Detailed IEP Planning Agenda** tools (see Chapter 9) include a simple protocol to support the connection between questions, data, and decisions.

online resources

- *Use visible note-taking to connect questions, data, and decisions.* We've created a **Visible Note-Taking Tool (Example)** that you can use or modify to ensure that information is visible and aligned clearly for all members of the team. This tool is linked in Chapter 9 and available on our companion website. We've included some sample language for a 504 team conversation. During the meeting, the team can identify one or more note-takers (e.g., parent and educator) at the start of the meeting. You can also share note-taking if many people express an interest in supporting documentation. The notes should be visible to everyone during the meeting so that corrections can be made by any team member at any time. Team members should check in with one another throughout the meeting by asking, "Is this correct in our notes?" or "Did I capture this well?" before moving on with the agenda.

online resources

Data Collection Strategies

During the planning and placement determination process, teams are referring to existing data in order to make decisions. This data was collected either through the most recent evaluation process or it has been collected and shared by team members. This is true for both Section 504 and IEP teams. A critical aspect of the work during the meeting is connected to the ability of the team to collect data in a shared way outside of the meeting. Data collection should be approached as an opportunity for team dialogue, whether team members are sitting together in the same room or they are dispersed and data is being shared via remote means (e.g., emails, phone calls, texts, shared documents or databases).

Figure 5.6 summarizes strategies that you might consider when approaching data collection with the team.

Figure 5.6 • Data Collection Strategies

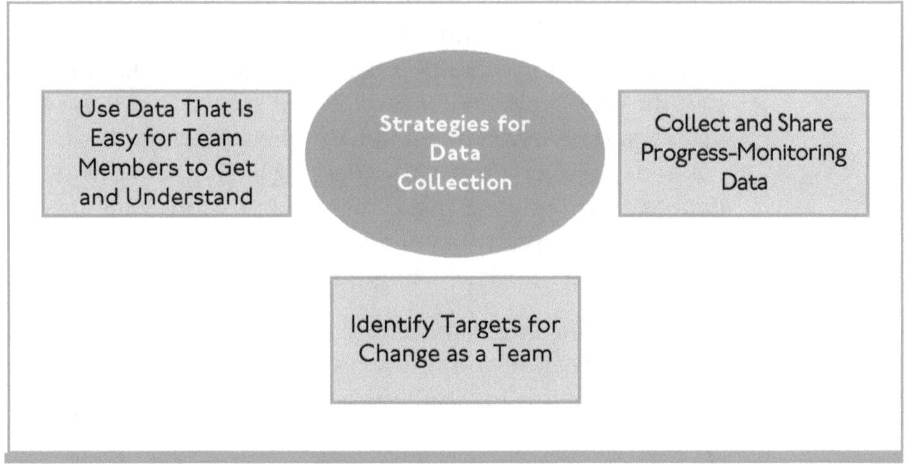

Here is a more detailed description of strategies that we recommend in order to build and sustain responsive teaming in preparation for team planning and placement determination:

- *Monitor progress by collecting and sharing data identified by the team.* At the planning and placement meeting, 504 and IEP teams should talk about the question, "How will we know the plan is working?" In an IEP meeting, this always happens when annual goals are developed and discussed; however, even IEP teams don't always "dig down" to identify specific types of data that will be collected and regularly shared with team members. For 504 teams, because there are no annual goals, the team has to take the initiative to talk about any supports provided through the planning process (e.g., accommodations, modifications, transportation, or other services) and should document both the target change that will result if the support works and the specific data the team can review to know it's successful.

  Rather than waiting to gather and share data at a particular time (e.g., progress report or report card dates), the team should use any available methods to make data visible as it's collected. Many schools are doing this with grades, making information about student assignments and teacher feedback visible through online data management systems. Now that we have technology such as shared Google Docs, Google Forms, and corresponding Google Sheets, as well as videos/photos at our fingertips, it is easy for team members to share images of student work samples, short videos of student participation (with prior consent), and even data sheets in real time with all members of the team. We recommend creating a system to identify data points for each accommodation, modification, and goal or service and ensure that these are visible and reviewed by team members before the team convenes or even during the meeting. Using schoolwide data (e.g., attendance, assignment submission, PBIS data, etc.) is always recommended for monitoring progress, and teams should prioritize using this data whenever possible.

- *Identify specific targets for change together as a team.* If we are investing time and resources in supporting access and effective progress for students with disabilities, we should all know and agree what success looks like. Involving students in these conversations along with the adults on the team is critical to support self-determination and to get student buy-in for the plan. If services and supports don't result in changes, they are ineffective in addressing the problem of the fit between learning and schooling. We recommend that teams describe in detail the type of changes that should result, using qualitative as well as quantitative measures. For example, if a student is passing all of their classes yet experiences anxiety to the point that they can only attend school for one or two days each week, there is a problem with the fit between learning and schooling. The target that a team would identify would be to increase attendance to at least four days per week. If the child has a 504 plan, the accommodation could be to adjust the schedule so a preferred activity happens upon arrival. A modification could be a slightly later start time and a slightly later end time for the school day. A service could be a morning and afternoon check-in. There are any number of possible interventions; however, the goal should be to increase attendance, and adjustments to the plan should be made regularly until progress is evident and acknowledged by everyone on the team.
- *Use data that is easily available and understood by all team members.* Data serves two purposes for 504 and IEP teams.
  - First, data is collected and used to measure success. As we've said before, teams have a problem: the problem of finding a good fit between student learning needs and schooling. Teams spend a lot of time inquiring about the problem—what the student knows and can do; what educators have tried; what's happened as a result.

We need to spend more time thinking about how we'll know when we're successful and agreeing about this. What does success look like, sound like, and feel like for all members of the team? How will we know when we've all arrived at a successful fit between the child and schooling? The more we can rely on data that is highly visible and important for all learners, the more confident we will be about the team's success in solving the problem.

- Second, data is collected and used to understand the student's connection with the larger community of learners. Any time we can use the data that we use for understanding the success of all students, we should. That means that we might pull specific learning standards used to guide instruction. We might use benchmarking data. We might look at PBIS data or whole-school initiatives for student conduct. We might even consider qualitative data, such as the ability of students to join an extracurricular activity or the ability of children to show how they prepare for an upcoming exam by videotaping themselves.

What matters is that the team agrees that the data is available, understandable, and would represent a clear, indisputable success to everyone. This agreement should happen before goals are finalized. All team members should agree about how the data can be gathered with input from the student, the family, and the school team. That way, all team members identify and agree on the sources of data, and everyone is actively looking for information that will tell us about the child's progress.

In order to support the team's ability to organize meaningful, available data that aligns with the learner profile and what's happening at school, we've created this **Tool for Responsive Teaming: Organizing Data.** We hope that this helps you to begin exploring the ways to put a more responsive approach into practice. This tool is linked in Chapter 9 and is available on our companion website. online resources

One additional consideration is to align goals with data that is readily available in the school. In order to accomplish this, team members must know and have available the types of data that are routinely collected and that relate to specific skills that students may need to strengthen. We recommend that school members of 504 and IEP teams engage in an activity to understand the data that is routinely collected at the whole-school level as well as the key assignments and activities used in classrooms. Here are some examples of data that could be described in 504 plans or IEPs:

- Attendance data (by the day or by the period)
- Sign-in/sign-out logs (for students who need to increase attention or time in the room)
- Question sets on quizzes/tests/exams (e.g., inferential questions on literature tests; questions requiring students to plot points on graphs in math; spelling tests; pre- and post-tests in science; social studies research paper citations)
- Assignments for which rubrics are used to give feedback (rubrics contain criteria and the numeric scores on rubrics can offer readily available data that can be incorporated into 504 plans and IEP goals)
- PBIS tools (social skill autopsies, collaborative problem solving templates, etc.)
- Projects that are part of community service or public presentations (e.g., science fair projects, grade-level mastery projects, etc.)
- Performances or work products along with the feedback offered by educators or juries

We're certain that you have other ideas now that you've seen these examples. You can brainstorm with the educators on your team to discover some of the routine data that is collected in your school to understand how students are developing and demonstrating the skills we want all students to master. You can also see examples of IEP goals written with the routine data collected in a school in the case study at the end of Chapter 6.

Decision-Making Strategies

Teams are most successful when they understand the process for making decisions together. Some teams operate using a "majority rule" approach. This approach is not recommended for Section 504 and IEP teams because there can be inequities that arise, based on the conflicting needs and identities of team members. Other teams operate on a "defer to the parent/caregiver" approach. This approach is also not recommended because parents/caregivers often lack information about practices that are effective for the child in a particular school or situation. Some teams approach planning with an understanding that one or more people on the team are "the authority" and they "know best" what should happen. This is another approach that we don't recommend, both because it violates the explicit requirements of Section 504 and IDEA regarding team-based decisions and because it contradicts the collaboration and consensus building at the heart of responsive teaming.

Figure 5.7 summarizes the strategies that we recommend to support responsive team decision-making.

Figure 5.7 • Strategies to Support Decision-Making

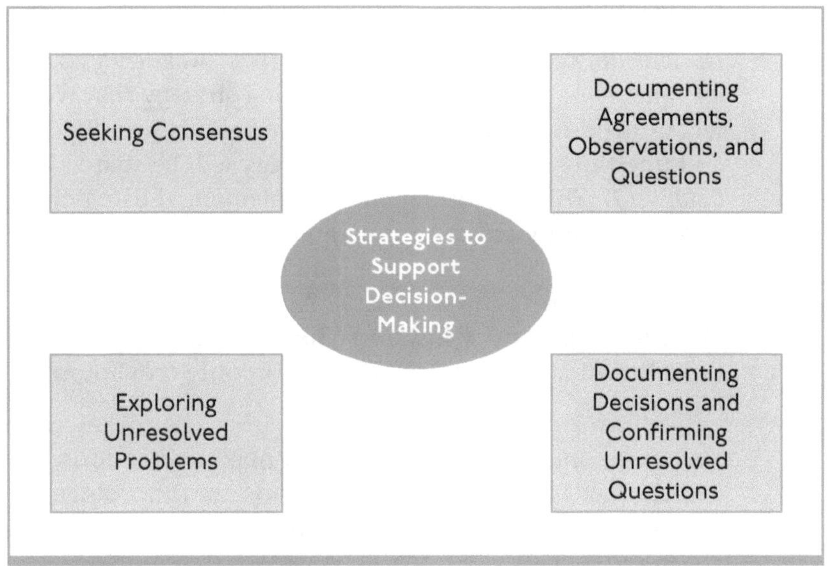

We recommend that teams engage in seeking consensus when making decisions. Consensus means an overall agreement about a decision by a group. Often in schools, decisions are made by others: by teachers, by families, by students, by administrators, by school boards, or even by government entities. When making decisions by consensus, all members of the group are asked to contribute and to share their thoughts and feelings about a particular decision.

- *Seeking consensus:* There is a fabulous resource that models consensus-based decision-making for IEP teams. The same approach can be applied to 504 teams, though the decisions made by a 504 team are different than those made by an IEP team. The process of getting to consensus is the same. The resource is called the Facilitated IEP Team Meeting, and it was developed by the Region 13 Education Service Center in Austin, Texas. We could not create a better resource, so we'll refer you to their website, where you'll find a 35-minute video as well as specific tools to support consensus-based decision-making (https://esc13.net/resources/a-facilitated-iep-meeting). One important point you'll notice if you review this resource is that consensus is a continuum. While several people on the team may be totally excited about a particular decision, others might have concerns or some fears associated with the decision. As long as everyone gets to the point where they can say, "It's OK with me if we try this," consensus has been reached.

- *Documenting agreements, observations (i.e., "wonderings"), and questions:* Another decision-making strategy that we recommend is documentation of agreements, wonderings, and questions. More about this strategy will be shared in Chapter 8. This approach can be implemented using chart paper or a Jamboard to capture agreements, wonderings, and questions. See the sample Jamboard with directions for implementing this approach: **Agreements, Wonderings, and Questions Jamboard.** This tool is linked in Chapter 9 and is available on our companion website.

online resources

- *Exploring unresolved problems:* When making decisions, teams often have unanswered questions and unresolved problems. We've heard this described by team members as "the team gets stuck." It makes sense that any group of people with high levels of commitment and differing perspectives might discover problems that take some time, thought, and trust to resolve. One strategy that we believe helps teams when there are differences in the level of comfort that individuals have about a particular decision is to document different perspectives as part of the meeting. A protocol and tool that we've adapted comes from the National School Reform Faculty data-driven dialogue protocol (see https://nsrfharmony.org/protocols/ for this and many other amazing protocols that you can use or adapt with school-based teams). Our adapted format that considers the schedule and availability of most school-based teams (i.e., can be accomplished in 15 minutes or less) is called the **Exploring Unresolved Problems Tool**. This tool is linked in Chapter 9 and is available on our companion website.

- *Documenting decisions and confirming unresolved questions:* After decisions have been reached, ask each team member to write down or share aloud these items:
    - One important agreement that they believe the team has made
    - One thing about the team's decisions or process that stands out (a pattern, an impression)
    - One question about the decisions that were made

  Team members can be invited to share these as a way to clarify their understanding about the decisions and their impressions of the process. This is not required—it's an offer. If questions that are shared can be answered by the team, go ahead and answer them. If they can't be answered, the team should acknowledge this, document and revisit these in the future, or make a plan for getting answers. Also, some questions may be offered to help keep the team on track. These can be used in future meetings as a way to remind team members of important priorities for decision-making. Team members can thank each other for the questions that are offered, too, especially if they resonate with other members of the team.

CASE STUDY: ALBERT'S TEAM

We will join Albert's 504 team in the middle of a meeting already in progress. As described earlier in this chapter, Albert's team has found him eligible for protection under Section 504 of the Rehabilitation Act. At this point, the team must determine placement, meaning that they must consider the elements of a free appropriate public education (FAPE) in the least restrictive environment (LRE) in order to allow Albert to experience a fit with education that mirrors the fit for children without disabilities in his school.

504 coordinator: Now that we've determined eligibility, it's our job as a team to look at the questions that guide planning under Section 504. We know that Albert is a student with a specific learning disability affecting reading and written output. Let's do a quick revisit of your strengths, Albert, particularly as we prepare for planning. I'm going to ask everyone to share one strength that perhaps you weren't thinking about when you came to the meeting today, but which could be important as we plan. I'll go first: Albert, one strength that I didn't know you had was the ability to inspire other kids in your class to use technology. Who wants to go next?

[Each team member shares one strength they feel is important to keep in mind when planning.]

Our next step is to consider these questions together: What adaptations will help Albert to access instruction as well as other students in the classroom? How can we offer adaptations that will give Albert the opportunity to learn in the general education classroom as often as other students are learning in the general education classroom? How will we help each other to be sure that the adaptations we suggest are working to improve the fit between Albert and schooling?

[Note-taker records questions so all team members can see them.]

Albert's father: Are we finally going to talk about what we're doing here for Albert?

School psychologist: In a way, we have been talking about this. Figuring out how to make school a better fit for Albert hasn't been quick or easy. We've gotten a lot of information about who Albert is as a learner. We're at the bottom of page 3 of our agenda for today. Can you share something from the data we've reviewed that might help us make decisions about accommodations or modifications we should consider?

Albert's father: Well, yeah! We know that he's staying in class and not going to guidance as much. Clearly, that's working.

Albert's teacher: I agree. Why do you think that's happening, Albert?

Albert: I guess it's because I don't feel so embarrassed every time you tell us to read or write. I'm glad that the other kids in my group are OK with using the Chromebook the way I do. They think the reading and writing programs are cool. They think we can use them because I'm in their group.

Albert's father: That's cheating! Are you kidding me?

Albert's teacher: Actually, it's not cheating. I know it's really different than when we were in school. Right now, all of the kids have Chromebooks, and they all have access to the word prediction and text-to-speech software that Albert's been learning about and using. I think some of the kids didn't know how to use it before, but all of the kids have always had it. Even colleges allow kids to use these programs to do their work. In fact, colleges in our state are required to use only texts and books that have a digital format so that any student can use software that makes access options available. This is really getting Albert and his friends more ready for college.

Albert's father: Wow. I guess I'll have to check that out. If it's true, Albert, you're actually helping the other kids out.

School psychologist: Exactly. You know, the guidance office can help you to connect with people at colleges to learn more about this. Would that be helpful?

Albert's father: No. I can figure it out. Thanks.

504 coordinator: So it sounds as if you're staying in the classroom more because the software is working in terms of reading and writing, Albert. Is that true?

Albert: Yes.

Albert's mother: The only reason Albert knows about the software and uses it is because he's gotten tutoring after school. I want to know if that's still going to be available for him now that he doesn't qualify for an IEP.

School psychologist: I'm so glad you said that! There are lots of misunderstandings about IEPs, and this is one of them. We actually offered the tutoring in the library after school because it's a support we offer to any student. Sometimes, it's hard to get kids to take advantage of it.

Albert's mother: Well, that's where we come in. Do you mean that he can keep getting this?

Albert: Oh, great. Now I have to keep going to tutoring even though I'm doing better?

Albert's father: You don't want to do better?

Albert's teacher: Albert, I'm relying on you. I know it means that you have to give up some after-school time, but you've really changed the dynamic in our ELA class. I know that this is happening in math too. Please, I hope you'll keep going to after-school tutoring and coming back to class to share what you learn about the Chromebooks. Other kids are listening to you and watching you—you have a lot more influence with them than I do!

Albert: Well, I guess I could do it for a while. The tutor mentioned some software for taking notes and putting in pictures or some way to get notes more understandable. I'm kind of interested in that for math and science.

504 coordinator: Great! It sounds as if we might agree about the tutoring and the software on the Chromebook. Tutoring is a support service, and the software is an accommodation. If everyone agrees, I can put this in the 504 plan as a way to document it. Let's see if we have consensus about this. Albert, we'll start with you. Let's say two hours of tutoring after school each week and software to support reading fluency,

	written output, and note-taking—we're saying this based on the data about your increased time in class and reduced time in guidance as well as the data from the classroom about written output and participation. On a scale of 1 to 5, with 1 being *Not at All Comfortable With This Decision* and 5 being *Very Comfortable With This Decision*, where are you?
Albert:	I want to know when the tutoring can stop, though.
Albert's father:	It stops when we say it stops.
504 coordinator:	Albert, it sounds like you're OK with this . . . do you think maybe a 3 or 4 on the scale? Can I ask people to go around and tell me what number represents your comfort with the plan if we can get clarity about how long to continue?
Albert:	I'm at 3, like you said.
Albert's father:	I'm good at a 4. Albert, I want you to do this, do you hear me?
Albert's mother:	Maybe we can think about some goals or some way to figure out how long tutoring should last. If we can do that, I'm at a 5.
Albert's teacher:	Let's think about this together. I really like the help, Albert, and I know it's a big sacrifice for you. I'm at a 5 if we can figure this out.
School psychologist:	I'm concerned that we come up with a plan that Albert supports. I think we can, so if we can work out the goals and duration for an initial trial period, I'm at a 4 if Albert is on board.
504 coordinator:	It sounds like we're at consensus. Thanks, everyone. Now, let's look back at the data and make sure we have a plan that answers all of our questions. I know we'll need to talk about the ways we monitor the effectiveness of the plan. That's the point at which we'll come up with specific data points to meet, and we can

tie one or more of these to the tutoring support so that we'll know how to decide together about ending the after-school tutoring. OK?

online resources

[Note-taker records these two agreements: one about the software and one about the tutoring, in the ***Visible Note-Taking Tool (Example)*** *available in Chapter 9 and on our companion website so everyone can see it before the team moves on.]*

You can see how this team used the agenda, the guiding questions, and the data to make decisions about Albert's 504 plan. You can see how note-taking and ensuring people have visual representations of questions, data, and decisions help to support trust and engagement. It's really important to note that the team will cycle back to another conversation about the third question, "How will we help each other to be sure that the adaptations we suggest are working to improve the fit between Albert and schooling?" in order to ensure that Albert's concern is addressed.

You can also see from this case study that the team uses the guiding questions from the "during-the-meeting" chart in a way that integrates with the questions from the agenda. It's not necessary to respond to each question individually. In Albert's case, the discussion about adaptations led to a conversation about accommodations and services. There was no need to discuss these questions from the agenda separately. In some meetings, it will be important to talk separately about accommodations, modifications, services, and removals from general education. In this case, it was not. What matters is that the team engaged in a discussion that was linked to the data, and the team made decisions that were compliant and collaborative. This is responsive teaming in action.

SUMMARY

Developing plans and determining placement involve not just compliance with regulations, but they also offer an opportunity for strengthening shared understanding and collaboration as a team. The purpose of planning and placement determination is for all members of the team to partner in making decisions about the supports and services a student needs to succeed at school. In order to accomplish this purpose, the team must have a shared understanding of the questions that guide team decisions and the data that is available to understand the fit between the student's profile and schooling; ultimately, the team must be able to come to consensus about the necessary decisions that result in a compliant plan and placement determination.

Guiding questions that can support teams in this process include the following:

- What are the changes we will see in the student's performance if adaptations work to create a better fit between the child and schooling?
- How will we measure these changes? What data will we collect, share, and review so that we are sure our plans are working?
- What are the needs of team members (student, family, educators, community providers) to keep this plan moving forward? How can we respond to one another in a way that builds trust and strengthens our partnership?
- What are the ways we're ensuring that this child experiences schooling in a way that does not separate them from other children or school experiences?

The team relies heavily on qualitative data in order to understand and create a plan that fits with the unique characteristics of the individual child in the unique context of their school and family culture. Responsive teams value the stories, perceptions, and experiences of the student along with data from home, school, and classroom settings in order to answer the guiding questions, develop a compliant plan that can be implemented at school, and decide where and how adaptations to schooling will be made.

In the end, 504 and IEP teams are charged with making different types of decisions, based on the differing requirements of state and federal regulations. Both 504 and IEP teams can engage in a responsive approach to planning and placement determination. By using protocols and tools to make questions, data, and decisions visible to all team members, 504 and IEP teams can meet procedural requirements in ways that strengthen relationships and respond to the needs of the student, the family, and the school.

CHAPTER SIX

After the Team Meeting

Implementing the Plan and Monitoring Progress

"There are some things in your messaging that you can control. Be persistent in your conversations.

It's OK to lead with, 'This is a legal document.' It's not OK to leave what is in an IEP undone.

You are fighting for the lives of children. It is that important."

—Marc Swygert, Principal

GUIDING QUESTIONS FOR THIS CHAPTER

- What are the critical considerations for responsive team members after planning is complete?
- What are the differences in monitoring "after the plan" activities for 504 teams and IEP teams?
- How can responsive team members approach "problems" by using questions that seek to understand different perspectives and embrace a mindset of inquiry?

Cultivating relationships among team members lies at the heart of responsive teaming. Responsive teams plan to initiate these relationships beginning with the referral (Chapter 3) and commit to nurturing these relationships after the eligibility meeting (Chapter 4). In the process of developing a plan and determining placement (Chapter 5), team members considered the key question, "How will we know the plan is working?" Team members collaborated to identify specific and measurable qualitative and quantitative criteria to answer this question. In so doing, all team members gain a vested interest in the success of the plan. What's at stake is nothing less than improving the fit between the child's learning profile and their schooling experience. Ultimately, "every child should have the chance to meet challenging objectives" (*Endrew F.*, 2017). A shared understanding of the criteria to gauge the success of the plan, as well as a shared understanding of the meaning of the data related to these criteria, is necessary during the process of reviews and reevaluations of IEPs and 504 plans, as well as during discussions of a change in eligibility (Chapter 8).

What happens after the planning and placement meeting can vary greatly, even if the meeting went well and team members left with clear understandings and agreements and feelings of connection. People can respond after the meeting with thoughts and feelings based on what happened at the meeting and their further reflection about what happened—for example, understanding or not understanding, remembering or not remembering accurately. People can also respond based on their feelings of confidence or anxiety. There is the very real possibility that one or more team members might feel lost or forgotten. There is the very real possibility that one or more team members left the meeting with a question or unresolved problem. There is the very real possibility that one or more team members are unsure of what will happen next. Responsive teams anticipate each of these possibilities with planful communication.

After the parents/caregivers accept the IEP or 504 plan, or portions of it, team members will collaborate in order to

- Implement the plan,
- Resolve any problems, and
- Monitor progress.

As you work to accomplish these three "to-do" items, remember that you are in an ongoing relationship with members of the team whom you don't see regularly. If you neglect this relationship, or relegate it to routine notes home and mass communication, your relationship with parents/caregivers will suffer. Parents/caregivers need a nurturing relationship. Even if school folks are always initiating the communication, and even if the parent/caregiver never initiates and/or never responds, regular and personal communication from the team liaison is necessary to nurture the relationship and the trust that began with the referral.

In the next section, we will look at specific strategies that can help all team members collaborate toward these purposes. It is this collaboration that nurtures and sustains responsive teaming.

STRATEGIES TO CONSIDER

After the meeting occurs, there are several ways to ensure that team members continue to communicate in a spirit of collaboration and trust. Figure 6.1 summarizes the types of strategies that you might use after 504 and IEP team meetings to sustain responsive teaming.

Figure 6.1 • Strategies to Use After Meetings

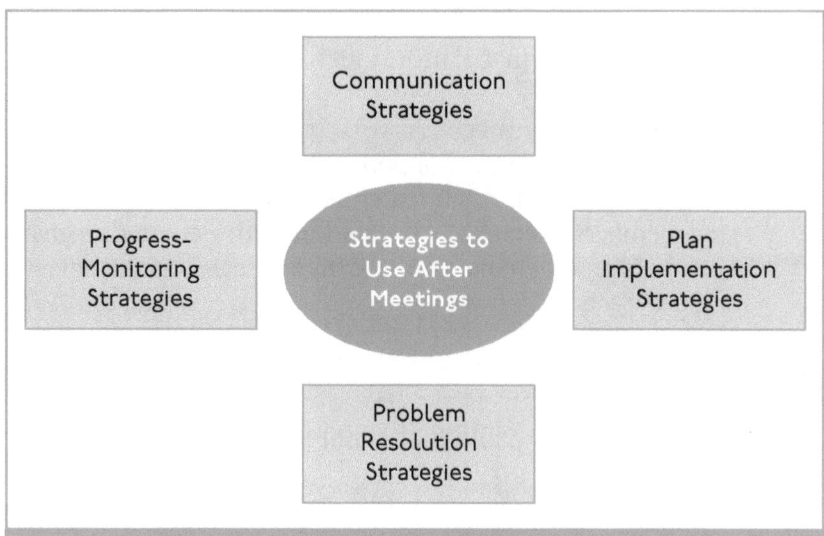

We've collected the following responsive practices from teams in the northeastern part of the United States to communicate, implement the plan, resolve problems, and monitor progress.

COMMUNICATION STRATEGIES

This section offers three kinds of considerations related to how team members communicate with one another. *Mode considerations* refer to oral versus written communication and various possible ways to engage a conversation. *Language considerations* describe nuances of language preference. *Time considerations* suggest that the details of when team members are available to send and receive oral communications matter. The section conclude with a table that connects mode, language, and time considerations.

Mode Considerations

Consider coupling oral and written communication. The repetition provides team members with multiple opportunities to receive and process information. Oral communication makes space for a conversation to clarify information (e.g., "What does this report mean?") and processes (e.g., "How can I be sure that my child is receiving the accommodations in his IEP?"). And by now, you know that we recommend oral communication to initiate and nurture relationships among all team members. In order to reach out for a conversation, you'll need to know if the team member prefers in-person communication, a phone call, or a virtual platform such as Zoom or Google Meet.

Providing parents/caregivers with the prior written notice (PWN) offers an excellent opportunity to couple oral and written communication. You'll remember that we recommend that team members initiate a conversation with parents/caregivers before and/or after a mandated written notice is sent. Table 6.1 compares Section 504 and IDEA regulations regarding the PWN.

TABLE 6.1 Prior Written Notice (PWN): Section 504 and IDEA Guidance

QUESTION ABOUT COMPLIANCE	SECTION 504 REGULATIONS	IDEA 2004 REGULATIONS
What does prior written notice require?	OCR guidance has interpreted Section 504 regulations as follows: *"45. What procedural safeguards are required under Section 504?* Recipient school districts are required to establish and implement procedural safeguards that include notice, an opportunity for parents to	(a) Notice. Written notice that meets the requirements of paragraph (b) of this section must be given to the parents of a child with a disability a reasonable time before the public agency— (I) Proposes to initiate or change the identification, evaluation, or educational placement of the child or the provision of FAPE to the child; or

QUESTION ABOUT COMPLIANCE	SECTION 504 REGULATIONS	IDEA 2004 REGULATIONS
	review relevant records, an impartial hearing with opportunity for participation by the student's parents or guardian, representation by counsel, and a review procedure. *46. What is a recipient school district's responsibility under Section 504 to provide information to parents and students about its evaluation and placement process?* Section 504 requires districts to provide notice to parents explaining any evaluation and placement decisions affecting their children and explaining the parents' right to review educational records and appeal any decision regarding evaluation and placement through an impartial hearing" (OCR, 2020).	(2) Refuses to initiate or change the identification, evaluation, or educational placement of the child or the provision of FAPE to the child. For additional details about the required content of these notices, see 34 C.F.R. 300.503. See also OSEP "Dear Colleague" letters about prior written notice at https://www2.ed.gov/policy/speced/guid/idea/letters/revpolicy/tppwnote.html.

Language Considerations

Each team member may use multiple heritage languages. Members of a responsive team know one another's preferred language for team communications. A student's preferred language may differ from their parent's/caregiver's preference. And the language preferred for written communication may differ from the language preferred for oral communication. We also need to acknowledge acronyms (e.g., OCR, FAPE, PWN) and "education speak" (e.g., "His F & P 'just right' level is J, so we're using Level K in guided reading groups") as language forms that can cloud meaning. We know that team members can often think, but rarely say, "I don't know what that means." The unaware and unintended impact of not understanding another team member's language can include embarrassment, feelings of inferiority, intimidation, and exclusion;

these, in turn, can provoke feelings of resentment and distrust. Responsive teams are mindful of using transparent language that includes everyone.

Time Considerations

Team members need to agree on the frequency of communication, keeping in mind the twin purposes of providing information and building relationships. Team members also need to know the days of the week and time of day when each team member is available to send and receive communication.

Table 6.2 summarizes our communication strategies. For each mode consideration, the table suggests actions related to language and time considerations.

TABLE 6.2 Mode, Language, and Time Considerations

MODE CONSIDERATION	ACTION (LANGUAGE AND TIME CONSIDERATIONS)
Transparent language matters in all modes of communication. It is particularly important in communication that occurs without visual contact because body language and other nonverbal cues will not be available to cue the speaker (or writer) to clarify the message.	Define acronyms so team members understand them when they encounter them elsewhere. Define "education speak" so team members understand it when they encounter it elsewhere.
The Visible Notes app (Google) is a tool to support shared understanding across modes of communication.	Create visual representations of a message, such as a step-by-step list, a bulleted list of key points, a timeline, a flowchart, or a photo, drawing, or other image. Record these visual representations in commonly and remotely accessible tools, such as Google Docs, Google Sheets, or Jamboard.
Coupled oral and written communication	Initiate oral communication before and/or after the written message arrives. Send a written message after an oral communication.

MODE CONSIDERATION	ACTION (LANGUAGE AND TIME CONSIDERATIONS)
Face-to-face communication	Record the locations, days, and times when team members are available. Note "drop-in" or by-appointment availability and how to make an appointment for in-person or remote meetings, including virtual "office hours." Note the preferred language for oral communication and the need for an interpreter.
Phone communication	Record the phone numbers, days, and times when team members are available in a **Communication Preferences Chart.** Note "just call" or by-appointment availability and how to make an appointment. Note the preferred language for oral communication and the need for an interpreter. Keep a **Home-School Contact Log,** particularly for communication between parents and school. All team members should have a log of all communication. These tools are linked in Chapter 9 and are available on our companion website. online resources
Virtual communication (e.g., Zoom, Google Meet)	Record the platforms, days, and times when team members are available. Note impromptu or by-appointment availability and how to make an appointment. Note the preferred language for oral communication and the need for an interpreter.
Written communication	Note preference for hard-copy or email communication. Record email addresses, if applicable, and send an email message to follow up a hard-copy communication. Note the preferred language for written communication and the need for a translation.

With a commitment to communication to maintain relationships among team members, the next section considers multiple dimensions of what is required to implement a plan with fidelity.

PLAN IMPLEMENTATION STRATEGIES

This section highlights key comparisons between 504 teams and IEP teams related to implementing the plan. We offer strategies to engage the student and parents/caregivers in implementing the plan, as well as strategies to support educators and parents/caregivers who will implement the plan. Finally, we suggest questions, data, and decisions to help teams and other educators implement a plan with fidelity.

We described in Chapter 5 the process of developing an IEP or 504 plan and determining placement. In an IEP plan, placement could include both general education and special education settings; in a 504 plan, placement typically refers to accommodations, modifications, and services to support successful participation in the schooling. It also happens that a 504 plan can specify removals from general education to meet a particular learning need:

> [S]chool districts must place students with disabilities in the regular education environment unless the school district demonstrates that educating the student with a disability in the regular education environment with the use of supplementary aids and services cannot be achieved satisfactorily. In implementing the decision of a group of knowledgeable persons to place a student in a setting other than the regular educational environment, the school must take into account the proximity of the alternate setting to the student's home (34 C.F.R. 104.34(a), cited in Office for Civil Rights, 2016, p. 24).

Table 6.3 compares Section 504 and IDEA regulations regarding plan implementation.

TABLE 6.3 Questions for Implementing a Plan

QUESTIONS	SECTION 504 TEAMS	IEP TEAMS
Is a written plan required?	"Though not explicitly required by the Department's Section 504 regulations, school districts often document the elements of an individual student's FAPE	IDEA requires a written plan that includes specific elements outlined in 34 C.F.R. 300.320.

QUESTIONS	SECTION 504 TEAMS	IEP TEAMS
	under Section 504 in a document, typically referred to as a *Section 504 Plan*" (OCR, 2016, p. 10, italics in original).	
How is implementation supported and documented?	In general, a Section 504 plan describes the general or special education and related aids and services a student needs and the appropriate setting in which to receive those services. "A written Section 504 plan is often a useful way to document that the school district engaged in a process to identify and address the needs of a student with a disability and to communicate, to school personnel, the information needed for successful implementation. OCR encourages schools to document a student's Section 504 services in a written plan to help avoid misunderstandings or confusion about what Section 504 services the school offered the student" (OCR, 2016, p. 10).	Decisions about the content of the plan are made by the IEP team. The IEP team must include members as described in 34 C.F.R. 300.321. Guidance regarding the development, review, and revision of IEPs is specified in 34 C.F.R. 300.324.

Note three key differences in implementing IDEA and Section 504:

- *Requirements for a written plan:* A Section 504 plan is not required. IDEA provides many requirements related to the written IEP regarding what is documented and how the documentation is accomplished.
- *Regulatory oversight:* Section 504 is a federal provision that delegates implementation to any public institution that receives federal dollars. Compliance monitoring typically occurs in response to a complaint made to the federal Office for Civil Rights (OCR), and this monitoring may include extensive hearings. IDEA is a federal provision that delegates implementation to the states, so public schools are accountable to their state departments of education for compliance.

- *Relationships to support implementation:* Because each public school has a relationship with the OCR, members of a 504 team can contact this office to ask questions and receive other support to implement Section 504 requirements. IEP team members have relationships with their state departments of education to ask questions and receive other support to implement an IEP.

We recommend a written Section 504 plan. Written plans to provide a student's FAPE support a shared understanding of the elements of a student's educational program and can promote buy-in from all team members to implement the plan. Though not required prior to implementation, getting signatures for a Section 504 plan emphasizes the official agreement. The signatures on an IEP indicate the provisions that are accepted by all parties as a legal contract. Table 6.4 contrasts frequent and responsive approaches to getting signatures.

TABLE 6.4 Getting Signatures: Frequent Versus Responsive Approaches

PRACTICE	FREQUENT APPROACH	RESPONSIVE APPROACH
Getting signatures	Documents are signed at the team meeting or sent by mail or electronic means for signature.	A "student-friendly" summary of the IEP or 504 plan and related documents (such as the procedural safeguards) is prepared and offered to supplement the IEP legal contract or the 504 plan that is signed by the district and the student/parent/caregiver. One or more representatives of the district review documents after the meeting with the student and parents/caregivers. Signatures are provided after the review of the final document and after any questions by either party are addressed and any problems are resolved (see **Signed/Unsigned Documents Tracker**). This tool is linked in Chapter 9 and is available on our companion website. online resources

Note that initial consent must be given before the IEP can be implemented. While signatures may or may not be required at regular intervals in your local jurisdiction, it is important, before services begin, to ensure that parents and caregivers know and understand the services that are being proposed and how these services will be delivered. When parents and caregivers have misunderstandings about these aspects of the educational program, the ability of the team to partner in support of the child is compromised. We recommend a review of the plan and a clear, documented understanding about parental agreement, whether this is required or not in your jurisdiction.

We also recommend that a 504 team create a written plan and that the parent/caregiver sign it, though this signature is not required prior to implementation. We suggest a "student-friendly" summary of the documents that the student needs to understand to participate in their educational program as an engaged stakeholder. Beginning with the referral for an IEP or 504 evaluation, we have recommended personalized communication to begin to seed trust and build relationships with the student and their parents/caregivers. This communication is especially important after the planning and placement meeting because team members can experience new thoughts and feelings, as we observed earlier.

In the third section of this chapter, "Problem Resolution Strategies," we will consider actions that the district and the parent/caregiver can take when an issue remains unresolved.

Now we will consider plan implementation strategies. Before we turn our attention to implementing the plan, let's take stock of what the responsive team has accomplished so far. The team has built a profile of the learner that identifies strengths/assets and current needs. The team has identified what in the learner's current experience is not working—that is, where the fit between the learner's profile and the current experience of schooling is not creating the conditions for a FAPE. Team members have collaborated to describe, as specifically as possible, what a successful schooling experience for this learner will look like, sound like, and feel like for the learner, educators, and parents/caregivers. We offered the **Tool for Responsive Teaming: Organizing Data** (mentioned in Chapter 5, linked in Chapter 9 and available on our companion website) to help team members do this work. Finally, the team collaborated to make thoughtful, data-driven decisions to develop the IEP or 504 plan and determine placement.

online resources

Implementing the plan begins when the signed documents are received in the district. High-quality implementation requires *engagement of team members* and *support of team members and others* who will implement the plan. Figure 6.2 illustrates these two groups of strategies.

Figure 6.2 • Strategies for Implementing the Plan

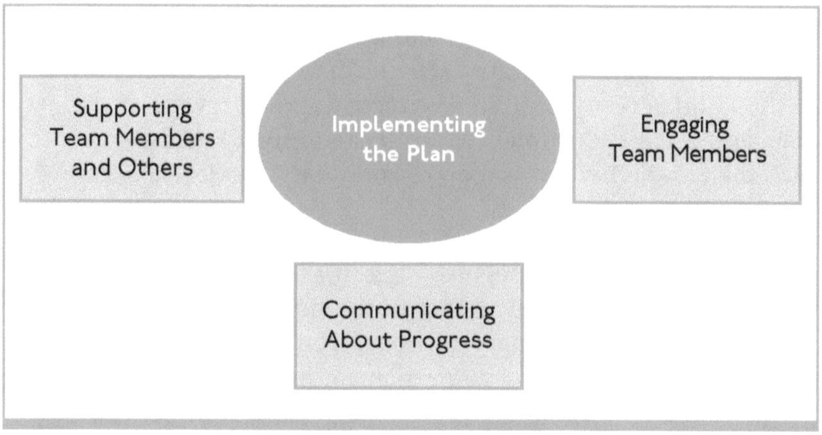

Engaging Team Members

- *Communication, communication, communication.* By now, you know that communication is a cornerstone of responsive practice. We have proposed the importance of intentional and systematic communication, beginning with the referral (Chapter 3) and continuing through evaluation and eligibility determination (Chapter 4) and the team meeting to develop the plan and determine placement (Chapter 5). We began this chapter on what happens after the team meeting with consideration of communication strategies (Figure 6.1). Communication maintains an experience of connectedness by showing care and concern, providing information, and responding to questions in a timely fashion and with empathy. Communication after the team meeting reminds everyone who is connected to a learner that they are not alone or forgotten and that the team continues to support the student's progress.
- *Engage the student.* Responsive teams engage the student as much as is developmentally appropriate, beginning with the referral. We suggested in Table 6.4 that the student receive a "student-friendly" summary to supplement the IEP or 504 plan and related legal documents. We also suggest that the team chair confer with the parent/caregiver to determine who will review the plan with the student so that the team can ensure that the student has a complete understanding of the plan. This decision made

collaboratively with the parent/caregiver is an important first step in engaging them in implementing the plan.

- *Engage the parents/caregivers.* The inclusion of parents as decision-makers in their children's school experience is a fundamental component of IDEA, and "[meaningful] collaboration between school personnel and a student's parents throughout the IEP process" is "vigorously protected by the courts" (Peabody College, 2021a). What forms can meaningful collaboration take?
  - Exchanging information: Using the communication strategies identified in Table 6.2, we propose communication initiated by team members or parents/caregivers to share this information:
    - Success in the student's learning or improvement in the fit between the student's learning profile and the schooling experience
    - New insight regarding the student's learning profile
  - Collaborating regarding the following:
    - Problem or barrier in implementation—and brainstorming solutions
    - Change, proposed or required by unforeseen circumstances, to the student's IEP
  - Co-training with educators to understand and/or implement an accommodation, modification, or service, particularly if implementation occurs at school and at home; co-training topics can include "special education, communication, collaboration, positive behavioral interventions, or other topics" (Technical Assistance ALLIANCE for Parent Centers, 2008, p. 5).
  - Monitoring the fidelity of plan implementation:
    - Identifying criteria and data
    - Participating in out-of-school data collection
  - Monitoring and reporting the student's progress:
    - Building a shared understanding of how educators will monitor and report progress
    - Monitoring and reporting out-of-school progress

Implementing the plan also requires intentional and sustained support of the educators who will be responsible for implementing the plan. Often, plans are not implemented as written because educators are not aware of the plan.

Albert was a high school Spanish teacher when he taught Tamara for about four weeks before learning about her IEP. Albert discovered the plan not because he was told about it, but because he was noticing Tamara's very significant written language difficulties that contrasted sharply with her oral language proficiency, which was developing satisfactorily. Wondering if Tamara might have a learning disability, Albert approached the school's special education coordinator to ask about the process for referring a student suspected of a learning disability. When he learned that Tamara was learning on an IEP, Albert reviewed the full document and copied the list of accommodations that he needed to implement to support Tamara's written expression.

While Albert and several of Tamara's other teachers understood the accommodations and were able to provide them to Tamara, he learned at a team meeting requested by Tamara's mother that these accommodations were being implemented unevenly in Tamara's other classes. To their credit, several teachers candidly acknowledged that they were not implementing certain accommodations because they did not understand them (e.g., sentence frames, note-taking scaffold) or because they did not know how to implement them (e.g., oral testing).

This illustration shows that all of a student's teachers need to be given the plan, *and they need to be supported to implement it* within their particular courses. Teachers' access to adequate support is particularly important in general education classrooms in which there can be many students who are learning with individualized adaptations or goals.

Supporting Team Members and Others Who Will Implement the Plan

- *Ensure access to the IEP or 504 plan and understanding of its implementation.* IEPs should be shared in hard copy or electronically with everyone who is responsible to provide services. When access doesn't occur, or is delayed, the student is denied adequate opportunity to learn; parents/caregivers lose trust in the district, school, or particular educators; and educators are left without the information and tools that the team has determined are necessary to support the student's learning. We offer **Ensuring Access**

to the IEP or 504 Plan and Understanding Its Implementation as a tool to document access to the student's plan as well as a shared understanding of responsibilities for plan implementation. This tool is linked in Chapter 9 and is available on our companion website.

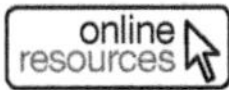

- *Ensure understanding of responsibilities for plan implementation.* Access alone is not enough to guarantee that an IEP or 504 plan is implemented with fidelity. Educators and parents/caregivers must understand the responsibilities for implementation related to their roles and settings. We recommend oral communication (in-person, phone, or other virtual platform) to build a shared understanding of the elements of implementation; providing accommodations, modifications, specialized instruction, or other services, and the settings in which these are provided; and collecting and reporting progress-monitoring data. Note that the tool provided in the previous paragraph can be used both to document access to the plan and also to ensure a shared understanding of implementation.

Now that the team has ensured access to the IEP or 504 plan and has verified that everyone who is involved in implementing the plan understands their roles and responsibilities, the task is to ensure that the plan is implemented with fidelity. The essential purpose of an IEP is to enable the student to "meet challenging objectives" (*Endrew F.*, 2017). The essential purpose of a 504 plan is to enable access to a FAPE so that "the individual educational needs of the handicapped student [are] being met as adequately as the needs of nonhandicapped students are met in academic and nonacademic settings" (34 C.F.R. 104.33). This means that there are educational outcomes expected for a student protected under Section 504, and these outcomes are indexed to the outcomes established for "nonhandicapped" students in the same school (Kowalski et al., 2005; Spiel et al., 2014).

To meet these purposes, the plan must be implemented with fidelity, meaning "the extent to which the services and supports outlined in [the plan] are correctly and fully implemented" (Peabody College, 2021b). Table 6.5 suggests questions, related data, and decisions regarding implementation with fidelity.

TABLE 6.5 Questions-Data-Decisions: Implementing the Plan With Fidelity

QUESTIONS	DATA	DECISIONS
Is everyone involved in implementing the plan fulfilling their responsibilities? Are accommodations, modifications, and services implemented in the settings and with the frequency (e.g., 3x/week), duration (e.g., 30 min.), and longevity (e.g., year-round) prescribed in the plan?	Access to the plan and understanding of its implementation as suggested in the tool **Ensuring Access to the IEP or 504 Plan and Understanding Its Implementation** Use **Implementing the IEP or 504 Plan With Fidelity** as a tool to collect: • "Spot check" observations of implementation • Interviews with the student to gauge their understanding of the accommodations, modifications, and services in the plan Review of documented service delivery, as in the **Provider Service Delivery Log** Student work samples that should evidence the supports prescribed in the plan if the supports are being implemented, as suggested in the tool **Work Sample Cover Sheet** *Note:* Tools listed in this column are linked in Chapter 9 and are available on our companion website. online resources	Commend individuals involved in implementing the plan and/or intervene as needed. Intervene as needed based on the reason(s) for partial implementation (e.g., insufficient time, materials, staffing, facilities, and/or readiness to implement the prescribed supports).
How often and by whom will data related to implementation fidelity be collected and analyzed?	Members of the IEP or 504 team Frequency of data collection and analysis that is viable and meaningful	Determine how often implementation data will be collected (e.g., within 4–6 weeks of the implementation date and periodically thereafter). Determine who will collect and analyze the data.
Who will respond to implementation fidelity and how?	Members of the IEP or 504 team School-based administrators Analysis of implementation fidelity data	Commend implementation with fidelity and/or address problems or barriers in implementation. Identify the individual(s) who will respond as suggested earlier.

We realize that the questions and related data collection in this table can overwhelm. Implementing a plan with fidelity and monitoring implementation are a lot. If your school or district is new to the work of monitoring implementation with fidelity, we recommend that you start by ensuring that all of a student's providers have access to the plan and understand how to implement it within their particular courses and settings. This *access* and *understanding* will go a long way to making sure that the student's plan is implemented as written. The first tool provided in Table 6.5, **Ensuring Access to the IEP or 504 Plan and Understanding Its Implementation**, will help you get started. This tool is linked in Chapter 9 and is available on our companion website.

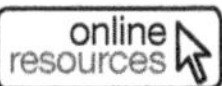

Thus far in this chapter, we suggested strategies to *engage* the student and parents/caregivers in implementing the plan, as well as strategies to *support* educators and parents/caregivers who will implement the plan. We also suggested questions, data, and decisions to help teams and other educators implement a plan with fidelity. Full engagement and optimal support to implement a plan with fidelity means that you will need to confront and resolve problems as they arise throughout the IEP or 504 process.

Communicating About Progress

In this section, we are not referring to progress-monitoring activities as much as making ongoing communication between team members a priority. We'll refer to progress-monitoring strategies later in this chapter.

One of the most important aspects of implementing plans is communication about how the plan is working to support the student's progress in school. When you think about the processes involved in identifying students with disabilities under Section 504 or under IDEA, it's easy to see that these are students for whom a team of people has determined that individualized approaches are necessary to support success in school. People have expressed concern about the fit between the student's profile as a learner and schooling. The way the team communicates with each other after a plan is in place may be more important for building trust and support than the work of planning together.

What everyone wants to know is, "Does this plan actually work?" In order to answer that question, team members need to communicate in an ongoing and focused way. Because a child with a disability is likely a child who has faced barriers to school success, it is also likely that there are adults who are keeping a close eye on what happens after a 504 or IEP team has convened. It's critical that the team have a shared knowledge and conversation about specific changes in outcomes for the child that the plan should support. For students with IEPs, this happens when measurable IEP goals are developed by the team. Section 504 of the Rehabilitation Act does not require the development of goals as part of the 504 process; however, we are recommending that responsive teams do well when there is discussion about how the success of the plan will be measured using readily available and reliable data. The reason for this is to anticipate and avoid discrepant claims about whether the plan is working. These are the types of claims that can lead to due process, which we will discuss later in this chapter.

In effect, responsive teams must think and act about not only the legal requirements for planning but also the interpersonal and social-emotional aspects of partnering to implement the plan. This means thinking beyond what is legally mandated and acting in ways that consider the needs of the adults who support the student with a disability. Current research has a great deal to offer about how teams can strengthen trust and build relationships. While this research is not focused specifically on the IEP or 504 team process, the findings apply to all teams of adults and can easily be generalized to the IEP or 504 team context:

- *Focus on achieving student outcomes together.* In a recent article by Gomes and McVilly (2019), the top-rated indicator for effective teams in disability services is the ability to focus on achieving outcomes together. In order to do this, outcomes must be discussed and clearly defined by the team. This may be an ongoing conversation, especially if the initial plan did not include goals (as with most 504 plans) or the goals need additional refinement to describe specific changes in the student or in the data that is collected to monitor progress so that members understand and agree what indicates progress.
- *Link decisions and discussions to multiple sources of data.* When talking about student successes and challenges, team members should always link conversations and claims to data. The data could be qualitative (e.g., an observation of an interaction between the student and

teacher), or it could be quantitative (e.g., the number of homework assignments submitted on or before the due date). The data that is collected to monitor progress must be understandable and regularly shared with all members of the team. Only if data is routinely available can *all* team members focus on achieving student outcomes together (Boscardin, 2007). Progress monitoring should be "frequent enough to provide the IEP team with meaningful data" and should "monitor academic and behavioral goals" (Etscheidt, 2006).

- *Prioritize excellent communication.* Because teams are dispersed and may not have regular contact, it is important to prioritize communication about student successes and challenges in relation to the outcomes that matter most (Gomes & McVilly, 2019). Sharing information in real time as much as possible (e.g., on the same day, within the same week) and including information about positive occurrences and setbacks that are connected to the identified outcomes are critical actions for building an effective team.

We also know that most disputes and concerns about children with disabilities arise after the evaluation and planning processes are complete. This is when a teacher, a parent, a student, or an administrator may observe the student's academic or behavioral performance and wonder whether the plan is working or not. Because the team may not be meeting regularly after the plan has been developed, there may be limited opportunities for the team to address these claims proactively or in person. This can lead to a reactive approach to communicating about progress, in which team members only talk when a student is at risk of failing or when other serious breaches, such as violations of the code of conduct, occur. This may be one of the most frequent practices that we see in schools, and it is one that we believe 504 and IEP team members can change.

Here are some strategies that you may want to consider to support proactive, ongoing communication about progress:

- *Identify specific, observable changes to monitor.* Whether you're on a 504 team or an IEP team, reach out to share information about the top one or two observable changes in the student you care most about. These may be included in a plan or not; but if all team members know what matters most to one another, this will provide a focus for communicating student successes and needs while also considering the needs and concerns of each team member. One tool that can be used to gather and share this information is a Jamboard. (see **Jamboard for Celebrating Progress**). You can link photos and comments to the Jamboard, and it can also be printed and shared for team members who prefer this method of communicating. A student may also want to contribute to this Jamboard to participate in sharing successes and challenges. This tool is linked in Chapter 9 and is available on our companion website.

online resources

- *Encourage communication from students.* Making time to sit with a student so that the student can share data and supplement information sharing with their own account is a powerful way to ensure that communication happens among all team members. This builds student self-determination skills and also strengthens the connections among team members. There are many ways to accomplish this on a daily or weekly basis. Having students text directly is a way to increase student awareness of successes and also empower students to share accurate information with others about difficulties. If you use this method, you can ask the student to send the text to the email addresses of team members from the school, or you can ask the student to copy and paste the text into an email. This is a good "exit ticket" or end-of-the-day check-in strategy. Students should be supported to connect their information to specific data points from different classes or situations that occurred during the day. If a student is too young to text or email, consider a "My Daily Review" (or "My Weekly Review") one-page collage, drawing, or short (one word, one phrase, or one sentence) report in relation to the priority outcomes identified by the team. Educators can take pictures of these products and send them along to the team after the student has created them. Educators can also partner with students to ensure that information is accurate and includes important insights and data from adults.
- *Create video notes.* These can come from teachers or from teachers and students together. Basically, a video note is a video that is under three minutes in length and that shares nonconfidential information related to outcomes. If you include a student in the video, you will need prior permission from the parent to videotape the student. If a teacher creates a video note, the focus should be only on the identified outcomes and on showing or telling one or two specific examples from the day or the week that speak

to the student's progress in relation to the team's priorities. This is *not* a progress report but, rather, a brief snapshot to capture one or two data points. The video can be placed in a protected folder and shared, or it could be attached to an electronic system to which team members have access. Video is a time-efficient and powerful tool when used well. Be sure to check with your building administrator and all team members before using this tool as there may be local guidance about when and how video is permissible. One additional possibility is to schedule a short video conference (limited to five minutes) with the team on a regular basis. This is not a team meeting, but an opportunity for those who choose to attend to communicate about progress. If you choose this option, be sure to have an agenda and a visual timer, and take care to remind team members of the importance of holding to a prompt start and end time.

PROBLEM RESOLUTION STRATEGIES

In spite of the responsive team's efforts toward strong collaboration and communication during the planning and placement process, disagreements and misunderstandings will arise. Different perspectives regarding the problem(s) to be addressed in the IEP or 504 plan and the effective solutions will persist. These differences become *problems* when they interfere with the team's ability to design and implement a plan that all team members believe will improve the fit between the student and schooling. We consider a problem to be resolved when team members perceive the decisions and actions to be "win-win" solutions that work for everyone (e.g., Fisher et al., 1991).

We distinguish between *problems* and *questions*. Problems refer to a present situation that needs to be resolved now. Solving a problem is urgent. Some questions refer to implementation: the *who, what, when,* or *how* of an accommodation, modification, or service. Other questions seek to understand a circumstance in ways that go beyond our current understanding; these questions cannot be answered (e.g., "What will happen to my child (who needs daily care) when I die?"). The present-moment response to a question that does not have an answer could be compassion and empathetic listening. Some questions about a circumstance should not be asked—"Did that child bring a gun to school because Dad is a member of the NRA?" or "Did that student bring 'pot' to school because his parents use it at home?" These are not questions to be asked; rather, they are questions to be expressed in ways that honor an intention for compassionate conversation searching for understanding and relationship.

This section considers research and strategies to help responsive teams resolve problems in the design and implementation of a plan. We also consider dispute resolution and due process procedures for problems that resist initial resolution efforts.

RESEARCH TO CONSIDER

Research in conflict and problem resolution points to several strategies that we will recommend for IEP and 504 team processes.

- *Communication:* Effective communication relies on trust. Beginning with the referral, responsive team members have worked to cultivate trust. Hammond (2015) identifies five "trust generators" that can be applied to teams: selective vulnerability, familiarity, similarity of interests, concern, and competence (p. 79). Effective listening and speaking skills build relationships and shared meaning, as well as overcome barriers to connection and shared understanding (University of Waterloo, n.d.).
- *Negotiation strategies:* More than 40 years of research in the principles and strategies of negotiation have yielded clear guidance for members of responsive IEP and 504 teams.
    - *Focus on relationships.* Separate the person from the problem because the person is not the problem (Fisher et al., 1991; Mind Tools Content Team, n.d.). Responsive team members have worked hard to build relationships with one another beginning with the initial referral. Through these relationships, team members can see that everyone holds a shared interest in supporting the student's access to the general education program and progress in achieving "challenging objectives" (*Endrew F.*, 2017). When this shared interest remains at the center of efforts to resolve a problem, possible solutions can appear more easily.
    - *Focus on interests, not positions.* Negotiating from a position (e.g., "I want this student to receive one-to-one instruction with the school's reading specialist at least three days per week") can narrow negotiation space and lead to impasse. Negotiating from an interest (e.g., "I want this student to learn to read with grade-level independence") can widen options for problem resolution as multiple alternatives to satisfy the interest are identified (Fisher et al., 1991; Program on Negotiation, 2019).

   - *Come prepared.* We have acknowledged that team members will come to the table with claims about the problems in the current fit between the student and their experience of schooling and what is needed to resolve these problems in order to improve this fit. We have encouraged team members to come prepared with data to support these claims. When an interest is supported by data, team members are more likely to understand and share it (Program on Negotiation, 2019).

- *Consensus-building techniques:* Consensus building, also known as "collaborative problem solving," is a conflict-resolution process widely used to respond to complex interests in multi-stakeholder disputes (Burgess & Spangler, 2003). Consensus building requires a clear definition of success at the outset and typically involves essential stages: defining the problem, convening and naming a facilitator or mediator, designing the process (e.g., determining ground rules, setting the agenda, joint fact finding), identifying "win-win" solutions (e.g., brainstorming), and decision-making and implementation (Burgess & Spangler, 2003; University of Colorado, 2015).

- *Facilitated IEP meetings:* The facilitated IEP meeting (FIEP) is a process developed by the Region 13 Education Service Center in Austin, Texas. It uses a consensus-building approach to developing the plan and determining placement (Chapter 5). We referred you to an excellent website developed by the Region 13 ESC (https://esc13.net/resources/a-facilitated-iep-meeting). If you review this resource, you'll find a 35-minute video as well as specific tools to support consensus-based decision-making. And you'll notice that consensus is described as a continuum. We know that people can "get behind" a decision with various degrees of enthusiasm; several team members might fully support a decision while others have concerns. Mueller and Vick (2019b) found that interviews with parents, advocates, educators, and facilitators "identified the FIEP as a promising collaborative practice . . . to prevent and resolve conflict [by] encouraging active parent participation through consensus building and maintaining the focus on the student" (p. 99).

STRATEGIES TO CONSIDER

- *Confirm and explore unresolved problems.* In Chapter 5, we described the processes of developing the plan and determining placement, and we acknowledged that team members may raise questions or problems that are not resolved in the initial planning and placement meeting. We suggested that teams not let problems linger unresolved. We urged team members to resolve problems as quickly as possible, and we offered a tool to help teams start on

(Continued)

(Continued)

the path to solutions: **Exploring Unresolved Problems Tool**. This tool is linked in Chapter 9 and is available on our companion website. online resources

- *Continue to nurture relationships.* Team members have been building relationships since the initial referral. Cultivating relationships takes time and needs ongoing nurture. Consider using Zaretta Hammond's "trust generators" to cultivate trust in an intentional way. Consider common barriers and effective strategies for listening and speaking from the University of Waterloo's Centre for Teaching Excellence (https://uwaterloo.ca/centre-for-teaching-excellence/teaching-resources/teaching-tips/communicating-students/telling/effective-communication-barriers-and-strategies) to interact with team members in more satisfying ways.
- *Negotiate.* Research suggests three strategies: (1) focus on relationships, (2) focus on interests versus positions, and (3) come prepared with data to corroborate claims about the problems the student is experiencing in the current fit between their learning profile and schooling, with ideas for supports that will improve this fit. We recommended the use of visible notes in the planning and placement meeting (Chapter 5) and offered a **Visible Note-Taking Tool (Example)** to ensure that information is visible and aligned in our "question–data–decision" model for all members of the team. We invite you to use visible notes in any negotiation process activity, such as brainstorming. This tool is linked in Chapter 9 and is available on our companion website. online resources
- *Engage consensus-building processes.* Consensus building seeks "win-win" solutions that satisfy the interests (not the positions) of all team members. A thoughtful process begins with defining what success will look like. Additional essential steps, as described in a model from Beyond Intractability (www.beyondintractability.org), include defining the problem, convening and naming a facilitator or mediator, designing the process (e.g., determining ground rules, setting the agenda, joint fact finding), identifying "win-win" solutions (e.g., brainstorming), and decision-making and implementation. You may also find the consensus-building techniques from the University of Colorado helpful.
- *Engage dispute resolution processes.* A continuum of dispute resolution processes is available to help team members resolve a thus-far intractable dispute. The Center for Appropriate Dispute Resolution in Special Education (CADRE) offers the "Quick Guide to Special Education Dispute Resolution Processes for Parents of Children & Youth (Ages 3-21)." One of these processes is the facilitated IEP meeting (FIEP), which we introduced in Chapter 5. We offered a resource to illustrate a FIEP's consensus-building processes, developed by the Region 13 Education Service Center in Austin, Texas, and available at https://esc13.net/resources/a-facilitated-iep-meeting.

If a problem remains unresolved and becomes a dispute, team members may engage due process procedures. Due process becomes necessary when a problem cannot be solved through alternative means, and we encourage team members to use it so that the problem does not persist. Table 6.6 compares Section 504 and IDEA due process provisions.

TABLE 6.6 Comparison of 504 and IEP Due Process Provisions

QUESTIONS	SECTION 504 TEAMS	IEP TEAMS
What can a district do if parents/ guardians refuse consent?	"If a parent refuses consent for an initial evaluation and a recipient school district suspects a student has a disability, the IDEA and Section 504 provide that school districts may use due process hearing procedures to seek to override the parents' denial of consent" (see Question 26 of OCR, 2020).	(3) A public agency may not use a parent's refusal to consent to one service or activity under paragraphs (a), (b), (c), or (d)(2) of this section to deny the parent or child any other service, benefit, or activity of the public agency, except as required by this part. (4)(i) If a parent of a child who is homeschooled or placed in a private school by the parents at their own expense does not provide consent for the initial evaluation or the reevaluation, or the parent fails to respond to a request to provide consent, the public agency may not use the consent override procedures (described in paragraphs (a)(3) and (c)(1) of this section); and (4)(ii) The public agency is not required to consider the child as eligible for services under §§300.132 through 300.144. (5) To meet the reasonable efforts requirement in paragraphs (a)(1)(iii), (a)(2)(i), (b)(2), and (c)(2)(i) of this section, the public agency must document its attempts to obtain parental consent using the procedures in §300.322(d). 34 C.F.R. 300.300(d)(3)–(5)
Under what conditions may a parent/ team member request a due process hearing?	Parents can pursue due process resolution if they are not in agreement with a 504 team eligibility determination (OCR, 2016, Question 27).	The IDEA's due process hearing right applies to "any matter relating to the identification, evaluation or educational placement of the child, or the provision of a free appropriate public education to such child" (20 U.S.C. §1415(b)(6)) and certain disciplinary matters (20 U.S.C. §1415(f)(1)). Other than the notice provisions expressly contained in the IDEA, no other notice provisions can be applied to limit the statutory right to a due process hearing" (IDEA, 2017).

(Continued)

(Continued)

QUESTIONS	SECTION 504 TEAMS	IEP TEAMS
What are the requirements and options if a parent/ team member disagrees with the district's decision?	The Office for Civil Rights addresses two specific circumstances in their FAQ regarding disagreements between 504 team members (typically the district and the parent): 26. *What should a recipient school district do if a parent refuses to consent to an initial evaluation under the Individuals with Disabilities Education Act (IDEA), but demands a Section 504 plan for a student without further evaluation?* A school district must evaluate a student prior to providing services under Section 504. Section 504 requires informed parental permission for initial evaluations. If a parent refuses consent for an initial evaluation and a recipient school district suspects a student has a disability, the IDEA and Section 504 provide that school districts may use due process hearing procedures to seek to override the parents' denial of consent. 31. *A student is receiving services that the school district maintains are necessary under Section 504 in order to provide the student with an appropriate education. The student's parent no longer wants the student to receive those services. If the parent wishes to withdraw the student from a Section 504 plan, what can the school district do to ensure continuation of services?* The school district may initiate a Section 504 due process hearing to resolve the dispute if the district believes the student needs the services in order to receive an appropriate education (U.S. Department of Education OCR, 2020).	The IEP is a legal contract between the district and the student/ parents/guardians. Prior written notice is required before any changes to the IEP occur. Distribution of notices of procedural safeguards to parents/guardians is also required annually. When one party disagrees with the decisions of another party regarding required consent or the elements of the contract, due process resolution options are available. Before exercising due process resolution, notice of the details of the complaint must be shared in writing with both parties. Due process resolution options include these: • Mediation • Impartial hearing • Appeals • Civil action 20 U.S.C. 1415

How do responsive teams approach due process? While team members might resist the prospect of a due process hearing, we invite responsive teams to view due process as a resource. Due process is an important tool to resolve a problem as quickly as possible after the team has tried unsuccessfully to achieve a resolution. Due process is neither the first problem-solving step nor a step to be avoided if it becomes necessary. It is important for responsive team members to remember that the team will continue to partner long after a due process resolution because responsive teams prioritize and preserve the long-term relationship even if they need third-party assistance to come to agreement. We suggest that it is a mistake to understand due process as a threat or to use the potential need for due process to threaten or intimidate other team members.

When team members developed the IEP or 504 plan and determined placement (Chapter 5), they posed the question, "How will we know the plan is working?" The team answered this question by specifying the measurable changes that would indicate an improved fit between the student and the schooling experience. These measurable changes, in turn, guided the team to identify the data points that would be accepted as evidence of the student's improved access to, and progress in, the general education program. Now, it is time to monitor the student's progress.

PROGRESS-MONITORING STRATEGIES

This section provides the requirements of Section 504 and IDEA regarding progress monitoring. It highlights research related to key aspects of progress monitoring and compares frequent and responsive approaches. The strategies we offer translate the research to practice and illustrate a responsive team's approaches.

As noted earlier, the team's purpose in designing and implementing a learning plan is to support the student's access to the general education program and progress in achieving "challenging objectives" (*Endrew F.,* 2017). In an IEP, these challenging objectives are stated as goals with corresponding objectives. We know that 504 plans are not required to include goals, and we do not recommend adding goals to

504 plans. So in a 504 plan, *goals* are usefully interpreted as *outcomes*. A 504 plan is designed to enable access to a FAPE so that "the individual educational needs of the handicapped student [are] being met as adequately as the needs of nonhandicapped students are met in academic and non-academic settings" (34 C.F.R. 104.33). As already noted, the educational outcomes expected for a student protected under Section 504 are aligned to the outcomes established for "nonhandicapped" students in the same school (Kowalski et al., 2005; Spiel et al., 2014). We hope that these educational outcomes are appropriately challenging. The purpose of progress monitoring is to track the student's success in meeting challenging IEP goals or challenging 504 outcomes. Table 6.7 compares progress monitoring of student access and progress as defined in a 504 plan or IEP.

TABLE 6.7 Comparison of 504 and IEP Progress Monitoring

QUESTIONS	SECTION 504 TEAMS	IEP TEAMS
What do the regulations generally require regarding progress monitoring?	Section 504 does not require teams to identify goals and benchmarks. Unless a student with disabilities has an IEP, progress is monitored for students with disabilities using the same tools and techniques used for students who are not disabled.	The IEP must include the following: (2) A statement of measurable annual goals, including academic and functional goals designed to— (A) Meet the child's needs that result from the child's disability to enable the child to be involved in and make progress in the general education curriculum; and (B) Meet each of the child's other educational needs that result from the child's disability; (ii) For children with disabilities who take alternate assessments aligned to alternate academic achievement standards, a description of benchmarks, or short-term objectives.

QUESTIONS	SECTION 504 TEAMS	IEP TEAMS
Against what specific criteria are we monitoring the student's access and progress?	Access and progress are monitored according to the accommodations, modifications, and services identified to improve the fit with the general education program.	Access and progress are monitored against the IEP goals and corresponding objectives.
What do the regulations generally require regarding progress reporting?	Progress is reported for students who are protected under Section 504 in the same way it is reported for all students: via report cards and, at the high school level, via transcripts. There are specific provisions about what information can be included in progress reports and transcripts of students with disabilities. See the Dear Colleague Letter from OCR issued in October 2008 for details and an FAQ document.	The IEP must include: (3) A description of— (i) How the child's progress toward meeting the annual goals described in paragraph (2) of this section will be measured; and (ii) When periodic reports on the progress the child is making toward meeting the annual goals (such as through the use of quarterly or other periodic reports, concurrent with the issuance of report cards) will be provided. 34 C.F.R. 300.320(a)(2)

Research related to monitoring and reporting progress, as well as our experience with IEP and 504 teams in the northeast United States, point to the strategies we invite you to consider in this chapter. What matters here is to remember that team members laid the groundwork for monitoring and reporting progress during the planning and placement process (Chapter 5) when they asked these questions: How will we know the plan is working? What are the measurable changes we will see? What data will show access, progress, or an improved fit between the child and schooling? Answers to these questions led the team to make decisions about monitoring the student's success, generally defined as access to the general education program and progress toward challenging educational outcomes.

RESEARCH TO CONSIDER

- *Essential nature of progress monitoring:* Progress monitoring is recognized as a "scientifically based practice . . . to assess students' academic and functional performance and evaluate the effectiveness of instruction" (Yell et al., 2012, p. 88). Despite the designation of progress monitoring as a scientifically based practice, Yell (2012) notes the low level of substantive compliance with this component of the IEP. The lack of progress monitoring with fidelity creates a legal problem. "If the goals and objectives of the IEP cannot be measured or evaluated, the IEP will not appropriately address the student's needs, which may result in the denial of FAPE" (Yell et al., 2012, p. 88). Decisions in multiple court cases "show that when a student doesn't make meaningful progress, *or an IEP team fails to collect data regarding student progress*, it is possible that a school district could be found in violation of . . . FAPE" (Yell et al., 2012, p. 89, italics added). Conversely, "when an IEP collects *legitimate data, and the data shows that a student has made progress*, the school district has clearly provided FAPE" (Yell et al., 2012, p. 89, italics added).

- *Uses of progress monitoring:* "Regular monitoring of student progress is an essential component of individualized education programs as well as response to intervention and other multi-tiered service systems" (Jenkins et al., 2017, p. 42). In the systematic practice of progress monitoring, "teachers use student performance data to continually evaluate the effectiveness of their teaching and make more informed instructional decisions" (Safer & Fleischman, 2005, p. 81). Specifically, progress monitoring can be used to create instructional groups; identify specific skill deficits; screen students for potential early school failure; provide accountability evidence to parents, teachers, and other educators about the impact of interventions; and evaluate the reintegration process for students moving from special to general education settings (Shapiro, 2008).

- *Data to monitor progress:* When we described the process of developing the plan and determining placement (Chapter 5), we encouraged teams to use routinely and easily collected data to show evidence of the impact of supports and services on the student. We noted the importance of schoolwide data (e.g., achievement testing, writing or reading benchmark assessments) that can show how well the student is learning in comparison to typically developing (nondisabled) peers.

  In addition to these group measures that provide only a "surface-level" view of the student's learning, research teaches us about the importance of getting "down to the ground to observe, listen to, and gather artifacts from the [student's] lived experiences" (Safir & Dugan, 2021, p. 57). Such a "ground-floor" view of "street data" gives us a more complete picture of the student's strengths, needs, and lived experience of the current fit with schooling. "Street data [show us] what's getting in the way of student . . . learning, illuminate where the learner is in relationship to a . . . set of goals, and determine what might come next" (Safir & Dugan, 2021, p. 57).

> The power of street data lies in the "systematic information" it can give us about how a student is *"performing* vis-à-vis developmental expectations, *feeling* about their learning environment and themselves, what might be *impeding* [their] ability to thrive, and what *instructional or leadership moves* should come next." (Safir & Dugan, 2021, p. 57, italics in original)

Earlier in this chapter, we offered the **Provider Service Delivery Log** that aligns specific data points with service delivery sessions. These data points are the street data that will give team members a "close-up" view of the student's current learning experience. Providers can include artifacts (e.g., student work samples, video of a performance assessment, audio recording of a student-to-student discussion [with prior approval]), stories/narratives (e.g., writing journal, interview), and observations (e.g., participation, nonverbal behavior, social interactions) documented with adequate supporting data (Safir & Dugan, 2021, p. 62). This tool is linked in Chapter 9 and is available on our companion website. online resources

Teams should note that courts have insisted on "systematic" data collection and have rejected "anecdotal" (e.g., anecdotal teacher observation without objective data) or sporadic data collection (Yell et al., 2012, p. 89). Also note that courts have accepted "teacher observation" as an adequate method of monitoring student progress *only when it is accompanied by "supporting data" that verify the observation* (Yell et al., 2012, p. 89, italics added).

- *Success criteria:* When team members designed the plan and determined placement (Chapter 5), they considered the criteria that define the success of the plan in terms of improving the fit between the student's learning profile and their current experience of schooling. When students collaborate in defining success criteria and use them to guide and strengthen their work, learning outcomes improve significantly (Fisher et al., 2021). Fisher and colleagues (2021) note that success criteria serve two important purposes. For the teacher, success criteria "signal student progress toward the learning [goals]" (p. 62). For the student, success criteria make the lesson's learning goals clear with specific descriptors that can highlight "expertise, skills, and background knowledge that they can leverage toward their . . . success" (p. 62). Success criteria can also support success by calling the learner's attention to "the possible difficulties [they] may encounter" (p. 62). Success criteria help a

(Continued)

(Continued)

student concretely answer the question, "How will you know when you've got it?" (Spencer-Iiams & Flosi, 2021, p. 72).

- *Frequency of progress monitoring for high-incidence disabilities:* Curriculum-based measurement (CBM) originated in special education as a tool that teachers could use to collect data on student learning to aid in monitoring and adjusting instruction for students with high-incidence disabilities (Deno, 2014). The Special Education Resource Project at Vanderbilt University defines curriculum-based measurement as "a simple set of standardized procedures that are a way to obtain reliable and valid measurement of a student's achievement" (Vanderbilt University, 2021). Curriculum-based measures in reading, for example, could include retelling, Maze passages, and word identification fluency, according to Jenkins et al. (2017). Jenkins and colleagues found that intermittent progress monitoring with CBM, in lieu of weekly monitoring, can "lighten assessment demands without undermining decision-making accuracy" (p. 42). Here, *decision-making accuracy* refers to using the results of CBM to maintain or adjust the accommodation, modification, or specialized instruction (e.g., focus, strategy, time, grouping). These findings align with the advice of the National Center on Response to Intervention (2012) to collect four to eight data points across a minimum of four weeks and the advice of the National Center on Intensive Intervention (n.d.) to collect at least six to nine CBMs for decision-making.

The research highlighted in this section, as well as our experience with IEP and 504 teams, influences our understanding of responsive approaches to progress monitoring. Table 6.8 compares frequent and responsive approaches to various dimensions of progress monitoring. You will see that the responsive approaches are made concrete in the "strategies to consider" that follow Table 6.8.

TABLE 6.8 Dimensions of Progress Monitoring: Frequent Versus Responsive Approaches

PRACTICE	FREQUENT APPROACH	RESPONSIVE APPROACH
Monitoring progress (ongoing)	Informal conversations happen between the student, parent/caregiver, and different members of the team. Sometimes, communication logs or regular data sheets are sent home with the student for parent review.	Data that was identified by the team is made available to all team members in real time. All team members know where and how to find data, as well as how to understand the connection between the data and the outcomes the team identified to strengthen areas of need. See Laurel's case study for details and tools.

PRACTICE	FREQUENT APPROACH	RESPONSIVE APPROACH
		All providers maintain accurate **Provider Service Delivery Logs** and can easily verify services that they have provided to each student on their caseload. This tool is linked in Chapter 9 and is available on our companion website. online resources Data review/progress meetings can be requested when a team member has questions or notices a pattern of progress that does not fit with the anticipated progress discussed by the team.
Issuing progress reports	Students with 504 plans receive a report card on the same schedule as students without disabilities. Students with IEPs receive a report card and an IEP progress report on the same schedule as students without disabilities. These documents are mailed home or sent home with students. Parent-teacher conferences occur two to four times a year for all parents in elementary and middle school, and they can be scheduled for high school students upon request. Annual review meetings happen once a year and include a report about the "present level of performance" (PLOP) for all students with IEPs. 504 plans are reviewed regularly. No schedule is set by regulation, and most schools do not have a regular schedule for review of 504 plans.	Because all team members have access to data in real time and agree about the changes in student performance that should happen, formal progress reporting summarizes the data and communications among team members. There are no surprises when progress reports or report cards arrive because the team communicates informally and has shared, real-time access to the data that is collected to show changes in students related to identified area of need/goals.
Identifying barriers to success	When a team member has a concern, that team member can request a meeting.	Because all team members know and can access data in real time that is connected to changes in student performance, there is ongoing communication between members of the team that focuses on what the data means. This occurs via phone calls, emails, or virtual meetings.

(Continued)

(Continued)

PRACTICE	FREQUENT APPROACH	RESPONSIVE APPROACH
		Because mailings are expensive and time consuming, schools regularly send materials home with students. Educators and families know that this method of communication can be unreliable, so we recommend considering releases to send documents electronically (e.g., email, private social media), in partnership with districts. Regular conversations with the student occur so that the student is involved in identifying barriers to success and offers suggestions about how and when to overcome these barriers.
Celebrating successes	Teams celebrate success at regularly scheduled initial meetings, annual reviews (for students with IEPs), or reevaluations (every three years for students with IEPs; regularly but with no mandated schedule for students with 504 plans).	Because all team members know and can access data in real time that is connected to changes in student performance, there is ongoing communication between members of the team that focuses on what the data means. This occurs via phone calls, emails, or virtual meetings. Because mailings are expensive and time consuming, schools regularly send materials home with students. Educators and families know that this method of communication can be unreliable, so we recommend considering releases to send documents electronically (e.g., email, private social media), in partnership with districts. **Student Reflection Logs** involve students in celebrating successes and making suggestions about how to sustain success. This tool is linked in Chapter 9 and is available on our companion website. online resources Team members express gratitude regularly to one another and talk to the student about successes regularly with intention and in connection to the student's goals. Students are clear about their own strengths and areas of growth and can express these with confidence. Planned celebrations with the student and all team members are part of the routine practice of the team.

The strategies that follow exemplify the responsive approaches described in Table 6.8.

STRATEGIES TO CONSIDER

- *Create a data collection system.* We recommended as part of the planning and placement process (Chapter 5) that teams identify the data that they would accept as evidence that the student is gaining improved access and/or making improved progress. For a student learning on an IEP, team members will want data that they are meeting the goals and corresponding objectives. For a student learning on a 504 plan, team members are seeking evidence that the accommodations, modifications, and services are enabling them to meet the educational outcomes aligned to the outcomes established for "nonhandicapped" students in their school. In considering the data that would be accepted as evidence of improved access and progress, we encouraged teams to know what data is routinely and easily collected in the school and use routinely and easily collected data to show evidence of the impact of supports and services on the student.

  Of course, the routinely and easily collected data identified by the team should also be easily understood by all team members. Providers can document and share data about each service delivery session using a tool such as the **Provider Service Delivery Log**. If team members created such a table or chart in a shared electronic format, such as a Google Doc, Google Form, or Google Sheet, team members and others who are responsible for implementing the plan can record the data point, and this growing body of evidence can be visible to everyone and available on an ongoing basis. This tool is linked in Chapter 9 and is available on our companion website. online resources

- *Record data from various types of assessment.* Data from schoolwide assessments (e.g., school/district benchmark assessments, state assessments), curriculum-based assessments (e.g., tests, quizzes, performance assessments), individualized assessments (e.g., repeated-trial measures in intensive instruction), and/or behavioral data (e.g., attendance, disciplinary referrals) will ensure that the student is gaining access and making progress against both individualized targets and outcomes established for "nonhandicapped" students in their school. You saw additional examples of these types of data in Chapter 5 (planning and placement), and you will see more examples in Chapter 8 (reviews, reevaluations, and changes in eligibility). Here, we gently caution you to report concrete data of a student's access or progress, not impressions or interpretations, and you will see this caution again in Chapter 8. A couple of examples of concrete data versus impressions or interpretations in your electronic data collection tool can help everyone who will be recording data.

(Continued)

(Continued)

- *Capture data in multiple modes.* We recommended that team members use visible notes in the planning and placement process (Chapter 5), and we recommend this practice throughout this book. Here, we suggest that visible data in the team's electronic data collection tool can include evidence in different modalities. For example, *visual data* can include a short video (with prior permission) or photograph of the student's work. *Graphic data* might chart a student's attendance or growing stamina for independent reading. An *aural recording* might describe a student's work sample or process, or capture an interview, presentation, or participation in a cooperative learning activity (with prior permission).
- *Develop a schedule for collecting and sharing data with all team members.* Sharing data promotes inclusiveness within a responsive team. Sharing data builds a common understanding of the student's current readiness and progress made. Developing a schedule for collecting and sharing data, and adhering to this schedule, promote trust and connection among team members. Collecting and sharing data according to the agreed-upon timeline positions team members to be able to report the student's progress. When we describe the process for leading teams through reviews, reevaluations, and changes in eligibility (Chapter 8), we consider electronic access to student information systems. Responsive teams can identify ways to attach data to student records and/or make data or data summaries available to all team members. If your school does not have an electronic database, you can use a simple form such as the **Student Profile Template**, linked in Chapter 9 and available on our companion website. online resources All educators can contribute links, including photos of work samples, to this sheet. It can be printed and shared with all team members. It could also be downloaded as a Word document and encrypted as a PDF if there is a need to protect this type of information before emailing or exchanging it via electronic communication.

  We recommend sharing data with all team members on a monthly basis, though some teams will choose to do this at the point when progress reports are due. By collecting, organizing, and sharing data in this way, the process of progress monitoring becomes transparent and much more efficient for educators.

  We noted earlier that developing a schedule for collecting and sharing data, and adhering to this schedule, promote trust and connection among team members. Trust and connection flourish to the degree that team members commit to avoiding unpleasant surprises for other team members. This means that if a student is not making satisfactory progress, and especially if a learning or behavioral challenge persists with severity, relevant data need to be shared and team members should be given a friendly "heads up" before progress reports, report cards, and other official notices are distributed. Sometimes, unpleasant news can land like a pail of cold water on the recipient's head, and responsive team members want to avoid this shock. The "pail of cold water" experience can also erode trust and cause resentment, which can weaken relationships among team members.

- *Report progress by interpreting data against specific targets for change.* In our discussion of the planning and placement process (Chapter 5), we recommended that team members, including the student, collaborate to identify specific targets for change (**Tool for Responsive Teaming: Organizing Data**). Here, we recommend that team members interpret the student's progress by comparing the data recorded in the **Provider Service Delivery Log** against the targets identified in the **Tool for Responsive Teaming** during the planning and placement discussion(s). If the tool contains data related to these targets, team members can see where the student is gaining access and making progress to date. If the tool does not yet contain data relevant to one or more targets, team members will see where data is still needed. These tools are linked in Chapter 9 and are available on our companion website. online resources
- *Report progress by interpreting data against the elements of the plan.* As team members see where the student is (not yet) gaining access and making progress, they can form impressions about which elements of the plan are contributing to the student's progress to date and which elements of the plan may need to be adjusted. Questions to ask at this point are questions the team will consider at the point of reviews, reevaluations, and changes in eligibility (Chapter 8):
  - What's working?
  - What's not working?
  - What's next?

If a team member proposes a change in an IEP or 504 plan, the data that have been collected and shared with reference to specific targets for the learner's growth will contribute to a compelling rationale for the proposed change.

CASE STUDY: LAUREL'S TEAM

We met Laurel and her team in Chapter 3. Let's fast forward through what happened after the initial referral and evaluation. Laurel's evaluation and subsequent eligibility determination resulted in her identification as a student with autism who requires specialized instruction and related services in order to make effective progress in the areas of social skill development, reading, and communication needs. Laurel's IEP goals for her fifth-grade year are written as follows:

- *Social skill development*: By the end of the IEP period, Laurel will be able to complete a **Social Skill Autopsy** with a peer and one trusted adult to understand how her "jokes" make others feel. With her peer and the trusted adult, Laurel will create a **Better Jokes Plan**, to which Laurel and her peer express consensus-based agreement (rating of "OK," "good," or "best" on the rating scale). These tools are linked in Chapter 9 and are available on our companion website.

online resources

- *Reading*: By the end of the IEP period, Laurel will read one chapter of an assigned whole-class text (e.g., read by all fifth graders in her English class) and accurately answer 90 percent of review questions requiring inferential thinking. Using a **Venn Diagram Exemplar**, Laurel will provide written summaries accurately comparing/contrasting the feelings and perspectives of at least two characters to support her answers (CCSS Literacy Standards 5.1 and 5.3). This tool is linked in Chapter 9 and is available on our companion website.

online resources

- *Communication*: By the end of the IEP period, Laurel will think of and ask three clarifying questions and one probing question during a reciprocal conversation to sustain a conversation with a peer on a topic of peer interest during a small-group speech and language session. Laurel will record her questions and her peer's responses in writing on a **Peer Dialogue Sheet** with 100 percent accuracy. This tool is linked in Chapter 9 and is available on our companion website.

online resources

You can see that Laurel's team took the time to identify data and agree about the tools that Laurel will complete to show her progress toward each goal. The Social Skill Autopsy is in use as the result of state-level guidance in Georgia, Laurel's home state. Her school has adopted graphic organizers to guide students through the social skill autopsy process as part of their positive behavioral supports initiative. All students know about social skill autopsies and routinely use the graphic organizers to solve interpersonal problems and resolve misunderstandings. The Better Jokes Plan is a modified version of the form in use by all students. This one includes language that Laurel has selected so that the form feels more personal and important to her. The Venn Diagram Exemplar was recommended because Laurel's fifth-grade teacher uses Venn diagrams on literature review tests. The Peer Dialogue Sheet is part of the routine practice of Laurel's speech and language pathologist and the board-certified behavior analyst (BCBA) who consults on Laurel's team.

It's a familiar tool used with many students in Laurel's school.

Setting up communication with the team will be easy for Laurel's liaison. The work of writing plans (IEPs or 504 plans) that use tools and strategies already in place for all students may take some thought and coordination before and during meetings; however, after the meeting, Laurel's team can simply create a protected folder so that documents used to monitor progress can be readily available to all members of Laurel's team. Laurel's folder should include three subfolders: one for each goal area (i.e., social skills, reading, and communication). Laurel's parents and school team members should be able to access the folder. Here are some options for strengthening team communication when this kind of system is in place:

- Laurel's educators can take pictures of the documents after each autopsy, chapter test, or speech and language session, making data visible and available to all team members.
- Laurel's liaison can scan folders for each student on her caseload and send an email every few weeks or call some parents each week to point out a highlight and encourage them to look at the folder.
- Laurel's parents can look in the folder, ask questions, and identify specific data/work samples that show any areas of concern.
- Laurel's team members can check to see whether Laurel's data/work samples indicate that the services, supports, or interventions are not working and can request a meeting to resolve problems.

I'm sure that you have many more ideas about how this responsive approach could assist the team to build strong, trusting, productive relationships after the team meeting is over. Just imagine how efficient the writing of progress reports will be when all of the data has been collected regularly throughout the marking period!

SUMMARY

What happens after the team meets to develop the plan and determine placement (Chapter 5) can vary greatly, even if this meeting went well. Nurturing relationships, particularly with members of the team whom you don't see regularly, is vital to accomplishing the post-team meeting work: implementing the plan, resolving problems, and monitoring progress. Relationships rely on communication, and we offered *mode*, *language*, and *time* considerations to help responsive teams plan to communicate in ways that strengthen connection and trust among team members.

We described key differences in implementing IDEA and Section 504 regarding the requirements for a written plan, regulatory oversight, and the official relationships that support implementation. High-quality implementation requires engagement of the student and parents/caregivers and support of all providers involved in implementing the plan, and we offered strategies and tools to accomplish both purposes. Engagement and support make possible the implementation of the plan with fidelity so that the student can meet challenging objectives. We provided a questions–data–decisions framework and tools to support implementation with fidelity.

In order for a plan to be implemented so that the student gains the greatest benefit from the supports and services in the plan, problems that arise must be resolved. We distinguish between *problems* and *questions* because problems need an urgent solution. Some questions can be easily answered. Others don't have an answer and require an empathetic presence. Still other questions should not be asked in their blunt form; instead, these wonderings can be expressed as bids toward compassionate understanding and relationship. We offered strategies and tools to resolve problems and suggested that team members view due process as a positive and powerful tool for third-party resolution if initial efforts have not yielded a satisfactory solution.

Progress is the lynchpin in the IEP or 504 process to ensure that the student meets challenging objectives. Research has shown the low level of substantive compliance with this component of the IEP and court decisions have invalidated an IEP because of inadequate progress-monitoring practices. We described requirements for communicating about progress and progress monitoring under Section 504 and IDEA, and we compared frequent and responsive approaches. The strategies and tools we offered translate the research to practice and illustrate a responsive team's approaches.

CHAPTER SEVEN

Additional Opportunities for Responsive Teaming

Reevaluations, Independent Educational Evaluations, and Manifestation Determinations

"The meeting needs to be a safe place to ask questions and maybe even restate what was said. So—communication is what makes things work."

—Margaret Madden, IEP Team Chairperson

GUIDING QUESTIONS FOR THIS CHAPTER

- What are some of the opportunities that responsive teams notice and use when conducting reevaluations, reviewing independent evaluations, or completing manifestation determinations?
- How do responsive teams navigate situations that involve tension, different understandings, and even conflict in ways that strengthen collaboration and compliance?

In this chapter, we approach a part of the work of 504 and IEP teams that can involve difficult conversations. We'll look together at three different processes for which teams are responsible: reevaluations, independent educational evaluations, and manifestation determinations. If you've read the previous chapters, we're sure you already have some useful ideas and strategies that will help you when the team engages in these processes. Let's begin with a brief discussion of the common conditions that responsive teams face when reevaluations, independent evaluations, and manifestation determinations are in process.

A reevaluation meeting is a time when the eligibility of a child is being revisited by the team. Reevaluation is required under Section 504. According to the U.S. Department of Education Office for Civil Rights (OCR; 2020) guidance,

> The Section 504 regulations require that re-evaluations be conducted periodically. Section 504 also requires a school district to conduct a re-evaluation prior to a significant change of placement. OCR considers an exclusion from the educational program of more than 10 school days a significant change of placement. OCR would also consider transferring a student from one type of program to another or terminating or significantly reducing a related service a significant change in placement.

Under IDEA, reevaluation is required at least once every three years or if the parent or teacher requests a reevaluation (34 C.F.R. 300.303). Two important exceptions to these requirements are allowed by the regulations: (1) the child cannot be reevaluated more than once each year unless the parent and district agree, and (2) the three-year reevaluation can be waived if the parent and district agree that it is unnecessary.

Regardless of the reason for a reevaluation, there is some uncertainty during the period when a child is being reevaluated. This impacts team members in different ways. For some people, there is a celebration of the child's successes and acknowledgement that a fit between the child and schooling has been achieved. For others, there is anxiety and fear of "losing supports" or entitlements that are essential to the child's success in school. Often, team members do not have an opportunity to share these feelings, so the underlying positions of different team members may be unclear, unrecognized, and unsupported before the day of the meeting.

When considering independent educational evaluations, teams frequently face uncertainty. Independent educational evaluations are "conducted by a qualified examiner who is not employed by the public agency responsible for the education of the child in question" (34 C.F.R. 300.502(a)(3)(i)). There are a number of reasons why a team is presented with an independent educational evaluation. We will discuss these later in this chapter; however, regardless of the reason, independent educational evaluations can also cause feelings of tension and uncertainty among members of 504 and IEP teams.

A manifestation determination (MD) meeting occurs only when there is a serious disruption in the fit between the child and schooling. In addition to the behavioral, social, and emotional needs that accompany situations in which a manifestation determination takes place, there are other conditions that a responsive team needs to notice and address. Team members may have different understandings about what a manifestation determination process entails. They may not know what's required for a compliant manifestation determination. They may not agree about what the outcomes of such a process should be for a particular student. It is also clear that there are significant disparities related to the rates and severity of disciplinary actions involving students of color, students with disabilities affecting emotional regulation, and students living in poverty.

The reason it's important to notice the common conditions of uncertainty, differences of understanding, and potential disagreements is that these conditions have an impact on the way people partner. Regardless of the type of meeting, responsive teams must prioritize different actions and make different assumptions when partnering under these conditions. Let's begin by considering a responsive approach to reevaluations.

RESPONSIVE TEAMS AND REEVALUATIONS

Whether a reevaluation is occurring as part of the regular review under Section 504 or as the result of a regular or requested review under IDEA, team members are engaged in revisiting the eligibility determination process as discussed in Chapter 4. Many of the strategies that were shared in Chapter 4 will be applicable to the reevaluation process. In this chapter, we want to consider opportunities for teams to strengthen relationships and communicate in a way that builds trust, even if there is a change in eligibility as the result of a reevaluation.

For 504 and IEP reevaluations, different types of data are collected over time. Before we discuss some of the opportunities and strategies that responsive teams can consider during the reevaluation process, we want to define a few terms so that our conversation that follows is clear. Here are the terms we use to describe different types of data:

- *Quantitative data*: Data that are recorded and shared using numbers or counts. An example is attendance data (number of days present out of number of days of school). Another example is a score on an achievement test.
- *Qualitative data*: Data that are recorded using descriptions or words that were shared with the evaluator by a person being interviewed or responding to a questionnaire. An example of qualitative data is the background information in many evaluation reports. Observations of students are often shared by using qualitative data.
- *Norm-referenced data*: Norm-referenced data compares the skills of a single person to the skills of a group of people who are at the same age or grade level. This data is important when a responsive team is targeting outcomes that "close skill gaps." It is also important in determining eligibility for some suspected areas of disability. Norm-referenced data cannot be used for progress monitoring when administration guidelines limit the frequency with which assessments can be repeated. An example of a norm-referenced assessment is the Wechsler Individual Achievement Test (WIAT).
- *Criterion-referenced data*: This data compares a student's performance to a standard or criteria for mastery. We use criterion-referenced data frequently in schools to monitor progress. An example of a criterion-referenced assessment is a spelling test. The student's success is determined based on the number of words that are spelled correctly. The "criterion" is the conventional spelling of a word, often referenced to the way the word is spelled in the dictionary.

Now that we have a shared understanding of some of the terminology we use when talking about the data collected during reevaluations, let's consider some of the ways that the reevaluation process provides opportunities for responsive teams to strengthen collaboration and engage in compliant practices. Here are some of the opportunities that come with reevaluations:

- *Student voice and leadership*: Because the student has been receiving services for a period of time, reevaluations offer responsive teams to involve the student as the primary agent in planning. The student who has been receiving services has valuable experience with accommodations, modifications, and services and can offer new perspectives to the team about next steps to strengthen the fit at school.

- *Looking at data trends*: Responsive teams look not just at the snapshot data that reevaluations provide, but they also compare trends over time by looking at progress-monitoring data, classroom and school data collected during the time the plan was in place, and current and past evaluation data. These data can be reviewed by the team to ensure that all team members understand the trajectory of the student's success in school. Teams can use the reevaluation process to dig deeply into what has worked and what hasn't worked for the student and support these claims with data collected across a number of years.
- *Reflecting on past successes*: A responsive team recognizes the opportunities to name, notice, and celebrate long-term gains as part of the reevaluation process.
- *Reimagining supports*: A responsive team approaches changes in eligibility and changes in the intensity of services as successes, a kind of "graduation" from more-intensive supports to less-intensive supports over time. Because all claims about reductions or changes in accommodations, modifications, or supplemental aids and services can be tied directly to specific, long-term data trends, responsive teams make these connections visible and celebrate changes together.
- *Identifying future outcomes*: Because the team has history together and has "longitudinal data" to review, reevaluations under Section 504 or under IDEA offer an opportunity to refine target outcomes with the student and discuss ways to measure a few meaningful changes to continue improving the fit between the student and schooling. This conversation can happen whether a child is found eligible or ineligible for continued services. Whether the child continues to be found eligible or not, whether the child's levels of service increase or decrease, responsive teams use these opportunities to prioritize celebration and to connect all decisions with data that has been gathered over time.

As you think about the opportunities that arise during the reevaluation process, you'll begin to see that responsive teams can employ many of the strategies from previous chapters to engage in a more robust and meaningful approach to reevaluation. We also want to recommend that responsive teams consider some out-of-the-box approaches that merge best practices in strategic planning and self-determination with the IEP and 504 team process. Some of the strategies that responsive teams might adopt include these:

- *Student-directed IEPs*: Involving students in directing their own meetings is an emerging best practice in the field. Student-directed IEP meetings can occur for students as young as elementary school and can continue throughout the child's school career. This approach is strongly associated with the development of self-determination skills, a practice that has been demonstrated to improve postschool outcomes for children with disabilities (Shogren & Ward, 2018). These skills and resources could be adapted for use by students with 504 plans. For more information and free curriculum resources, see the sources in the following table:

The Zarrow Center Self-Directed IEP	
I'm Determined: Student-Led IEPs	
I'm Determined: Resource for Parents About Student-Led IEPs	
Spartanburg School District 6	
Mrs. D's Corner (Elementary Resource)	

- *Visual representations of trends and comparisons of past and present data*: Responsive teams understand that representing data visually—using charts, graphs, bell curves (for norm-referenced data), and trendlines (for criterion-referenced data)—is critical to the team's ability to understand and use data together. Reevaluations offer an opportunity to see progress when data is shared visually before, during, and after meetings. Here are some examples of how to represent reevaluation data visually:

Data Visualization (examples of different types of visual representations)	
Pearson UK Visual Representation of WISC-V results (see graphs at the bottom of p. 15 and 16): This type of representation can include current and past results. Representations such as this can be created using Microsoft Excel for evaluation results from any norm-referenced assessment (e.g., CELF-5, WIAT, Woodcock Johnson ACH/COG, etc.).	
If you need a tutorial about how to create visual representations, a good starting example is available from Technology for Teachers and Students.	
Progress-monitoring (criterion-referenced) data with a trendline (scroll down to the chart embedded in this site)	

We propose that no data should be shared without an accompanying visual representation during the reevaluation process. Otherwise, there is so much data by the time a child is reevaluated that it can be difficult for the team to use the data available to identify trends and patterns related to the student's profile as a learner and the fit with schooling.

- *Person-centered planning*: Person-centered planning gathers the ideas and input of the team in a way that is strategic and focused on the student. Because the reevaluation is a time of reflecting and visioning, person-centered approaches to gathering or sharing data fit with the requirements of the reevaluation process and strengthen connections between team members. Using person-centered planning as part of a reevaluation pulls the team together to consider what is positive and possible for the student. For more information, see the following table:

Person-Centered Planning and Early Childhood	
Georgia Department of Education	
PACER Center	

- *Family-centered planning*: Some students may have stronger and more interdependent relationships with their families throughout their lives. For these students, family-centered planning may be a better approach. This is recommended because the needs of the student and the needs of the family intersect. What works for the student must work for the family, and vice versa. The Charting the LifeCourse project at the University of Missouri–Kansas City has developed tools and training resources, which are available at no cost for teams wishing to begin a family-centered approach to planning. For more information, see www.lifecoursetools.com.

As you can see, responsive teams approach the reevaluation process as an opportunity. Teams can come together using tools that empower students. Responsive teams can also review data, using approaches that promote creativity, visioning, and stakeholder engagement in strategic planning and decision-making. We do not recommend that a team adopt all of the strategies mentioned on behalf of one student, but rather, we offer these strategies as a way for teams to embrace a more positive approach to reevaluation. Teams that adopt one or more of these approaches will embed compliant practices in a context that emphasizes partnership, student centeredness, and celebration.

RESPONSIVE TEAMS AND INDEPENDENT EVALUATIONS

Independent evaluations are a right afforded to students and families under IDEA 2004. The right to a district-funded independent evaluation is not expressly allowed under Section 504 of the Rehabilitation Act. Guidance from the U.S. Department of Education OCR (2020) states,

> At the elementary and secondary education level, the amount of information required is determined by the multi-disciplinary committee gathered to evaluate the student. The committee should include persons knowledgeable about the student, the meaning of the evaluation data, and the placement options. The committee members must determine if they have enough information to make a knowledgeable decision as to whether or not the student has a disability.

Because the team determines whether they have enough data to determine eligibility and placement under Section 504, it is possible for a parent or caregiver to bring an independent evaluation for team consideration. In fact, we have heard of circumstances in which schools required parents to bring verification of disability before the school agreed to evaluate a child under Section 504. We want to emphasize that requiring parents to get an outside evaluation or diagnosis as part of the evaluation process is not a compliant practice. Districts are responsible to offer all required evaluations and gather all required data to make a knowledgeable decision about whether the student has a disability. Parents may offer to bring information from a doctor, clinician, or other person outside the school for team consideration, but it cannot be required.

Independent evaluations are a right offered to parents and caregivers under IDEA 2004 (34 C.F.R. 300.502). Parents can request that the IEP team consider evaluation data from independent evaluations for which they have privately paid. If parents disagree with the results of evaluations completed by district-arranged providers, they can request an independent evaluation to be paid for by the district. There are specific conditions for these independent evaluations that are spelled out in the regulations at 34 C.F.R. 300.502. Districts can respond to the parents' request by "providing the independent educational evaluation at public expense or filing a due process complaint to request a due process hearing to defend the public evaluation" (34 C.F.R. 300.502(b)(4)).

When we consider how responsive teams approach the review and discussion of independent evaluations, we need to start by thinking about the reason why independent evaluations occur. Typically, information from independent providers is sought to round out the information that is available in school-based evaluations. Frequently, this information is sought because parents have questions or concerns about district-provided evaluations. Frequently, the impact of independent evaluations on school-based members of the team is not positive and can cause feelings of uncertainty and stress. Parent assumptions about what this information suggests and how the district is required to respond can lead to tension among team members. In addition, independent evaluations are often conducted by people who are not as deeply familiar with the school setting. Often, independent evaluations are conducted by evaluators who have not observed the student at school or have not spent any time in the school in which services are being delivered. This doesn't diminish the value of insights that might be offered; however, the conditions under which evaluations are conducted may impact how the team understands and interprets the results.

As you already know from previous chapters, responsive teams are aware of the human side of our work. Responsive teams are also focused on inquiry and are therefore in a position to receive any information about a student with an eye to learning more about how to strengthen the fit between the student and schooling. For this reason, responsive teams acknowledge some of the opportunities and some of the limitations that may come with adding data from independent evaluations to team considerations of eligibility and planning.

Opportunities

- *Comparison of data from different perspectives*: The primary opportunity that comes with independent evaluations is the opportunity to compare quantitative and qualitative information about the student's profile and recommendations for schooling from the perspective of multiple evaluators. In our experience, it is rare to get an independent evaluation that does not yield at least one new important insight about the student as a learner.
- *Clarification of responsibilities*: Independent evaluations can include recommendations that go above and beyond the responsibility of the school to provide a free appropriate public education (FAPE) in the least restrictive environment (LRE). Reviewing recommendations systematically allows a responsive team to clarify the role and the responsibilities of the district by looking together at regulations describing these responsibilities. This opportunity allows teams to share claims, look at data together (including regulatory descriptions of FAPE, LRE, disability definitions, and definitions of specialized instruction and related services), and make decisions about which recommendations fit with the legal entitlements under IDEA and Section 504. In addition, responsive teams can brainstorm ideas about how community agencies, families, the student, and other stakeholders can take on responsibilities related to recommendations that are beyond the entitlements afforded by law to students with disabilities.
- *Strengthening trust and care*: Independent evaluations often come into play when there is distrust or uncertainty about data and decisions. Responsive teams are aware that there are opportunities to act with transparency. When a team receives an independent evaluation, a review is required under IDEA. This allows the IEP team to slow down and clarify the connection between data and the claims team members are making about the student's profile and appropriate schooling. Responsive teams take this time to engage in a deliberate, open, and straightforward conversation about differing opinions. These conversations can be difficult at the time. If the team can move through difficult conversations with respect and arrive at consensus, with clear targets for changes in student outcomes and agreement about the data that will

be used to monitor progress, then team member relationships and trust can grow.

In order to take advantage of these opportunities, we recommend the following strategies when receiving and reviewing independent evaluations:

- *Use protocols to review or compare evaluation data.* When reviewing independent evaluations, use a protocol such as the evaluation protocol developed by the Los Angeles Unified School District.

- *Create visual representations to compare and contrast evaluation results.* Whether you create charts to make evaluation results visible or you use a Venn diagram, compare and contrast the results of school evaluations and independent evaluations. The protocol for sharing information could be adapted from the Expeditionary Learning protocol for interactive word walls (see p. 18).

Team members could select data points from evaluations and sort them into categories (e.g., student strengths/areas of disability-related need) and then talk about why they selected and placed data from the evaluations into the categories they chose.

- *Make a "basic rights" video.* Create two videos that can be used at any time by responsive teams to remind everyone of the legal requirements for the provision of FAPE in LRE. Videos should be short (under five minutes is best) and clarify legal requirements that IEP teams need to consider. One video should address eligibility determination and the definition of specially designed instruction as well as the criteria used by teams to determine when this is necessary. One should address the criteria used to ensure that the educational program and placement represent FAPE in LRE. You may want to add captioning and enable translation so that all team members can access this information. You can use these videos as a point of reference when questions or differences of opinion about district obligations arise. You can also create videos about Section 504 provisions.
- *Address "parking lot" concerns.* Even if a child is not found eligible or a concern raised by the team is not included in a 504 plan or IEP, a responsive team addresses concerns that were raised during the meeting. It's important for the team to identify how concerns will be addressed, whether or not they are met in a 504 Plan or IEP. It may be that people who are not on the team become involved in these solutions. It is important for the team to identify next

steps so that all team members leave the meeting with clarity about how concerns will be resolved.

- *Close the review with a clear summary of agreements and differing opinions.* Make sure that everyone on the team is heard and the differing opinions that are offered are documented. You can do this by closing the meeting with a clear summary of agreements, differing opinions that were expressed, and the next steps that team members can expect. Even if there is not agreement, it is critical that all team members leave the meeting with a clear sense of what was decided and what will be offered.
- *Express gratitude.* Thanking people for specific contributions to the meeting and to maintaining relationships is a critical part of closing the meeting well, especially if consensus is not fully reached. Gretchen Rubin offers a wonderful activity that teams can use to close meetings. It's called "Writing Your Acceptance Speech," and Rubin invites people to spend just a minute or two composing a brief "acknowledgements" statement, similar to the one they would offer if they'd just received an award. Here's a description of the activity:

  The guiding questions are at the bottom of this blog (www.gretchenrubin.com). Teams could compose just a sentence or two (not a whole page or a speech) to thank specific people who supported the team process.

We believe that independent evaluations do not need to be approached in a way that escalates distrust or division among members of a responsive team. There are many other strategies that can be employed to support honest and respectful conversations when one or more members of the team disagree. In the next section, we'll look more deeply into the ways teams can continue to work in good faith, responding to one another as good people, even when there is tension or disagreement. We'll consider the circumstances surrounding manifestation determinations and student behavior that does not (yet) fit within the school's discipline code.

RESPONSIVE TEAMS AND MANIFESTATION DETERMINATION

As we begin thinking about the manifestation determination process, we want to share some resources and ideas that will set the stage for a more in-depth exploration throughout this chapter. One resource that we recommend is the School Discipline Support Initiative website (www.supportiveschool-discipline.org). The School Discipline Support Initiative provides strategies, practices, and tools to identify and redress disparities in school discipline. In Chapter 3, we described a multi-tiered system of support for academic, behavioral, and social-emotional outcomes. When a child is referred to the student support team, we recommended asking this question: "Has the child had an adequate opportunity to learn (the skill in question)?" A responsive approach is concerned with adequate opportunity to learn in the Tier 1 setting. The same is true for discipline: We recommend that a responsive team engaged in a manifestation determination ask, "Has the child had adequate access to alternatives to disciplinary action within the school community?"

In October 2021, the Association for Supervision and Curriculum Development (ASCD) dedicated an entire issue of their magazine, *Educational Leadership*, to "compassionate discipline." In this publication, there are 15 articles about alternative approaches to school discipline. Clearly, approaches to school discipline and manifestation determination are recognized as areas in need of improvement.

Responsive teams need to consider alternative approaches to strengthening the fit between the student and the school discipline code. Removals often reinforce behavior that we're trying to replace. Research-based approaches, including schoolwide positive behavioral incentive systems, individual behavior intervention plans, group contingency programs, and restorative justice initiatives, can be implemented in a way that affirms the child's membership and belonging at school while addressing the behavior and/or disciplinary responses that need to change.

Let's begin our conversation about a more responsive approach to manifestation determination by building a shared understanding about some of the terms and requirements.

WHAT IS A MANIFESTATION DETERMINATION (MD)?

Manifestation determinations happen when a student's behavior does not fit with the school's discipline code, and the child is removed from the classroom as a result. Specifically, a manifestation determination is required before a change in placement for a child with a disability. A change of placement is defined in IDEA 2004 as a removal that "would exceed 10 school days" within a school year (20 U.S.C. 1415(k)(1)(B) and (C).

These protections can also extend to children who have not yet been evaluated. If parents, educators, or school staff have raised concerns about the child previously or if the child was referred for an evaluation, the child may be protected even if they haven't been found eligible under Section 504 or IDEA 2004.

Manifestation determinations are described in federal law. The term "manifestation determination" is defined in the IDEA 2004 law as follows:

> (E)(i) . . . within 10 school days of any decision to change the placement of a child with a disability because of a violation of a code of student conduct, the local educational agency, the parent, and relevant members of the IEP team (as determined by the parent and the local educational agency) shall review all relevant information in the student's file, including the child's IEP, any teacher observations, and any relevant information provided by the parents to determine—
>
> (I) if the conduct in question was caused by, or had a direct and substantial relationship to, the child's disability; or
>
> (II) if the conduct in question was the direct result of the local educational agency's failure to implement the IEP.
>
> (ii) Manifestation. If the local educational agency, the parent, and relevant members of the IEP team determine that either subclause (I) or (II) of clause (i) is applicable for the child, the conduct shall be determined to be a manifestation of the child's disability" 20 U.S.C. §1415(k)(1)(E).

This law is also cited in guidance developed by the U.S. Department of Education's Office for Civil Rights (OCR; 2016) and has been interpreted by OCR to apply to students protected under Section 504 of the Rehabilitation Act.

You can see that manifestation determinations are based on two yes/no questions:

1. Is the conduct in question caused by the child's disability? (Yes/No)
2. Is the conduct in question the result of lack of implementation of a plan? (Yes/No)

It can be tempting to think that manifestation determination meetings should be short, sweet, and simple. We would caution against this, for reasons you'll discover as you proceed through this chapter.

We also believe that it's important for all team members to know the legal language that defines and describes manifestation determination before meeting together to answer these questions. The full requirements are described in 20 U.S.C. §1415(k). We also know that legal language can be a barrier to full team understanding and participation. Given this, we encourage districts and team members, in consultation with qualified legal advisors and leaders, to offer access to the full legal language along with a summary of legal requirements in the **500 most commonly used words in the English language by Summer Boarding Courses International**. Here is an example of such a summary:

online resources

> The words "manifestation determination (MD)" are from the law (IDEA, 2004). IEP or 504 teams must make MDs when children with 504 plans or IEPs are kept out of school because their behavior doesn't fit with school rules. An MD happens at a meeting of the team. Parents and the school decide together who should be on the team. The team meets to talk about whether the behavior is tied to the child's disability or the way the plan was done. The team decides about this together. If parents don't agree with what the team decides, they can ask for a hearing.

This type of summary is not legally accurate, nor do we offer it as a legal recommendation; however, in combination with legal language, it can support team use of legal requirements in a way that is more accessible for team members who have not had comprehensive legal training or who are using English as an additional language.

WHAT ARE THE REQUIREMENTS FOR MANIFESTATION DETERMINATION (MD)?

Manifestation determination can be a confusing process. Regulations, guidance documents, and precedent cases have shaped the way this process has evolved over time. Table 7.1 offers a summary of regulations and guidance that all team members should be aware of before participating in a manifestation determination meeting.

TABLE 7.1 Summary of Regulations and Guidance Informing Manifestation Determination

QUESTION	SECTION 504	SPECIAL EDUCATION
Why is the team involved in disciplinary removals for students with disabilities?	"OCR considers an exclusion from the educational program (for example, an out-of-school suspension) of more than 10 consecutive school days to be a significant change in placement. "OCR also considers a series of short-term exclusions (each 10 school days or fewer) from the educational program to be a significant change in placement if the short-term exclusions total more than 10 school days and create a pattern of removal. "OCR also considers a school's transferring a student from one type of program to another (for example, from a general education class with pull-out special education services to a self-contained special education class) or terminating or significantly reducing a related service to be a significant change in placement." U.S. Department of Education OCR, 2016, pp. 22–23	Section 504 conditions apply to all students with disabilities, including all students who are identified as eligible for special education services. "Within 10 school days of any decision to change the placement of a child with a disability because of a violation of a code of student conduct, the local educational agency, the parent, and relevant members of the IEP team (as determined by the parent and the local educational agency) shall review all relevant information in the student's file, including the child's IEP, any teacher observations, and any relevant information provided by the parents to determine— (I) if the conduct in question was caused by, or had a direct and substantial relationship to, the child's disability; or (II) if the conduct in question was the direct result of the local educational agency's failure to implement the IEP." 20 U.S.C. §1415(k)(1)(E)

(Continued)

(Continued)

QUESTION	SECTION 504	SPECIAL EDUCATION
Before suspending a student with a disability for more than 10 days (change of placement), what is required of the team?	"Section 504 also requires school districts to conduct reevaluations prior to significant changes in placement." 34 C.F.R. 104.35(a) "Under Section 504, OCR's determination of whether a series of exclusions creates a pattern of removal is made on a case-by-case basis, and may include consideration of several factors, including the length of each removal, the proximity of the removals to each other, and the total amount of time the child is excluded from school. See also 34 C.F.R. § 300.536 (IDEA regulations)." U.S. Department of Education OCR, 2016, pp. 22–23	(F) *Determination that behavior was a manifestation.* If the local educational agency, the parent, and relevant members of the IEP team make the determination that the conduct was a manifestation of the child's disability, the IEP team shall— (i) Conduct a functional behavioral assessment and implement a behavioral intervention plan for such child, provided that the local educational agency had not conducted such assessment prior to such determination before the behavior that resulted in a change in placement described in subparagraph (C) or (G); (ii) In the situation where a behavioral intervention plan has been developed, review the behavioral intervention plan if the child already has such a behavioral intervention plan, and modify it, as necessary, to address the behavior; and (iii) Except as provided in subparagraph (G), return the child to the placement from which the child was removed, unless the parent and the local educational agency agree to a change of placement as part of the modification of the behavioral intervention plan. *(G) Special circumstances.* School personnel may remove a student to an interim alternative educational setting for not more than 45 school days without regard to whether the behavior is determined to be a manifestation of the child's disability, in cases where a child— (i) Carries or possesses a weapon to or at school, on school premises, or to or at a school

QUESTION	SECTION 504	SPECIAL EDUCATION
		function under the jurisdiction of a state or local educational agency; (ii) Knowingly possesses or uses illegal drugs, or sells or solicits the sale of a controlled substance, while at school, on school premises, or at a school function under the jurisdiction of a state or local educational agency; or (iii) Has inflicted serious bodily injury upon another person while at school, on school premises, or at a school function under the jurisdiction of a state or local educational agency. *(H) Notification.* Not later than the date on which the decision to take disciplinary action is made, the local educational agency shall notify the parents of that decision, and of all procedural safeguards accorded under this section. (2) Determination of setting. The interim alternative educational setting in subparagraphs (C) and (G) of paragraph (1) shall be determined by the IEP team. 20 U.S.C. §1415(k)(1)(F)-(2)
What are the required supports and services during a disciplinary removal of a child with a disability?	"[W]hen addressing discipline for students with disabilities, it is important that schools comply with applicable legal requirements governing the discipline of a child for misconduct caused by, or related to, the child's disability." U.S. Department of Education OCR, 2016, p. 23	(1) A child with a disability who is removed from the child's current placement pursuant to paragraphs (c) or (g) of this section must— (i) Continue to receive educational services, as provided in §300.101(a) so as to enable the child to continue to participate in the general education curriculum, although in another setting, and to progress toward meeting the goals set out in the child's IEP; and (ii) Receive, as appropriate, a functional behavioral assessment, and behavioral intervention services and modifications, that are designed to address the behavior violation so that it does not recur.

(Continued)

(Continued)

QUESTION	SECTION 504	SPECIAL EDUCATION
		(2) The services required by paragraph (d)(1), (d)(3), (d)(4), and (d)(5) of this section may be provided in an interim alternative educational setting. (3) A public agency is only required to provide services during periods of removal to a child with a disability who has been removed from his or her current placement for 10 school days or less in that school year, if it provides services to a child without disabilities who is similarly removed. 34 C.F.R. 300.530(d)
What are the required steps when a child is removed for 10 or more school days within one school year?	"Although the Section 504 regulations do not set a specific timeframe within which students with disabilities must be reevaluated to make sure that they are receiving the appropriate services, Section 504 requires schools to conduct reevaluations periodically, and before a significant change in placement. OCR considers an exclusion from the educational program of more than 10 consecutive school days to be a significant change in placement." 34 C.F.R. 104.35(a) "[T]he school must reevaluate . . . , prior to imposing the 11th day of suspension, to determine whether [the] misconduct is caused by or related to [the] disability (manifestation determination), and if so to further evaluate to determine if [the] current placement is appropriate." U.S. Department of Education OCR, 2016, p. 23	(4) After a child with a disability has been removed from his or her current placement for 10 school days in the same school year, if the current removal is for not more than 10 consecutive school days and is not a change of placement under §300.536, school personnel, in consultation with at least one of the child's teachers, determine the extent to which services are needed, as provided in §300.101(a), so as to enable the child to continue to participate in the general education curriculum, although in another setting, and to progress toward meeting the goals set out in the child's IEP. (5) If the removal is a change of placement under §300.536, the child's IEP team determines appropriate services under paragraph (d)(1) of this section. 34 C.F.R. 300.530(d)

As you can see from Table 7.1, the process of responding to students with disabilities involves consideration of different types of guidance. Team members involved in disciplinary responses should be familiar with Section 504 and IDEA regulations about placement determination and the provision of a FAPE.

In addition, guidance documents and training materials released by the OCR provide important information for responsive teams. These documents explain the interpretation of regulations and describe the requirements for teams if students with disabilities are removed from regularly scheduled or available activities for short-term or long-term suspensions. Finally, a review or summary of the *Honig v. Doe* decision (Brennan & Supreme Court of the United States, 1987) is strongly recommended, particularly for team members who may be new to the intersection of suspensions or removals and the rights of students with disabilities.

Other Manifestation Determination Meeting Requirements

In addition to the two questions addressed in the previous sections, we want to highlight a few other requirements that we believe team members should know and communicate about well before a manifestation determination meeting occurs.

- *Composition of the team:* Parents and the district need to agree about the "relevant members" of the team that participate in the MD (20 U.S.C. 1415(k)(1)(E)(i)).
- *Services:* Regardless of the outcome of the MD, the child with a disability must continue to receive services during a removal from school so that they can participate in the general curriculum and make progress toward their IEP goals (20 U.S.C. 1415(k)(1)(D)(i)).
- *Behavioral supports:* Regardless of the outcome of the MD, a child with a disability should receive (as appropriate) "a functional behavioral assessment, behavior intervention services and modifications that are designed to address the behavioral violation so it does not recur" (20 U.S.C. 1415(k)(1)(D)(ii)).

- *Interim alternative educational setting (IAES):* When schools exercise their right to send a child to an IAES, parental consent is not required prior to changing the location of services. If the behavior in question involves possession of a weapon or knowingly possessing, buying, or selling illegal drugs, or if it results in serious bodily injury to another person *and* it happened at school or a school-sponsored event, the child may be removed for up to 45 days to an IAES. Often, there are questions about where services will be provided when behaviors that are considered dangerous are happening at school. There is urgency about relocating the child as soon as possible. The team, and not the district, determines the location of the alternative setting. The team should convene to discuss and agree about the IAES location before the child is placed there (20 U.S.C. 1415(k)(2)).

- *Appeal:* If parents disagree with any decision associated with the MD, they have a right to appeal to a hearing officer (20 U.S.C. 1415(k)(3)(A)).

WHAT IS DIFFERENT ABOUT A RESPONSIVE TEAM APPROACH TO MANIFESTATION DETERMINATION (MD)?

School responses to student discipline have changed significantly for all students during the past 40 years. Research and support for positive behavioral incentive systems, social-emotional learning, functional behavioral assessment, restorative practices, and culturally responsive teaching have shaped our understanding about the strong connections between responses to student behavior and access to education. We know that availability for learning happens when students and adults experience teaching and learning as safe, supportive, relevant, and engaging. A responsive team brings a mindset to school discipline that seeks to understand the fit between the child and schooling. The team is seeking to support a better fit for all involved, not to punish, blame, or exclude a child from the learning community. Accordingly, responsive team members will be curious about the child's history of accessing alternatives to disciplinary action that can meet the need(s) or teach the skill(s) suggested by the behavior.

The challenge that responsive teams face is that a manifestation determination occurs when the disruption in the fit between the child and learning is big. When removals are considered by a school, people are often angry, afraid, or ashamed. There is always a great deal of anxiety and uncertainty. There may be pain, property damage, or threats experienced by multiple members of the team. These conditions cause physiological and cognitive changes in children and adults, and the impact of our physiology leads to responses that can be difficult to recognize or overcome. We're in fight, flight, or freeze mode.

Zaretta Hammond talks about this in her book *Culturally Responsive Teaching and the Brain* (2015). She says that "the brain takes its social needs very seriously and is fierce in protecting an individual's sense of well-being, self-determination, and self-worth along with its connection to community" and that "we cannot downplay students' need to feel safe and valued in the classroom" (p. 47). We believe Hammond's insights and advice apply to every person—students and adults—on teams that support students with disabilities. When human brains and bodies sense there is a threat, our availability for problem-solving, curiosity, and creative thinking decreases significantly. You can imagine that, for a student experiencing removals, all aspects of well-being and connection are threatened. We also believe that the well-being, empowerment, self-worth, and connection to the school community are disrupted for educators, parents, administrators, and adults during disciplinary actions.

A responsive team knows this and approaches manifestation determination by focusing intentionally—and *intently*—on questions that promote the well-being, self-worth, and connection of all team members, as well as compliance. Responsive teams understand the manifestation determination process as an opportunity to reexamine the fit between the student's profile and the way schooling is happening. They also know that people have already made attempts to address this fit, and so more creative options may need to be identified and explored. Responsive team members care for one another and draw closer so that all team members can experience community and connection and avoid (as much as possible) the physiology of perceived threats and exclusion. This keeps team members available for brainstorming, dialogue, and thoughtful problem-solving together. Responsive teams know that the outcome of a successful manifestation determination is a better connection between the student and schooling that results from deeper connections among members of the team.

WHAT ARE THE STEPS IN A RESPONSIVE TEAM'S MANIFESTATION DETERMINATION?

Step #1: *Identify guiding questions for the manifestation determination as a team.*

While there are requirements in federal law about some of the questions the team must answer during a manifestation determination, there is also a reminder in federal law about the importance of making determinations on a case-by-case basis, considering the unique circumstances that led to the removal of the child from school (20 U.S.C. 1415(k)(1)(A)). As a place to begin, the team should identify specific questions together so that all team members have a shared understanding about what the team needs to accomplish.

Another reason we recommend identifying guiding questions together is that it can build team trust and rapport at a time of disruption in schooling. The Right Question Institute, mentioned in Chapter 5, has a video that describes how generating questions together supports strong relationships. Their process is called the question formulation technique (QFT), and we recommend that all team members view the *Using QFT With Adults* video (https://rightquestion.org/what-is-the-qft-2/) so that you can see how the process can work and can support connections between team members, particularly in situations that are confusing or could involve differences of opinion and perspective.

If you watch this video, you will notice the recommendation to allow people to identify questions by turning ideas or statements into questions. This is a very helpful strategy for teams that may anticipate difficult conversations. It is important that a team stay focused only on the generation of questions during the allocated time for this activity, as it can be easy for people to want to jump ahead and make analyses or defend specific ideas. We have provided a **List of Brainstormed MD Questions,** linked in Chapter 9 and available on our companion website, to give you a sense about what kinds of questions

could come up. Teams are likely to experience a much more thorough, trusting, and productive manifestation determination if team members give time and focus only to generating and selecting questions during this step in the process.

Case Study: Elijah's Team

Here is an example about the way Step #1 could work, shown to us by Elijah's team.

Team chair: Welcome, everyone. Thanks for making time for this meeting. Today, we're here to talk about the fit between Elijah and what's happening at school, with a focus on one unsolved problem: the problem of injuries to other people.

Elijah's mom: I get that this is a problem, but Elijah can't help it! He has autism, and he can't even talk—how is he supposed to tell us what's going on? How can you expect him to behave the way other kids do? [*She starts to cry.*]

[Silence for two minutes. It's a little awkward, but people offer tissues, nod, and some even join in the crying.]

Team chair: This is hard. [*There is more silence—maybe for even another minute or two.*]

Behaviorist: [*After a nod from the team chair*] This is hard, and it feels important to do something together to try to solve this problem. You already asked two really important questions.

Elijah's dad: Well, no kidding! Since the year started, he's been home with us for six days that we thought he'd be in school! Do you know how hard it is for me to get six days off work? Plus, look at my wife! She's exhausted! We need help! Elijah needs help! Sending him home from school isn't helping him or us!

[Pause for a moment—silences are a bit awkward, but important.]

Behaviorist: You know, as I listen to both of you, I have to say that maybe I haven't thought enough about what this means for you, as Elijah's parents. I'm so sorry. I should have reached out before this. You're right about how keeping Elijah home isn't helping. I guess I wish I'd thought more about how it wasn't working for you. This is not going to continue. I agree, we can't do this anymore.

Team chair: [*Seeing others nod in agreement*] Thanks for saying that. I can see that you're not the only one who feels this way. I agree. I'm wondering whether people feel ready to think together about what questions we need to answer to make sure that Elijah gets what he needs, his parents get what they need, and people at school get what we need. I think if we can come up with a good list of questions to address as a team, that will help us come together to solve this problem.

Elijah's mom: OK . . . I'm ready.

Elijah's dad: We can start there . . . but I don't know how it will help.

Behaviorist: I'm with Elijah's dad—ready but not sure if thinking about questions will work.

Assistant principal: We should try it and see. We can change our approach if we need to do that to get something in place for Elijah.

Special education teacher: I'm in.

General education teacher: Me, too.

Team chair: All right, let's start. We're going to brainstorm a list of questions that we need to try to answer using data. Our focus is on people getting hurt at school. You all have the information about what's been going on, and we've talked with Elijah's parents. Does anyone not understand what's happened and why Elijah has been sent home for six days this year?

[People shake their heads—they seem to know from previous conversations.]

Team chair: We all know each other pretty well, and we all seem to understand the reason we're here, so we're not going to do formal introductions or read reports today. What we are going to do is review information that is important by generating questions. I can help with this if anyone gets stuck. We'll keep brainstorming questions until everyone feels as if we have all of the questions that are relevant to this problem. No question is a bad question, so if it comes into your head, say it and we'll be sure to record it. I've asked Juana [*the assistant principal*] to write questions as they are shared, using the exact words that people say. Lucky for us, Juana is a fast typist. You'll be able to see the questions on the chart paper as she records them.

Here are three example questions to get us started: How do we know when people won't get hurt by Elijah? Do we think that when people get hurt by Elijah, it has something to do with his autism spectrum disorder—that is, his communication or social skill differences? How do we know when it seems likely that someone could get hurt?

Do these questions spark any questions for you? Please feel free to jump in and share your questions. We all know each other, and we can try to help each other do this in an orderly way. Please make sure Juana gets the current question down before someone else talks. Oh, and please let the group know if you have trouble coming up with a question but you think there's some important information from the record that we should consider.

Elijah's dad: My question is, "Why does Elijah do this?"

Assistant principal: That's my question, too—I got it!

Elijah's mom: I wonder how we can stop Elijah from hitting people and biting.

Team chair: That's an important observation. Can you say it as a question?

Elijah's mom: Oh—I thought it was a question. Let me think about it. [*One minute of silence—awkward, but important.*] How about, "How do we stop Elijah from hitting people and biting them?"

Elijah's dad: [*As the behaviorist claps and the team chair smiles*] Well done! I have another one: "How can we tell if the hitting and biting are getting better?"

Behaviorist: I love that question! I have some great ideas about that. For example . . .

Team chair: I have to interrupt. Sorry! We are going to talk about decisions later on. I don't mean to be rude. If you can write down your ideas, that will help us later. Also, if you can think of a question, I'd love to hear it.

Behaviorist: Oh, sorry! This is harder than I thought! [*Some people chuckle.*] Um . . . I guess my question would be, "What data will help us feel confident that the hitting and biting are under control so that Elijah doesn't get sent home by anyone anymore?"

[Now, Elijah's parents clap.]

You can see how the team continues. The process of generating questions can be short (five minutes) or long (20–30 minutes). It's important that, at some point, the team generates questions that are required by regulations. Any question that closely represents these requirements will work for the MD process. In Elijah's meeting, the team chair's second question ("Do we think that when people get hurt by Elijah, it has something to do with his autism spectrum disorder—that is, his communication or social skill differences?") is actually a close approximation of one of the required questions for MDs.

Once the team has generated a list of questions that feels comprehensive, the team chair will identify the required questions and then invite each team member to "vote" for the top three questions that the team should consider. Voting can happen by letting team members get up and draw a smiley face or place a check mark beside the top three questions they want the team to discuss. It can happen by giving each team member three stickers to place beside the top three questions. Team members can place multiple checks/smiley faces/stickers beside one question if they feel it is really important. In the end, the three questions with the most votes will be discussed, in addition to the two questions that must be answered according to the regulations. This can be done using emojis or other characters (asterisks, @ signs, etc.) if the team is working in a virtual/remote modality using shared electronic documents. We have provided an example of a team's **End of Step #1: List of Brainstormed MD Questions—Prioritized** so that you can see how this looks. This tool is linked in Chapter 9 and is available on our companion website.

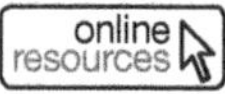

Step #2: *Review all relevant information (data).*

In this step, the person who is taking notes places one question at the top of separate pieces of chart paper. This can also be done by creating a Jamboard, with one slide for each question. It can be done using a Google Doc (or any other type of electronic document), with one page for each question. This may take a few minutes, so the team can take a short break for movement, personal comfort, or other needs. An example of how the **Beginning of Step #2: List of Brainstormed MD Questions—Prioritized** would look when laid out on a Jamboard is linked in Chapter 9 and is available on our companion website.

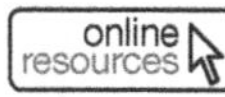

Team members can also be invited to review data that they want to highlight or share as important for answering the questions. Because questions that were brainstormed and prioritized are already visible for all team members, people can begin to think about data on their own while the person who takes notes creates the necessary documents for this step.

When the charts/electronic materials are ready, team members share information and ensure that everyone has access to current data that is relevant. Parents should go first, sharing any information (specific stories, situations, observations) that they would like the team to consider regarding the selected questions. Teachers also share observations as required by law. Team members should take notes about any information that is shared orally and not offered in a written document. Behavioral data related to the behavior(s) that led to removal is also shared.

The sharing of data that is on graphs, charts, or written documents can simply involve passing out copies. People should not read reports to one another during this meeting. Incident reports would have been sent home and made available prior to the meeting. There is no need to read or review these, but they will need to be available for the next part of the meeting.

Once all of the data is current and available, team members are invited to connect specific data points to the questions. There are many ways to facilitate this process and engage all team members. One of the key aspects of connecting data to decisions is allowing team members time to share, review, and think together about which data points are most relevant and inform the decisions that lie ahead.

STRATEGIES TO CONSIDER

- *Think-Pair-Share:* Pair up team members and give them a specific set of data to review (e.g., teacher observations, behavior intervention data, incident report data, attendance data, etc.). Invite each team to highlight at least three data points that relate to each question. Remember, the team will have only five questions to consider at most. After people have reviewed their data set, they should write their data points on Post-its (or add them in a specific color of text to the electronic document) and place them under the appropriate questions. In the end, you will have your five questions with a variety of data from different sources under each question. After adding their data points, team members can look at others' data points and talk together about the patterns that are important for the team to consider. When everyone is finished, each team member is invited to share one or two important connections between the questions and the data.
- *Scavenger Hunt:* Team members can work individually or in pairs if you use this approach. Each person or pair is assigned one question of the five prioritized questions. Depending on the size of your team, some people might be looking at the same question, or some people might have to do more than one question. If a team member has a strong preference about the question they are assigned, allow that team member to focus on that question. After each team member is clear about which question they are focusing on, they are given time to highlight the three or four most important data points for the team to review under the assigned question. Team members are given 15 to 20 minutes for this task. After that time, team members will go in order, sharing the three or four most important data points related to the question.

- *Whole-Group Data Mining:* Each group member is given the chance to record the two data points that matter most in relation to the problem the team is addressing. Ten minutes is allowed for this. Team members are asked to write their two data points on Post-it notes or document them in some way that can be shared. After 10 minutes, team members share their data points, and the team decides together which data points should be aligned with each question; do this until all data points are sorted.

In this phase, the team is only looking at data. No interpretations, analyses, or opinions are expressed. Data is simply reviewed and selected, based on what each team member (or pairs of team members) find that seems most relevant or important to answering the question at hand. Keeping team members focused on looking at and sorting data before making decisions is another critical element of managing the big feelings and challenges that can happen when a child experiences removals from school due to behavioral needs. One resource that may help you to understand how teams can do this together is the Data Wise Project at Harvard University. Harvard offers a free massive open online course (MOOC) at www.edX.org (www.edx.org/course/introduction-to-data-wise-a-collaborative-process). This course, called "Introduction to Data Wise: A Collaborative Process to Improve Learning & Teaching," includes free tools and videos that show how teams can use the "ladder of inquiry" as a tool for looking carefully at data before interpreting or analyzing the results.

Case Study: Elijah's Team

Team chair: We have five questions to think about together. Thanks for all of the work you've already done to start solving this problem. Our focus is on the problem of people getting hurt. It seems from our conversation so far that this happens when Elijah hits or bites people. It's important that we've gotten so clear about the problem because we know that having a clearly agreed-upon problem makes it more likely that we'll come up with a solution.

Our next step is to look at current data that we feel is relevant to this problem. In order to do this, we're going to use a strategy called *whole-group data mining*. Here's how it works: Every person is going to review the data that we've shared, including what Elijah's parents told us, what his teachers observed, and the printed behavior data about hitting and biting, as well as the incident reports that were submitted before the six days of Elijah's suspensions. Please use highlighters to find the two most important pieces of data (something specific that was shared or that you see in the documents) to help us understand and make decisions about the five questions we've prioritized. You'll have 10 minutes to find the two data points you want us to discuss. Everyone will share their two most important data points when we're done.

Does anyone have any questions about what to do?

Elijah's mom:	I don't know about this. I read really slowly. I'm not sure I can do this.
Behaviorist:	I'm glad you told us that! Can we work together?
Team leader:	It's totally great for people to do this alone or in pairs. Whatever works for you will be helpful to our team.
Elijah's dad:	I want to work alone.
Elijah's mom:	Will we pick two data points if we do it as a group or four data points? I don't want to miss the chance to pick what I think matters—I just might need help to find it quickly.
Team leader:	Great question! You can choose four data points if you work in pairs. Does anyone else want to work in pairs?
Assistant principal:	I would like to work with someone who knows the data better than I do.
General education teacher:	I'll work with you.
Special education teacher:	Can I join someone? I think better when I can talk about what I'm seeing.
Team leader:	We can work together. I like to talk about what I'm seeing too.

[*The team starts looking at data, highlighting, talking. Elijah's mom and the behaviorist go to the library because the room is too noisy. They come back in 15 minutes, and the team chair asks everyone to finish highlighting their one or two most important data points to share.*]

Team leader: Does everyone have the most important data points that you want to share? [*People nod.*] OK. Next, I'm going to ask you to write each data point you found on a Post-it. Every data point gets its own sticky note, so everyone should have two notes when we're done. As you write down your data points, think about which question you think they help us to understand. I'll ask you to share your data point and your idea about which question it should go with when we're done writing.

[*People write their ideas on Post-its. When they are done, the team leader invites Elijah's mom to go first.*]

Team leader: Will you share one data point and your idea about which question it will help us to answer?

Elijah's mom: OK . . . though I'm not sure this is right.

Team leader: It's OK—we'll talk about it together. These decisions are team decisions, but you're getting us started.

Elijah's mom: All right. Here's one of my data points: The behavior graph for biting shows 12 incidents in the morning and 36 incidents in the afternoon for the month before the suspensions.

Behaviorist: That was *great*! I noticed that too!

Elijah's mom: I think this helps us to understand the question, "What data will help us to know when the problem is getting better?" We should see a lot fewer bitings in the afternoon.

Team leader: Thanks for sharing your idea about which question this data point helps us to understand. Does anyone have a different idea about which question we should put this data point under?

Behaviorist: I have to say that I want to support Elijah's mom. I think she has pointed out something really important.

Assistant principal: I agree.

Elijah's dad: Well, I'm not sure how significant this is—it seems like a no-brainer. Of course we want to see less biting!

Elijah's mom: Why do you say that? I think knowing exactly how much biting is happening and figuring out how to get it to be less is really why we're here. So it's definitely significant.

[*Awkward silence for half a minute—it's important to let people think and settle in before whatever comes next!*]

Team leader: I'm thinking about how hard this is. We're definitely making some progress here, and I know this is a bit different than what people might have experienced at other meetings. Is it OK to keep going? I really want to hear everyone's data points and get organized for making decisions. Is it OK?

Elijah's dad: Yeah.

[Others nod, murmur agreement.]

Team leader: OK, I'm going to go to another team member, and we'll just go around the room. Share one data point that you noted on one of your sticky notes and tell us which question you think it will help us to answer. I'll try to keep us moving forward smoothly. [*Turning to the assistant principal*] Will you go next, and then I'll come to Elijah's dad for his first data point?

[Step #2 continues until everyone has shared their data points and the team has agreed about the questions for which each data point has relevance.]

You can see that this phase is only about sharing and sorting questions. It's likely that this process will take about 30 minutes because people may be feeling a bit overwhelmed by the data or unsure about the process. That's something to be expected. We want to encourage teams to stick with this process and remind each other that the decision-making step will happen as soon as this preparation work is done. Organizing relevant data under questions that will guide team decisions makes the decision-making process clear and quite efficient. It can also help to keep teams focused on what they've already decided matters most. When teams experience doubt at this phase, it's important to help people trust the process and notice how far they've already come as a team in exploring new ideas and reviewing important information together.

At the end of this step, you should have charts that look something like our tool **End of Step #2: List of Brainstormed MD Questions With Relevant Data Points**, which is linked in Chapter 9 and available on our companion website.

Step #3: *Make decisions and clarify agreements/disagreements.*

In Step #3, responsive teams are ready to make decisions using the questions and data points that were organized in Steps #1 and #2. This part of the meeting involves answering and agreeing about the responses to the five questions that the team has prioritized. It can be very quick, especially if the team is feeling connected and trustful of one another.

At this point, because all of the questions and data have been developed, prioritized, and reviewed by the team, team members are very familiar with the information. This helps to calm fears and alleviate anxiety, making people available and ready for the cognitive demands that are part of group decision-making. The team leader simply starts with the two required questions—Is the behavior disability-connected? Did it happen because the plan wasn't implemented well?—then moves on to the remaining questions, inviting team members to share their answer to the question while others listen respectfully and take notes. Once all team members have answered the questions, the team can revisit any questions about which team members disagreed.

In the end, the team has made decisions that can be used to inform any changes in plans or next steps for improving the fit between the child and how schooling happens. Often, people are relieved at this point and feel encouraged about moving forward together.

We need to point out one thing before we return to Elijah's team. There are many MDs at which a student is present. Elijah was not present at his MD because he is a student who has autism and is functionally nonverbal. A meeting that relies so heavily on language, dialogue, sitting, remaining quiet, and listening is not an accessible venue for him. It may be possible for a student with Elijah's profile to be "present" through the use of videotaped examples. If a team chooses this method of representation, it's important to include short videos of Elijah's success with the target behaviors as well as short videos of times when the conduct in question occurs. A responsive team never looks only at what needs to be corrected or changed; a responsive team considers what is working and tries to learn from this. When a responsive team looks at problem behaviors or failures to implement a plan as developed, this is done with a mindset of curiosity and a desire to understand what is happening and how it can be addressed. A responsive team is not trying to blame or find fault or punish; a responsive team is trying to use information and ideas to make the fit better. In doing this, team members refuse to get distracted or derailed by falling into habits of blame or punishment.

If Elijah could be present and contribute, he would be invited to do so. Most students should be invited to attend MDs and should be treated as equal, contributing team members when they are able to attend. Even when students seem reluctant to participate, they should be engaged in some way, particularly as they enter middle and high school. Helping students to brainstorm questions and learn that problems—even problems that result in removal from school—can be solved is a critical part of preparing for the transition to adulthood. Decisions should not be made *for* children when they can be made *with* children. And as much as it is possible, children should be encouraged and prepared to take an active role in a responsive MD process. We want to encourage you again to look at the Right Question Institute website, as they include a video of students engaging in the question formulation technique (https://rightquestion.org/what-is-the-qft-2/) that has informed our approach to manifestation determinations.

Now, let's go to Elijah's case study one more time and see how this team wraps up a responsive team MD.

Case Study: Elijah's Team

Team leader: Thanks, everyone, for doing such a thorough review of the relevant data. We've reached the point in our meeting where we'll answer our five questions and make decisions together about next steps. Does anyone need a break? Water? Anything before we continue?

[Team members shake their heads.]

Elijah's dad: I just want to get this over with and get Elijah back to school.

[Team members nod, murmur agreement and support.]

Team leader: Well, let's do that now. We're going to start with the required questions for our manifestation determination. These are the questions IDEA 2004 requires us to answer. Based on what we've shared and the data that's up there, I'm thinking we're going to get through these quickly. I'll ask each person to answer the question with a "yes" or "no" and share at least one data point that you feel supports your answer. If you can use the data points we sorted under this question, that's great. If you have another data point that you're thinking of, you can share that too. If we hear new data points, we'll add them to our chart so we have a good record of the data that we used to support each decision. Is everyone clear about what we're doing?

[People nod, indicate agreement.]

[*Looks at Elijah's dad*] OK, will you start us off? Do you believe that the biting and hitting that have caused injuries to people at school are connected to Elijah's disability?

Elijah's dad: Yes. I believe that the data about Elijah's communication and how many words he's saying in a week—what is it, about 100 in five days? [*Behaviorist nods*]—leaves him frustrated, and he hits and bites to tell us when something is really bothering him.

Team leader: Great. Now we'll just go around the table. Please answer my question. [*Looks at Elijah's mom*] You're next.

Elijah's mom: I agree. It's because he can't communicate in any other way, and that's about his autism.

[Team leader looks at the behaviorist.]

Behaviorist: Yes, it's a manifestation of his autism. I think it could be a combination of communication limitations and anxiety, including not understanding the social expectations. It could be about sensory needs as well . . . actually, I'm looking at the data from OT about using the chewy noodles and gum, and now I'm thinking his behavior might be communication. That data shows that Elijah likes to bite objects, too, so yes—definitely related to his disability.

[Other team members concur.]

Team leader: Thanks, everyone, It seems like we are in agreement that hitting and biting are manifestations of Elijah's disability. The next required question is whether the hitting and biting are connected to a failure to implement the IEP as written. This is a hard question, especially for us at school. I know everyone works to help Elijah. I know everyone is doing what they can do to make school a good fit. So I'm going to ask people to be really honest and reflect deeply before you answer this question. [*Turns to Elijah's dad*] I'll ask you to go first this time too.

Elijah's dad: Well, to be honest, I have wondered about this. For example, the behavior intervention plan says that Elijah will have access to gum, mints, and chewy noodles all the time at school. I wonder about this now that we've talked about the OT data. Thinking about our time at home, if I had to do this, I have no idea how I could be sure that Elijah would have access to those things all the time. So how could you possibly do it at school? Then again, Elijah doesn't bite or hit at home.

Elijah's mom: Well . . . he doesn't bite or hit *you*. I have to admit that I've been bitten and hit, but not as often as it's happening at school, that's for sure.

Elijah's dad: That's what I mean. Home is better.

Team leader: These are important data points, and I really appreciate your honest reflection. What's your answer to this question?

Elijah's dad: Well, I guess my answer is "I don't know."

Team leader: I appreciate how fair you're being and how honest this answer is. [*Looks at Elijah's mom*] Would you like to go next?

Elijah's mom: Sure. Actually, I think people are implementing the IEP as well as they can. Elijah is making progress, and we can see that his words are increasing and that he's up and ready to go to school every day. The kids here really seem to know him and like him too. So I think the IEP is being implemented, but we haven't figured out the biting and hitting based on the data from the behaviorist.

Team leader: Thanks for sharing specifics about the data to support your answer!

Behaviorist: I think we're doing what we can too. I would say the progress reports show that Elijah is making improvements in most areas, including his behavior. He's able to sit on his mat for circle time, point to pictures in response to circle time questions, and he never hits or bites anyone during circle time. In fact, most of the time he's in the classroom working with the kids, he's happy and enjoys learning.

Team leader: Thanks.

Assistant principal: I'm with Elijah's dad. I want to think we're implementing the IEP, but I'm not sure. It's not that I think people are slacking—

it's just that I wonder whether we might want to structure recess and passing in the halls and lunch. It seems like the data is showing us that the hitting and biting are happening when learning is not happening.

Team leader: Remember, this question is about implementing the current IEP. We might end up making some changes to take care of that as we look at our next three questions.

Assistant principal: Yes, OK, sorry. I'm still with Elijah's dad. My answer is 'I don't know.' I think the progress report data does show progress, and I think the hitting and biting data don't show progress. I don't know why.

Team leader: Thanks—another very honest answer!

[The team continues until everyone has shared. There is disagreement about this question.]

Team leader: Since we have some differing opinions about this question, I'm going to ask us to use consensus-based decision-making. On a scale of 1 to 5, how comfortable are you with answering this question about implementation of the IEP by saying that the school has implemented the IEP? One is *Not at All Comfortable*. Five is *Very Comfortable*. We use this during our IEP meetings, so I'm guessing people are pretty familiar with it. If you said "I don't know" earlier, I guess I'm asking if you're comfortable with a "yes" response. We didn't have any "no" responses—but there were quite a few "I don't knows."

Elijah's dad: I'm at a 3. So I guess OK to say "yes" for me.

Elijah's mom: I'm at a 5.

Assistant principal: I'm a 2 or 3. I'll go with 3 since it seems like we're really on the fence.

[*Others get to 3 or higher, indicating consensus about the school's implementation of the plan. Remember, a "no" here would not change the manifestation determination because the team already determined that the behavior is a manifestation of the disability.*]

Team leader: Thanks for trying so hard to get to consensus! I know it's not always comfortable to adjust and try to agree. In this case, we already know that the behavior is a manifestation of the disability because we answered "yes" to our first question. It's good that we were able to agree about the answers to both of these questions.

Given that this team has decided that the hitting and biting events are a manifestation of Elijah's disability, this team has some specific requirements to meet. We have to conduct a functional behavioral assessment (FBA) and implement a behavior intervention plan (BIP) unless this was previously in place. Elijah does have a BIP to address hitting and biting—that's why we've been getting such accurate data about these behaviors. Since this is true, we need to review the BIP and modify it to address the hitting and biting. We also have to return Elijah to his regular schedule unless we agree to change his placement as part of the BIP.

We'll decide how to address these items as we talk about our next three priority questions.

[*The meeting continues in a similar process, addressing the three remaining questions.*]

I'm sure you're thinking about what happens next. How does the team ensure that the requirements around the FBA, BIP, and IEP review are met? How can answering questions prioritized at the meeting by the team be guaranteed to lead to a compliant process?

Truly, this is the place where team members can become uncomfortable and where we have a chance to build our trust in one another and the responsive team process. We often feel a need to deal with compliance in a direct way, making a list of agenda items and reminding each other of the rules. There are some advantages to this approach, and there are also limitations. Our purpose in writing this book is to offer choices. We want to remind you that the typical approach to compliance is not the only approach. Actually, we think that the more options teams can explore in terms of how to address and resolve problems, the more likely the team is to come to consensus.

So what happens next in Elijah's team is that the items, including consideration of an FBA, a review of the BIP, and changes to the plan or placement, are noted on the chart paper or Jamboard as items to be discussed in the context of answering the remaining questions. What's really amazing is that in these types of meetings, if team members can be available for brainstorming and prioritizing questions, the final set of questions is always aligned with the concerns that led to the student's removal. It's not a linear process, and yet it leads to the same end as a more traditional approach to manifestation determination. It is a process that considers and supports both the tasks that the team must accomplish and the social and emotional needs of team members. That's the primary difference between the responsive team approach to manifestation determination and a more typical approach. The outcome is not only a compliant review of the data but also a sense of trust and hope for positive change after the very difficult experience of removing a child from school due to an unresolved gap between the child's behavior and the discipline code.

After a responsive team completes the MD process, the team chairperson offers a written summary of the team's answers to the five prioritized questions. The notes include the important data points that were selected by the team in support of the answers. The notes also include any decisions that are not based on team consensus, and instead, represent an offer from the district to the parents as a next step.

Remember, it's not required that the team agree. It is required and very helpful to have an accurate account about individual team members' input, including the answers to the questions and the reasons why. Using data to support claims made by individual team members can help everyone feel confident that they have been heard and that disagreements have been shared and understood, even if they could not be resolved at this particular stage in the team's process. We believe that it can be advantageous to identify disagreements clearly and proceed to due process resolution. Doing this after clearly communicating and documenting reasons for disagreement allows people to preserve relationships with one another by acknowledging that it is possible for reasonable people to disagree. Getting help from an outside party (mediator, hearing officer, facilitator) is often the best path to solving unresolved problems quickly and in a way that allows the team to come back together and continue supporting a child in partnership. Responsive teams hold on to this mindset, even when tensions arise. Responsive teams do not compromise about the outcomes of a manifestation determination. The outcomes must be a better fit between the child and schooling so the behavior does not recur *and* the preservation of a respectful, collaborating team that will continue to partner in the future to support the child's success.

SUMMARY

In this chapter, we introduced some opportunities and strategies for responsive teams engaging in completing reevaluations, reviewing independent evaluations, and conducting manifestation determinations. When any of these three activities is required, responsive teams are careful to share data in ways that can be understood by all team members. Responsive teams know when and how to make time for longer discussions and prioritize team relationships. Because there are many opportunities for improving educational plans during these processes, responsive teams approach their work with an eye to inquiry and a spirit of curiosity rather than a posture of defensiveness. Responsive teams are intentional and strategic; they care for one another and listen to understand and consider change.

Responsive teams also approach student discipline through a different lens. In this chapter, we've described some strategies, tools, and examples to help you rethink discipline in general and shift the approach to disciplinary determinations for students who have IEPs and 504 plans. We hope this chapter helps you to think about how the school community approaches the removal of children from school as an opportunity to strengthen relationships by solving problems together.

The reason for our proposed shift is based on our understanding of the philosophy and practices related to approaches to change and school discipline as cultural institutions. After reading this chapter, we hope you come away with new ideas and tools to use before, during, and after reevaluations, initial evaluations, and manifestation determination meetings. Ultimately, our commitment has to be to support the child and the team by using each of these processes to find a better fit between the needs of the child and the way schooling happens.

CHAPTER EIGHT

Leading Teams Through Reviews and Changes in Eligibility

"What's not working for me in team meetings? The language in evaluations.

There's so much jargon. I don't know what it means for the child and for me in the classroom."

—Anna Marchefka, General Educator

GUIDING QUESTIONS FOR THIS CHAPTER

- How can responsive teams anticipate changes in a way that celebrates student growth?
- What are the six steps to consider when reconvening 504 and IEP teams to consider changes in eligibility?
- What are the strategies that responsive teams can embrace to strengthen collaboration and compliance when considering changes in eligibility?

By this point, we're sure that you have a good sense of the elements of a responsive approach to partnering as 504 or IEP teams. By identifying guiding questions, reviewing data to explore answers to these questions, and then making decisions together as a team, it's possible to work together in a way that is compliant and collaborative.

In this chapter, we will consider the types of meetings that are required after a child has been determined eligible. These meetings happen frequently for school members of teams, but they happen much less frequently for individual students, families, and team members from outside the school community. It's important to notice this difference and think about how it may impact teamwork if you want to be part of an efficient, responsive team.

We'll also look at research and strategies that guide the way teams can approach change together, particularly changes in the location of services, placement, or eligibility. We know that change can cause uncertainty and anxiety. Responsive teams acknowledge this and consider not only the need to organize information and communicate well but also the need to recognize the feelings of team members as changes are coming and respond in a supportive way.

REQUIRED STEPS FOR REVIEWS AND REEVALUATIONS

When teams meet for reviews of 504 plans or IEPs, or redeterminations of eligibility, there are tasks that are required by regulation. Table 8.1 summarizes these steps.

TABLE 8.1 Required Tasks for Reviewing 504 Plans and IEPs

GUIDING QUESTION	SECTION 504	SPECIAL EDUCATION
What are the required tasks for reviewing plans?	The Office for Civil Rights has offered guidance about reviews in an FAQ updated in January 2020. *"28. Once a student is identified as eligible for services under Section 504, is there an annual or triennial review requirement? If so, what is the appropriate process to be used? Or is it appropriate to keep the same Section 504 plan in place indefinitely after a student has been identified?*	(4) Review and revision of IEP (A) In general The local educational agency shall ensure that, subject to subparagraph (B), the IEP team— (ii) revises the IEP as appropriate to address— (I) any lack of expected progress toward the annual goals and in the general education curriculum, where appropriate;

GUIDING QUESTION	SECTION 504	SPECIAL EDUCATION
	Periodic re-evaluation is required. This may be conducted in accordance with the IDEA regulations, which require re-evaluation at three-year intervals (unless the parent and public agency agree that re-evaluation is unnecessary) or more frequently if conditions warrant, or if the child's parent or teacher requests a re-evaluation, but not more than once a year (unless the parent and public agency agree otherwise). U.S. Department of Education OCR, 2020, Question 28	(II) the results of any reevaluation conducted under this section; (III) information about the child provided to, or by, the parents, as described in subsection (c)(1)(B); (IV) the child's anticipated needs; or (V) other matters. 20 U.S.C. 1414(d)(4)(A)(ii)
How is progress monitored (FAPE requirement)?	The FAPE requirement is different under Section 504. The standard requires "the provision of regular or special education and related aids and services that are designed to meet individual educational needs of handicapped persons as adequately as the needs of nonhandicapped persons are met." 34 C.F.R. 104.33 Under Section 504, progress is monitored for eligible students in the same way that progress is monitored for nondisabled students.	The local educational agency shall ensure that, subject to subparagraph (B), the IEP team— (i) reviews the child's IEP periodically, but not less frequently than annually, to determine whether the annual goals for the child are being achieved. 20 U.S.C. 1414(d)(4)(A)(i)
What are the requirements of the team when reevaluating?	(d) *Reevaluation*. A recipient to which this section applies shall establish procedures, in accordance with paragraph (b) of this section, for periodic reevaluation of students who have been provided special education and related services. A reevaluation procedure consistent with the Education	(c) Additional requirements for evaluation and reevaluations (1) Review of existing evaluation data As part of an initial evaluation (if appropriate) and as part of any reevaluation under this section, the IEP team and other qualified professionals, as appropriate, shall—

(Continued)

(Continued)

GUIDING QUESTION	SECTION 504	SPECIAL EDUCATION
	for the Handicapped Act is one means of meeting this requirement. 34 C.F.R. 104.35(d)	(A) review existing evaluation data on the child, including— (i) evaluations and information provided by the parents of the child; (ii) current classroom-based, local, or state assessments and classroom-based observations; and (iii) observations by teachers and related services providers; and (2) Source of data The local educational agency shall administer such assessments and other evaluation measures as may be needed to produce the data identified by the IEP team under paragraph (1)(B). (3) Parental consent Each local educational agency shall obtain informed parental consent, in accordance with subsection (a)(1)(D) prior to conducting any reevaluation of a child with a disability, except that such informed parental consent need not be obtained if the local educational agency can demonstrate that it had taken reasonable measures to obtain such consent and the child's parent has failed to respond. (4) Requirements if additional data are not needed If the IEP team and other qualified professionals, as appropriate, determine that no additional data are needed to determine whether the child continues to be a child with a disability and to determine the child's educational needs, the local educational agency—

GUIDING QUESTION	SECTION 504	SPECIAL EDUCATION
		(A) shall notify the child's parents of— (i) that determination and the reasons for the determination; and (ii) the right of such parents to request an assessment to determine whether the child continues to be a child with a disability and to determine the child's educational needs; and (B) shall not be required to conduct such an assessment unless requested to by the child's parents. 20 U.S.C. 1414(c)
What are the requirements when redetermining eligibility?	The Office for Civil Rights has offered guidance about reevaluations and redeterminations of eligibility in an FAQ updated in January 2020. *29. Is a Section 504 re-evaluation similar to an IDEA re-evaluation? How often should it be done?* "Yes. Section 504 specifies that re-evaluations in accordance with the IDEA are one means of compliance with Section 504. The Section 504 regulations require that re-evaluations be conducted periodically. Section 504 also requires a school district to conduct a re-evaluation prior to a significant change of placement. OCR considers an exclusion from the educational program of more than 10 school days a significant change of placement. OCR would also consider transferring a student from one type of program to another or terminating or significantly reducing a related service a significant change in placement."	(B) On the basis of that review, and input from the child's parents, identify what additional data, if any, are needed to determine— (i) whether the child is a child with a disability as defined in Section 1401(3) of this title, and the educational needs of the child, or, in case of a reevaluation of a child, whether the child continues to have such a disability and such educational needs; (ii) the present levels of academic achievement and related developmental needs of the child; (iii) whether the child needs special education and related services, or in the case of a reevaluation of a child, whether the child continues to need special education and related services; and (iv) whether any additions or modifications to the special education and related services

(Continued)

(Continued)

GUIDING QUESTION	SECTION 504	SPECIAL EDUCATION
	U.S. Department of Education OCR, 2020, Question 29	are needed to enable the child to meet the measurable annual goals set out in the individualized education program of the child and to participate, as appropriate, in the general education curriculum. 20 U.S.C. 1414(c)
What are the requirements if a child is found not eligible?	There is no guidance about finding a child no longer eligible under Section 504. One important aspect of Section 504 protections that schools should be aware of is that the definition of people who are protected under Section 504 includes those who have a record of impairment. This suggests that some students who have been found eligible may continue to be protected under Section 504 even if a written plan is not in place. 34 C.F.R. 104.3(j)	(5) Evaluations before change in eligibility (A) In general Except as provided in subparagraph (B), a local educational agency shall evaluate a child with a disability in accordance with this section before determining that the child is no longer a child with a disability. (B) Exception (i) In general The evaluation described in subparagraph (A) shall not be required before the termination of a child's eligibility under this subchapter due to graduation from secondary school with a regular diploma, or due to exceeding the age eligibility for a free appropriate public education under state law. (ii) Summary of performance For a child whose eligibility under this subchapter terminates under circumstances described in clause (i), a local educational agency shall provide the child with a summary of the child's academic achievement and functional performance, which shall include recommendations on how to assist the child in meeting the child's postsecondary goals. 20 U.S.C. 1414(d)(5)

GUIDING QUESTION	SECTION 504	SPECIAL EDUCATION
What are the requirements and options if a parent or team member disagrees with the district's decision?	The OCR addresses two specific circumstances in their FAQ regarding disagreements between 504 team members (typically the district and the parent). "26. *What should a recipient school district do if a parent refuses to consent to an initial evaluation under the Individuals with Disabilities Education Act (IDEA), but demands a Section 504 plan for a student without further evaluation?* A school district must evaluate a student prior to providing services under Section 504. Section 504 requires informed parental permission for initial evaluations. If a parent refuses consent for an initial evaluation and a recipient school district suspects a student has a disability, the IDEA and Section 504 provide that school districts may use due process hearing procedures to seek to override the parents' denial of consent." "31. *A student is receiving services that the school district maintains are necessary under Section 504 in order to provide the student with an appropriate education. The student's parent no longer wants the student to receive those services. If the parent wishes to withdraw the student from a Section 504 plan, what can the school district do to ensure continuation of services?* The school district may initiate a Section 504 due process hearing to resolve the dispute if the district believes the student needs the services in order to receive an appropriate education." U.S. Department of Education OCR, 2020, Questions 26 and 31	The IEP is a legal contract between the district and the student/parents/guardians. Prior written notice is required before any changes to the IEP occur. Distribution of notices of procedural safeguards to parents/guardians is also required annually. When one party disagrees with the decisions of another party regarding required consent or the elements of the contract, due process resolution options are available. Before exercising due process resolution, notice of the details of the complaint must be shared in writing with both parties. Due process resolution options include: • Mediation • Impartial hearing • Appeals • Civil action 20 U.S.C. 1415

There are several important points that you should notice as you consider the regulations and guidance mentioned in Table 8.1.

1. Why are reviews conducted? Reviews are conducted to ensure that 504 plans or IEPs do not need to be altered in order to offer FAPE to a child with a disability.
2. When are we required to reevaluate a child? The regulations about when teams must offer reevaluations are different for Section 504 and IDEA. Under Section 504, reevaluations must happen when a change that could impact services occurs. For example, if a child with a 504 plan is changing schools, a reevaluation would be required. For children with IEPs, reevaluations must occur at least once every three years.
3. What is required when a team reconvenes? When teams meet, they need to review the following items:
   - Student strengths (including progress data)
   - Current challenges (including any lack of progress that the data shows and parent/student concerns)
   - For students with IEPs only, updates to goals to meet current challenges
   - Adjustments to adaptations to address challenges (including accommodations, modifications, services)
   - Least restrictive environment (LRE)/placement
   - Any other items required by state regulations

It's also very important that all team members keep in mind that the purpose of individualizing education for students with disabilities is to strengthen the fit between the child and schooling. If a child has been found eligible, individualization of the supports and services is necessary in order to provide access or support progress in school. Responsive team members can anticipate changes in what the child knows, understands, and can do. Responsive team members must also anticipate changes in the way schooling is provided as part of their preparation for reviews, reevaluations, and redeterminations of eligibility.

RESEARCH TO CONSIDER

Reviewing progress and revisiting eligibility are activities that happen after the plan that a team has developed has been tried. When reviewing, reevaluating, or even reconvening to discuss disputes, the team encounters many opportunities to improve plans and to strengthen relationships. These opportunities happen only after a plan has been implemented:

- The opportunity to celebrate and express gratitude for specific achievements and successes
- The opportunity to ask questions to support improvements:
    - What's working?
    - What's not working?
    - What's next?
- The opportunity to share data targeting specific outcomes from multiple settings:
    - How do we know the fit between schooling and the child is better?
    - How do we know what's not working to support a fit between the child and schooling?
- The opportunity to affirm decisions that support a good fit and make new decisions where the team finds the fit not good enough based on this data.

Current research suggests that the way teams approach these opportunities can strengthen or erode the effectiveness of the team. Here are a few important takeaways from current research that inform the strategies we will suggest in the rest of this chapter:

- *Question goals.* Discuss and improve goals to ensure that they are measurable and meaningful (Kowalski et al., 2005; Spiel et al., 2014; Yell et al., 2020).
- *Question adaptations and service.* Discuss and improve adaptations and services to ensure they are actively supporting a better fit between the student and schooling (Goran et al., 2020; Yell et al., 2020).
- *Communicate about data.* Collect and share data from the classroom to support ongoing communication with all members of the team (American Institutes for Research, n.d.; Francis et al., 2017; Kurz et al., 2015; Sullivan-Walker et al., 2017).
- *Collaborate when making decisions.* Approach problems or differences of opinion in a way that is respectful of multiple opinions and open-minded about options (Geller, 2017; Malhotra, 2016; Sinai-Gavrilov et al., 2019).

(Continued)

(Continued)

A word about goals: We know that 504 plans are not required to include goals. In fact, we don't recommend adding goals to 504 plans. When we talk about goals in the context of 504 plans, we hope team members are thinking of these as outcomes. We use the word "goals" here because goals are a required part of every IEP. When it comes to planning for students under Section 504, the "goals" conversation should be framed in the context of offering a free appropriate public education (FAPE) under Section 504, which uses this as a guiding question: "Are the individual educational needs of the handicapped student being met as adequately as the needs of nonhandicapped students are met in academic and nonacademic settings?" (34 C.F.R. 104.33). We will talk more about this later on in this chapter. What matters here is that, even if a child is protected under Section 504, there are educational outcomes that are expected for that student, and they are indexed to the outcomes that are being sought for "nonhandicapped" students in the same school (Kowalski et al., 2005; Spiel et al., 2014).

STRATEGIES TO CONSIDER

By this point, you're probably wondering, "How can we do this?" There are many strategies that can be used to strengthen team collaboration and compliance during reviews, reevaluations, and changes in eligibility or times when team members disagree. In this chapter, we are encouraging you to develop intentional routines around reconvening 504 and IEP teams. We are also encouraging you to care actively for people as part of the process of developing responsive team routines. Actively caring is a critical aspect of creating a safe environment for team members to collaborate (Geller, 2017). We believe that many of the routines, practices, and strategies that are employed by 504 and IEP teams are designed to facilitate an effective and compliant process; however, we also believe that many of these routines, practices, and strategies have been adopted without an equal emphasis on caring for people, particularly those who may feel unheard, unsafe, or unwelcome as collaborators in the 504 and IEP team planning process.

In order to correct this, we recommend a step-by-step approach when reconvening the 504 or IEP team. We also recommend reconvening teams at least once a year. This is required by IDEA 2004 for students who have IEPs; however, there is no timeline set for reconvening 504 teams. When reconvening a team, meetings do not have to be long or drawn out; in fact, they should be brief—even as short as 10 to 15 minutes—especially if everyone arrives on time and is prepared. Now that we are able to convene teams using remote tools such as Google Meet and Zoom, meetings don't even have to involve travel. This is a significant advantage for us as team members, and it allows us to use the opportunity to reconvene as a way to check in more frequently about compliance and build our connections with each other. Figure 8.1 provides a summary of the steps in the process for reconvening responsive teams.

Figure 8.1 • Summary of Steps for Reconvening Responsive Teams

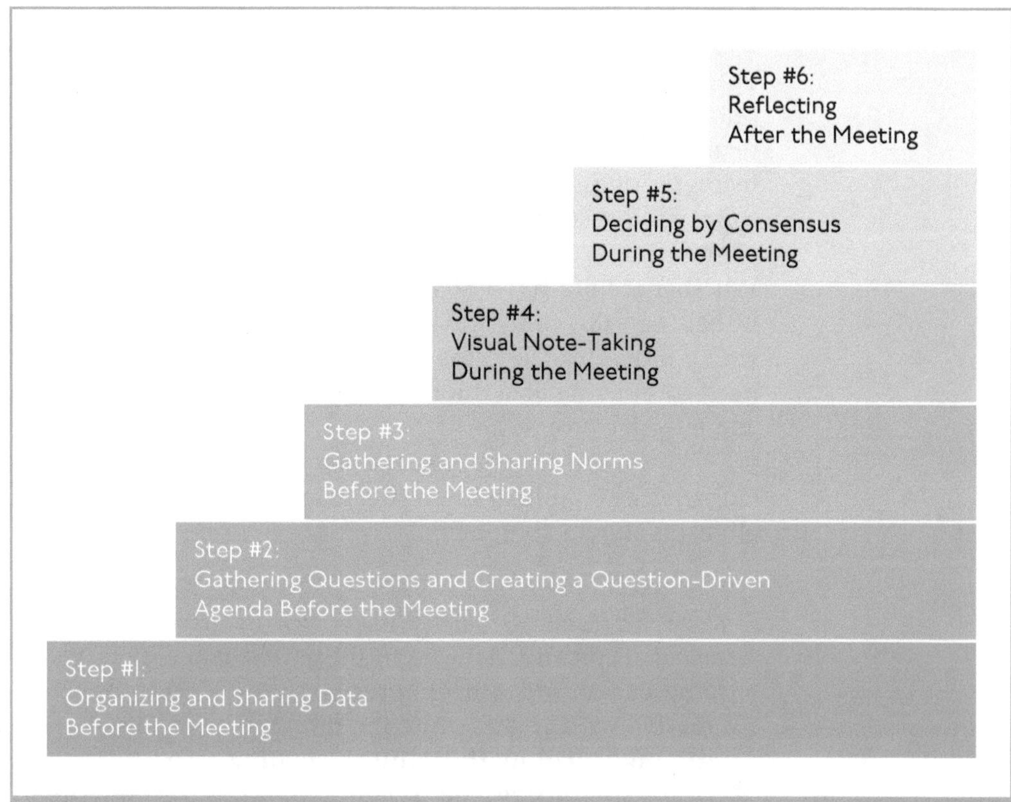

We hope you'll notice that most of the work of reviewing and reconvening happens before the team comes together to make decisions. By following these steps as the team reviews or reconvenes, including meetings in which there may be unresolved questions or differing claims by team members, we believe the team will have the clarity that is needed to maintain collaboration, even if due process resolution is necessary. We want to emphasize that responsive teams understand that reasonable people can disagree without disrespecting one another. Unresolved problems do not have to lead to broken relationships, especially if all team members are clear about the differences that they face and the data that is being used to support different claims. While we all strive to reach consensus about decisions, responsive teams understand that preserving a trusting long-term relationship between students, families, and educators is one outcome that can never be compromised, whether a team is able to agree at a particular time about a particular decision or not.

Let's look more closely at each of these steps.

Step #1: *Organize and share data before the meeting.*

This may be the most important step for responsive teams to prioritize. The data that should be organized and shared on a regular schedule with all team members should be identified at team meetings. This data should provide visible evidence that supports and services are being provided as well as evidence of their impact on the fit between the child and schooling. Whether a child has a 504 plan or an IEP, we know that the fit between the child and schooling has gotten to a point at which individualization is required. That means that we also need to individualize the reporting of data that shows access and effective progress.

Our advice about how to do this involves several actions that all teams should complete:

- *Know what data is routinely and easily collected in the school.* Typically, data including attendance data, work samples (end-of-unit/chapter tests, book reviews, creative writing assignments, lab reports or observation write ups, mad math minutes, spelling tests, vocabulary quizzes, etc.), benchmarking assessments (AIMSweb, DIBELS, etc.), and positive behavioral supports data are routinely collected for all students across settings.

- *Use routinely and easily collected data to show evidence of the impact of supports and services on the child.* If the child has a 504 plan, the team should identify specific types of data to collect to show the impact of accommodations, modifications, and services on the child's access to schooling. If the child has an IEP, the team should identify specific types of data and predict changes that should be evident by looking at samples of routinely and easily collected data. IEP goals should be written in a way that relies on this kind of data and describes the changes in this data as a way to monitor progress.

- *Develop a system and schedule for collecting and sharing data with all team members.* Now that technology allows schools to link data to student records and affords electronic access to these records, the infrastructure exists to easily share data.

Using tools such as PowerSchool, Frontline, Sparkler, ESPED, ASPEN, or other databases, responsive teams can identify ways to attach data to student records and make data or data summaries available to all team members. We recommend doing this on a monthly basis, though some teams will choose to do this at the point when progress reports are due. By collecting, organizing, and sharing data in this way, the process of progress monitoring becomes transparent and much more efficient for educators.

If your school does not have an electronic database, you can use a simple form such as the **Student Profile Template** mentioned in several earlier chapters. This tool is linked in Chapter 9 and is available on our companion website.

All educators can contribute links (including photos of work samples) to this sheet. It can be printed and shared with all team members. It could also be downloaded as a Word document and encrypted as a PDF if there is a need for protecting this type of information before emailing or exchanging it via electronic communication.

Step #2: *Gather questions and create a question-driven agenda before the meeting.*

This step involves communicating with team members about two weeks before the meeting. Typically, the team chairperson would initiate this communication; however, any team member could initiate with the team via email or other electronic communication. Team members are asked to review and prioritize questions that drive the agenda at least five days prior to the scheduled meeting date. They are also invited to submit questions to be added to the agenda. If team members do not respond, that is all right. It simply means that the agenda is developed based on the input of those who do respond. What matters is that all members are invited to participate in the development of the agenda.

In this step, team members identify questions that they want to prioritize during the upcoming meeting. Some questions are required by regulations when conducting a review for a 504 plan or IEP. There are also required questions for reevaluations that are included in Chapter 4. The team should be clear about which questions are required and should also identify any additional questions well before the time that the team meets. In addition, the team can prioritize the amount of time that will be allocated to each question, whether it is a required question or not. This allows team members to anticipate the time that will be agreed upon for discussion and helps team members to know what to expect. Time limits are not meant to be rigidly enforced, but rather, they offer a guide and an estimate for prioritizing and planning.

One tool that may be helpful for this step is the **Question-Driven Agenda.** This agenda could be sent to team members two weeks before a meeting, with a deadline for input five days before the team meets. Using questions helps the team to come together with a focus on discovery and inquiry. Responsive teams recognize that the process of finding a fit between the child and schooling is one of ongoing investigation. It's important to remember that no one has all of the answers when it comes to educating a child with a unique learning profile. Using tools to keep the team curious about options and possibilities while also keeping the team on track with compliance is essential for getting to positive outcomes for students. This tool is linked in Chapter 9 and is available on our companion website.

Step #3: *Gather and share norms before the meeting.*

Most teams are familiar with the use of norms. In many schools, norms are developed by administrators and shared with team leaders and other members of the team. Often, these norms are the result of deep thought and research, so we strongly recommend that team members consider norms that are developed in this way as a starting point for meetings.

When there are differences of opinion or unresolved issues, we recommend reviewing and rethinking the norms well before the team meets. The reason for this is that teams operate best when all team members feel empowered to contribute. If team members are given an opportunity to look at norms ahead of time and make changes or express their agreement with norms well before the day of the meeting, the team has already engaged in successful collaboration and has several agreements before people have walked in the door.

Norms are often easier to agree to than plans and placements. By revisiting norms and reminding each other that it is possible to partner effectively, teams can come together with shared expectations, ready to engage in brainstorming and problem-solving efficiently when team members are face-to-face.

We offer the tool **Proposed Norms for Team Meetings** for reviewing and revising. This tool is linked in Chapter 9 and is available on our companion website.

Step #4: *Use visible note-taking during the meeting.*

Many of the strategies that we discussed in Chapter 4 and Chapter 5 will apply when teams reconvene for reviews or eligibility redetermination. Some of the strategies offered in Chapter 7 will also apply, particularly if the team faces difficult conversations or conflict. In addition to these strategies, we want to encourage teams to offer one set of notes that is visible for all team members. Remember, these notes may not be the "official notes" that go in the student record. The purpose of using visible notes is so that all team members have a way to refer to what has been said and to use information that is gathered throughout the meeting to support decisions.

We strongly recommend that the visible notes include graphics or incorporate multiple colors or highlighting as well as other visual tools that support organization and memory. Any team member who has skill with listening, capturing the exact words spoken by team members, summarizing important ideas, or using color/drawings/graphic representations to organize information would be a good person to capture visible notes. If these notes are not the "official team meeting notes," the team chairperson should make this clear either before or during the meeting.

There should be no confusion among team members about the different purposes of "visible notes," which help team members to capture and recall information during a meeting, and "official meeting notes," which capture the decisions and supporting reasons for each decision made by the team for the student record. Parents/guardians may want to take pictures of visible notes to refer to during future meetings. This is certainly allowable. It's critical that all team members understand that the visible notes are not the "team meeting notes" that are part of the student's record. It's also important to remind team members who are not parents/guardians that keeping photos of confidential student information on personal devices or unsecured locations is not allowed.

We offer Examples of **Visible Notes** to show some different ways to record information at a team meeting (we simply used markers and chart paper during a meeting). It is linked in Chapter 9 and is available on our companion website. A Google image search using the key term "visible note-taking" will yield many examples if you're interested in other tools and strategies for visible note-taking. One tool for capturing visible notes when teams convene virtually is Jamboard, a free tool available from Google. In Chapter 9, you will find a link to an example using Jamboard to show a **Visible Note for Student Strengths**.

If team members have barriers to accessing visible notes, it is important to identify supports to accommodate their access to information. For example, if a person cannot see or read the notes, it's important to use tools such as high-contrast materials, large print, seating arrangements, or drawings to supplement materials that might not be accessible. If a team member reads a language that is different than the one in which notes are taken, using drawings or symbols, having an interpreter take notes in the heritage language of that team member (e.g., two sets of visible notes), or using a tool such as the multi-language translation tool mentioned in Chapter 4 may help with making information visible and available during meetings. If a student uses symbols to communicate, a program such as Widgit's Writing With Symbols (www.widgit.com) could allow for visible note-taking that will automatically generate symbols above key words so that everyone can use and understand the information being provided.

Step #5: *Decide by consensus during the meeting.*

Because responsive teams know that agreement may not be easy to achieve, consensus-based decision-making is critical for maintaining trust and clarity about team member input. Consensus-based decision-making involves individual responses to team decisions. Here are the steps in a consensus-based approach to decisions:

1. Clarify the decision that the team is facing. What is being proposed?

2. Invite each person to answer the following question about the proposal: At this time, are you able to give us the go ahead for this proposal? Why or why not?
3. Remind people that consensus does not mean enthusiastic support but rather a willingness to accept the proposal or give the team a chance to try it out under certain conditions.
4. If a team member indicates that they are not able to give the go-ahead at this time, others on the team can inquire further by asking one or more of the following questions:
   - On a scale of 1 to 5, how comfortable are you with this decision? (1 is *Not at All Comfortable*; 5 is *Extremely Comfortable*.)
   - Is there any change we could make to this proposal so that you could give us the go-ahead? If so, what is that change?
   - Can you help us to understand the data that connects with your discomfort? What data are you thinking of, and what would you like to see change with this data point?

If consensus can't be reached, the process of engaging in consensus-based decision-making should result in team members having a shared understanding about where each person stands in supporting a specific proposal or decision. The responses of team members should be documented in the official meeting notes. After a team has tried to reach consensus, team members may disagree, but clarity and respect for one another should be intact. This is critical for supporting the child. It is also very beneficial if a due process resolution is needed because the team goes into due process with a well-defined problem for the third-party mediator or hearing officer to decide.

If consensus can't be reached, the likely outcome will be due process for a 504 plan. It is important for teams to understand that

> Section 504 neither prohibits nor requires a school district to initiate a due process hearing to override a parental refusal to consent with respect to the initial provision of special education and related services. Nonetheless, school districts should consider that IDEA no longer permits school districts to initiate a

> due process hearing to override a parental refusal to consent to the initial provision of services. (U.S. Department of Education OCR, 2020, Question 44)

If consensus can't be reached by an IEP team, the plan or placement is likely to be rejected by the parent. One important outcome when consensus-based decision-making occurs is that teams can proceed to due process quickly so that the dispute can be resolved quickly. The team will go into due process resolution with a clear understanding about what is in dispute and why. Unless new data is collected and presented, a due process resolution is a good option for teams to use so that the relationship between team members does not erode. Failure to use due process resolution to wrap up issues that are in dispute leads to repeated meetings about the same questions, using the same data to support the same opinions. Clearly, this is a recipe for frustration. Responsive teams understand that disagreements should be resolved quickly and definitively so that the team can continue partnering in support of the student.

Step #6: *Reflect after the meeting.*

What happens after meetings is essential for supporting continued trust and connection among team members. During reviews and reevaluations, it's important to name and notice accomplishments and celebrations. At the end of the meeting, the team should spend a few minutes together, reviewing the child's strengths and the data that shows where the child has made progress or continued to successfully access the general curriculum and schooling. Reviewing specific contributions of team members and inviting team members to express gratitude and appreciation for contributions made during the meeting are other important elements of keeping a team strong and united.

If there are unresolved issues at the close of a meeting, these should be reviewed, noting the differing opinions and ideas and confirming the next steps that all team members can expect to happen. One of these next steps may be to implement a 504 plan. One may be to offer a consent for additional evaluations. One may be to offer services and supports that are available to all students in the school. One may be to offer an IEP that could subsequently be rejected. Team members should be reminded that due process options exist so that the team does not get bogged down in disagreements. If due process is needed, it should be welcomed as a way to get resolution and move forward together as a team.

For all teams, post-meeting feedback and connection is critical. Even if there are disagreements or feelings of discomfort at the end of a meeting, team members should be offered the opportunity to give their feedback, either orally or by using a confidential survey. This should be done before people leave the room or the virtual meeting so that feedback is authentic and connected to each team member's experience during the meeting. Feedback should be reviewed by district members of the team in order to understand how responsive teaming is impacting team members. Feedback about a particular team's work over time might be reviewed by that team too. This could help a specific team track progress with effective partnership and accomplishments, even if agreement about plans or decisions is hard to achieve.

A sample **Responsive Team Meeting Feedback Survey** linked in Chapter 9 and available on our companion website may be helpful for evaluating the impact of responsive team practices.

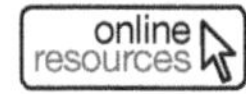

CASE STUDY: LAUREL'S TEAM

Let's take a look at a responsive team in action. We'll go back to Laurel's team that was introduced in Chapter 3 and revisited in Chapter 5. As you can imagine, this team has experienced some highs and lows in terms of collaboration. Laurel's team initially evaluated her in fourth grade as a child suspected of having autism. We considered the ways her team communicated after she was found eligible under IDEA 2004 as a student with autism. Let's fast forward to sixth grade. Laurel is now in middle school with an IEP addressing social skill development, reading, and communication needs; however, the team has had ongoing concerns about her behavior and social-emotional needs. We'll join Laurel's team as they reconvene at a meeting requested by her parents.

Laurel's mom: Thanks for meeting with me again. You must be getting sick of me calling these meetings, but I just can't figure out what's going on with her. I'm so worried about what happened in the industrial arts class. I also wonder why she's refusing to do anything with friends outside of school at this point. I'm totally fed up!

Team chair: It sounds as if you're really concerned about Laurel. So are we! I'm going to ask Mr. Grim, our assistant principal, to start some notes on chart paper for us. These aren't the official notes; they're just "visible notes" so that we can keep track of information easily today. Ms. Ortiz, Laurel's special education teacher, will take the official team meeting notes, and we'll share a copy with you at the end of the meeting. We'll tear up the "visible notes" when we're done so the information is confidential; however, we recognize that Laurel's parents might want to get pictures of these notes for future reference.

Special education teacher: OK, I'll make a note about our agenda items. Can you remind me about the questions we're answering today?

Laurel's mom: Yes, we got the agenda questions by email last week. I think we just have three questions for today: Why is Laurel failing industrial arts? Why is she crying about her industrial arts assignments? Are Laurel's "pranks" interfering with her relationships with kids in her class? Did I get that right?

Special education teacher: Thanks. I think those are the questions we settled on.

Assistant principal: I'll make one chart for each question. I'll take notes as we note data that ties to these questions.

School psychologist: Did you get a chance to look at the self-rating scales we've had Laurel filling out? Here's a graph of the ratings she's given herself over the past six weeks.

Laurel's mom: No, I'm sorry. I haven't had a minute to spare. Can we look at this now?

School psychologist: No need to apologize! That's why I graphed her answers to the questions for us. It should be easy to see what's happening. [*The school psychologist projects the following graph for the team.*]

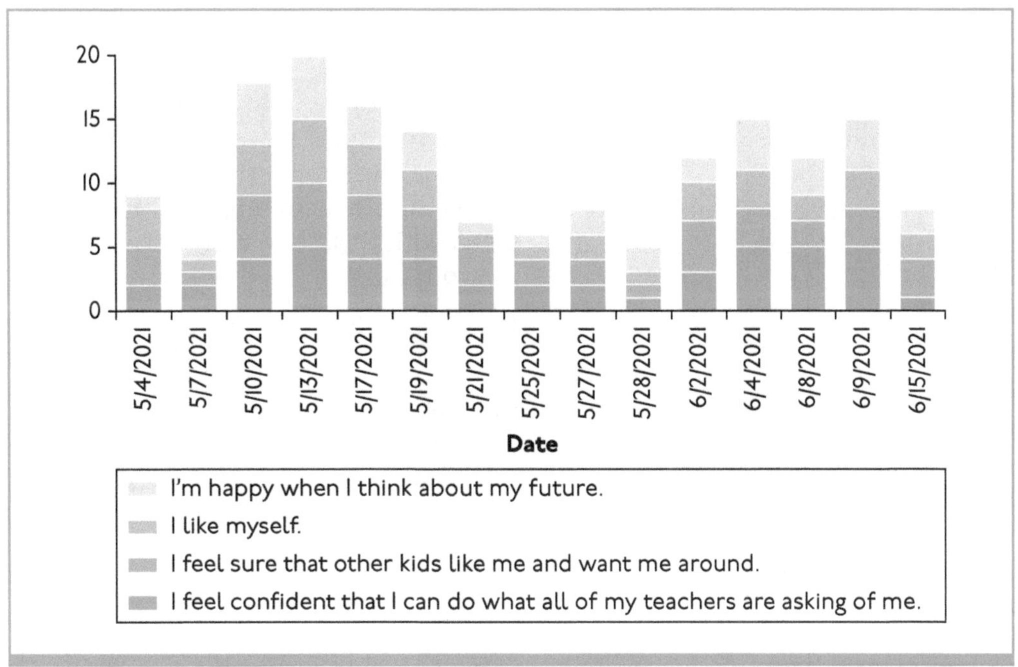

Team chair:	So this is what Laurel is saying about herself? What does this mean when we look at the questions for today?
School psychologist:	The bands of color show Laurel's responses to the four questions on her self-rating scale. She completes the scale at least twice each week. She designed the questions with me. They are things that Laurel thinks cause her to feel anxious and then engage in the "pranking" behaviors or disrupt her sleep or mood.
Laurel's mom:	Well, I can tell you that she had a major project due on May 26 for industrial arts. She had to sew an apron using a sewing machine. It was a disaster. She cried and cried.
Special education teacher:	I remember that week. I think Laurel actually cried in school, which she never does. Interestingly, there were three separate incidents involving other students' lockers during the week of May 24 to 28.

Industrial arts teacher: I had no idea she was crying about the sewing project! I'm so sorry!

Laurel's mom: Don't apologize. This happens. Laurel definitely struggles when she feels anxious. She's working on it, so having assignments that are hard might help her to get better with this. I just wish she wasn't failing your class.

Industrial arts teacher: We can certainly talk about that.

Assistant principal: Can I check in for a minute? I'm not sure where we are with the agenda. Can someone help me so I can get some notes for us?

Team chair: You're right. Let me get us back on track. The first question we're here to discuss is, "Why is Laurel failing industrial arts?" I'm going to ask Mrs. Ido, the industrial arts teacher, to share data with us to answer this question. After Mrs. Ido goes, I'll ask other team members for input about additional data.

Industrial arts teacher: Well, Laurel seems to think that industrial arts class doesn't matter because it's not an academic subject. She's always happy to read and do seatwork, but when we start doing any kind of project, she is very resistant. She puts her head down. She wanders around and talks to other students, sometimes distracting them or doing "pranks" to get their attention. It's clear that she's not interested in this class, and she's trying to get other students to be less interested too.

Special education teacher: I want to be careful here. Remember, we want to talk about data before we interpret data. I heard you say that she reads assignments and completes seatwork, right?

Industrial arts teacher: Yes. She has an average of 96 percent on the chapter quizzes and on written class assignments. But the sewing project, the cutting board project, and the metal mouse decoration project are all failing grades for Laurel. She earned a 20 percent on the sewing project, 50 percent on the cutting board project, and did not get credit for the metal mouse because she did not attempt to complete it. We have a cooking project next, and I'm really concerned about Laurel. I can't imagine that she'll be willing to cook a three-course meal!

Assistant principal: This is really good data. I'll add the data about her strengths with reading and seatwork and the data about her grades on these three projects to our visible notes.

Laurel's mom: Yes. That's helpful. We can all see why she's failing.

Team chair: Let's be sure we're in agreement about the answer to the question, "Why is Laurel failing industrial arts?"

Laurel's mom: Because of the grades on the projects.

[Other team members nod heads, murmur agreement.]

Team chair: Does anyone have another answer to this question? [*Waits one minute with no other responses coming*]

Assistant principal: OK, I'll note on the chart paper that we agree that Laurel is failing industrial arts because of her grades on the projects. I have to ask: Do we think there is a disability-related need that's impacting Laurel's ability to perform here?

School psychologist: I have to say, I've been wondering about that question too. I think it's about her anxiety. She's such a strong reader and writer, but maybe she's not feeling as confident about her ability to do the hands-on parts of industrial arts.

Industrial arts teacher: This is interesting. I didn't know that Laurel was so upset about the class. Does she really cry about it?

Laurel's mom: Almost every night. I know Ms. Ortiz says she was crying in school about it, too, which is really unusual for her.

Special education teacher: Yes, just that last week of May. I caught her in the corner reading a book, and when I got closer, I could see she was crying. I waited until the other kids were headed out of the room and asked Laurel if she was OK. She said she wasn't sure she could do the sewing, and a few tears came out of her eyes while she talked to me. I asked her if I could talk to Mrs. Ido, and she begged me not to. She told me that she was worried that Mrs. Ido would not like her if I told her she was worried.

Industrial arts teacher: I wish you had told me! I feel terrible about this! I thought Laurel didn't care. It seems like maybe she cares too much.

Laurel's mom: Well, I don't know about that. I do know that she worries a lot about doing what teachers expect. She sometimes tells teachers that she'll get in trouble at home if she doesn't get As. That's not true—but it's what she believes.

Team chair: OK. We know that Laurel is failing industrial arts and that it could be due to her anxiety, as well as the need to communicate better among team members so we have a better fit. We'll need to make a decision about what to do next here. Can you note this in the chart, Mr. Grim?

Assistant principal: Yes. I think we have data that answers our first two questions. Are there any more data we should consider before we decide what our next step will be to support a better fit between Laurel and what's happening in industrial arts?

Laurel's team continues to address each question. You should notice that having the questions in advance helped the team to regroup when they got offtrack. Also, this team was able to come prepared with data from the industrial arts class (grades and observations), the special education class (observations), home (observations), and from the student (self-rating scales). The data was documented using visible note-taking and recorded in narrative format by the "official note-taker." Having visible notes allowed the team to make connections between the questions from the agenda and the data that was presented by different team members. Reconvening with a question-driven meeting allowed the team to respond to one another in a way that revealed some gaps in communication. It was especially important that the qualitative data shared from home and the special education classroom about Laurel's distress shifted the industrial arts teacher's understanding about Laurel's attitude and investment in learning. This is a frequent outcome of a responsive approach to teaming, especially when the plans for a student are not yet resulting in the kind of fit the team hopes to see between the child and schooling.

SUMMARY

In this chapter, we have recommended a six-step process that can be followed when teams reconvene for reviews, reevaluations, or resolution of problems. By identifying and sharing questions, using data to understand what is happening at school, and making decisions based on what the data reveals, team members can respond in a supportive and curious manner, even when problems or disagreements arise.

When working as a team, even with the guidance from state and federal sources, collaboration is hard. Responsive teams are aware of this and recognize that:

- Reasonable people disagree.
- People have big feelings and care deeply about the child and outcomes.
- Anxiety and conflict, apathy and intimidation—all of this can happen and lead to decisions that are not truly shaped by the data or by input from the entire team.
- Time, availability for planning, and the desire to be efficient is another factor that can impact team decisions.

By following the six steps in this chapter, teams can continue to partner effectively even when these obstacles arise.

Finally, we want to close this chapter by proposing a responsive teaming theory of action:

We believe that if teams spend time before, during, and after team meetings, making sure that all team members

- Know the questions the team will address,
- Agree that all decisions are made by the entire team,
- Agree that all decisions are connected to specific data points that have been collected and shared with the team, and
- Agree to focus on answering specific questions about the fit between the child and schooling,

then team members will

- Report that they were able to have input into the planning process,
- Document that the process was compliant, and
- Know what the likely next steps will be related to the IEP/serving the student.

In the end, the best thing that teams can do for students with disabilities is refuse to be divided by the differences that inevitably arise.

CHAPTER NINE

Summary

> *"What leaves me satisfied at the end of the meetings is that a collaborative plan has been put in place that will focus on what the student needs in order to help the student begin to (hopefully) succeed."*
>
> —Miriam Robinson, ESL Teacher

GUIDING QUESTION FOR THIS CHAPTER

- What are the highlights, key takeaways, and tools that responsive teams can use?

This book proposes an approach to IEP and 504 teams that emphasizes relationships, connection, and trust to promote a satisfying experience for all team members. This is responsive teaming. This summary offers chapter-by-chapter highlights—key takeaways to help you begin your journey with responsive teams or to nourish the efforts you've already been making with responsive practice. Chapter 1 and Chapter 2 introduced the idea and practice of responsive teaming. Chapters 3 through 8 described and illustrated responsive team processes from the initial referral through reviews, reevaluations, and changes in eligibility. In the chapter-by-chapter summary that follows, you will find points to remember, actions to take, and tools to use. "Points to Remember" highlights key ideas in the chapter. "Actions to Take" points you toward concrete steps to begin or deepen your practice of responsive teaming that were suggested within the chapter. And "Tools to Use" conveniently provides the responsive teaming tools that we offered within the chapter. We conclude our summary by reflecting on the question, "So what?"

CHAPTER 1: INTRODUCTION

This chapter introduced our perspective on responsive IEP and 504 teams with a case study about Elijah.

Points to Remember

- Hidden factors impact team dynamics.
- The problem addressed by a team is not a student or a student's profile as a learner. The problem that the team is working to solve is the fit between the student and the student's experience of schooling.
- The responsive teaming cycle creates a pattern or routine for conversations and decisions at every step of a team's work. This *questions–data–decisions* cycle is applied in Chapters 2 through 8 to illustrate how a responsive team does its work at each stage of the team's process.
- Each chapter compares specific provisions of Section 504 of the Rehabilitation Act ("Section 504") and IDEA 2004 ("IDEA"), two distinct federal laws that differ in the legal protections they afford and the populations of students who are protected.
- This book is a "how-to" manual that offers a consistent and responsive approach to a team's decision-making.

Actions to Take

- Use the *questions–data–decisions* cycle at each stage of the team's work.

Tools to Use

Summary of Important Information: Section 504	See Appendix
Summary of Important Information: IDEA 2004	See Appendix

CHAPTER 2: WHY DO WE NEED RESPONSIVE TEAMS?

This chapter introduced the commitments and practices of responsive teaming with a case study about Albert.

Points to Remember

- Responsive teaming means that team members listen actively, with curiosity and respect, to one another's perspectives and priorities. The purpose of listening is to understand and empathize in order to identify questions, look at data that responds to these questions, and then collaborate to make decisions that respond to the data (questions–data–decisions cycle).
- Responsive teaming means that all voices are heard, team members feel understood, and the decisions made reflect available data and a robust vision of the child as a learner and a unique person, both in and out of school.
- Responsive teaming emphasizes shared understanding to enable collaboration.
- Responsive teaming processes comply with the relevant regulations.
- Responsive teams work to build relationships beginning with the referral, and they actively cultivate these relationships throughout the life of the team.
- Within the questions–data–decisions cycle, teams identify questions in response to specific criteria. All members of the team need equitable access to the data used to respond to questions and inform decisions. Claims about problems and ideas about solutions are based on the data in order to make decisions.
- Teams use facilitation techniques and a problem-solving approach to review data and map the student's learning profile before making decisions about eligibility, instructional planning, and placement.
- Section 504 and IDEA define the roles and responsibilities of the respective teams.

Actions to Take

- Use the strategies suggested to build a shared understanding of key criteria among all team members.
- Use the strategies suggested to strengthen communication and build trust among team members.
- Use the strategies suggested to make the relevant data about a particular student accessible to all team members.
- Use the strategies suggested to create and share a detailed meeting agenda.
- Use the suggested approach to reviewing data.
- Use the suggested strategy to map the student's learning profile.

Tools to Use

Responsive Teaming Survey	[QR code]
Summary of Evaluation Data Template	[QR code]
Student Profile Template	[QR code]
Sample Meeting Agendas	[QR code]
Establishing a Responsive Team Checklist	See Appendix

CHAPTER 3: REFERRING STUDENTS AND OBTAINING PARENTAL CONSENT

This chapter surveyed the processes related to referral with a case study about Laurel.

Points to Remember

- Responsive teams consider the concerns and social-emotional needs of all team members.
- Responsive teams know that team members will bring potentially different perspectives to the difficulty that prompted the referral.
- The responsive teaming cycle (questions–data–decisions) guides teams through the processes related to referral.
- The process before referral includes identifying and locating students who may be at risk for an IDEA- or Section 504–eligible disability ("child find"). Section 504 and IDEA give different requirements for child find. Teams take a responsive approach to child find.
- The process before referral also includes strategies to respond to learners' academic and social-emotional needs with multi-tiered systems of supports. A student's "adequate opportunity to learn" in the general education program depends upon access to the supports that will meet the particular need.
- A responsive approach to the initial referral increases accessibility to the required procedures and seeks to connect the concern(s) prompting the referral to IDEA- or Section 504–eligible disabilities.
- Section 504 and IDEA define "compliance" in the referral process.
- In the "response to referral" phase, responsive teams take specific actions when they decline to evaluate and when they offer to evaluate.
- Section 504 and IDEA provide guidance regarding parental consent.

Actions to Take

- Use the questions, data, and decisions in Table 3.3 to strengthen your district's responsive approach to child find.
- Use the questions, data, and decisions in Table 3.4 to determine if a student has had an adequate opportunity to learn a particular skill in the general education program.
- Use the responsive approach in Table 3.7 to strengthen your district's responsive approach to compliance in the referral process.
- Use the questions, data, and decisions in Table 3.8 to strengthen your district's responsive approach to the referral process as a whole.
- Use the questions, data, and decisions in Table 3.10 to strengthen responsive communication among team members.
- Use the responsive approach in Table 3.11 and the questions, data, and decisions in Table 3.12 to work with team members when the team declines to evaluate.
- Use the responsive approach in Table 3.14 and the questions, data, and decisions in Table 3.15 to work with team members when the team offers to evaluate.
- Use the responsive approach in Table 3.16 and the questions, data, and decisions in Table 3.17 to engage all team members in collaborating to identify suspected areas of disability and understand the eligibility determination process.

Tools to Use

Responsive Teaming Questions-Data-Decisions Tool	
Student Profile Template	

CHAPTER 4: EVALUATING STUDENTS AND DETERMINING INITIAL ELIGIBILITY

This chapter considered how responsive teams approached the question, "Does this student have a disability?" with a case study of Elijah's team.

Points to Remember

- Think about the evaluation and eligibility determination process as an investigation. Teams can approach the child's learning and the way education is working for that child with curiosity. This fit is something teams are trying to understand because it hasn't yet been fully figured out.
- Intentional practices encourage collaboration, the use of various types of formal and informal data, and an asset-based view of the learner.
- Intentional practices reflect on the fit between the learner's profile and schooling, consider prior interventions and the student's adequate opportunity to learn, and investigate how schooling processes can be adapted to the needs of the learner if there is evidence that the learner needs such adaptations in order to access schooling or make effective progress in the general curriculum.
- All members of the team need a shared understanding of the eligibility process before beginning an evaluation.
- Section 504 and IDEA offer distinct regulations regarding eligibility determination.
- Teams can gather, organize, and share information throughout the evaluation process in a way that helps team members; in this way, all team members can participate in the investigation of the child's learning profile. Sharing and organizing information while evaluations are happening brings two additional benefits: first, time for team members to review and think about information before coming together to make decisions; and second, the opportunity to have small chunks of information translated or interpreted over time. This opportunity is important to allow increased access and

eliminate the information overload that can happen when the language of evaluations is difficult for one or more members of the team to understand.

- Team members who work in schools know that the evaluation period involves much time engaged with the student. For parents/caregivers, this period of waiting and silence can be a time for worrying about the student's learning challenges and the possible outcomes of the eligibility determination meeting.
- Team members should have previewed all of the information needed to complete the responsive teaming decision-making cycle (questions–data–decisions) before the eligibility meeting. Team members should have access to all reports as well as usable summaries at least a few days before they gather for eligibility determination.
- Regardless of the outcome of the eligibility determination, team members remain present to support the student's access to the educational program and schooling. Once an eligibility determination is made, the team continues as a group of people who are connected in their commitment to the success of the student and responsive to the concerns that team members have raised.

Actions to Take

- Use the responsive approach in Table 4.1 to comply with regulations and build strong relationships among team members in the evaluation and eligibility determination process.
- Use Table 4.3 and Table 4.4 to ensure that all team members understand the questions, data, and decisions that the team is addressing during the evaluation process.
- Use the "strategies to consider" before beginning an evaluation.
- Use the "strategies to consider" to strengthen responsive teaming while evaluations are happening.
- Use the questions, data, and decisions in Table 4.5 to consider and discuss the questions that can arise at the eligibility determination meeting as the date of this meeting approaches. This is particularly important when differences of opinion or values are identified early in the process.

- Use case conferencing and intentional communication and address time-related issues before the eligibility determination meeting.
- Use the questions, data, and decisions in Table 4.6 to guide a team's deliberation during an eligibility determination.
- Use the questions, data, and decisions in Table 4.7 to guide the team whether or not the student has been found eligible under Section 504 or IDEA.
- Use the "strategies to consider" (commitments of care, commitments of service and support, commitments to the vision for the future) to demonstrate that the team continues as a group of people who remain invested in the student's success.

Tools to Use

Student Profile Template	
IEP Team Video	
Autism Definition Summary	
Multilanguage Translation Tool by Michelle Austin (mkaustinl@gmail.com)	
Annotated IEP Eligibility Meeting Agenda	

(Continued)

(Continued)

Abbreviated Eligibility Meeting Agenda	
Evaluation Summary	
Eligibility Infographic	
Sample Case Conference Agenda (Slides)	
Tool for Identifying Questions for Eligibility Determination	
Visuals for Aligning Evaluation Data to Questions (Jamboard)	
Learner Profile Jamboard	
Documenting Team Commitments Tool	

CHAPTER 5: DEVELOPING THE PLAN AND DETERMINING PLACEMENT

This chapter considered planning for 504– and IEP-eligible students with a case study of Albert's team.

Points to Remember

- The bulk of responsive teaming occurs before and after team meetings.
- Before the team meets to make decisions regarding planning and placement, it is important to identify the questions that all team members will use to guide this collaboration.
- The critical aspects of providing a free appropriate public education (FAPE) to students protected under Section 504 are
  - clear alignment between disability-related needs and barriers to access; and
  - documentation that the adaptations identified by the team are consistently available and afford equitable access to education.
- The critical aspects of providing FAPE to students protected under IDEA are the development of measurable annual goals that are used to monitor the student's progress, as well as the clear identification of data that will be used to monitor progress related to these goals.
- The four elements of a compliant and responsive team process for both IDEA and Section 504 include (1) determining needs and services, (2) prioritizing the least restrictive environment (LRE), (3) offering a free appropriate public education (FAPE), and (4) ensuring parent and student input. A responsive team process occurs when these elements are defined and identified as questions for decision-making, data are reviewed and interpreted by the team in clear and explicit alignment with these questions, and decisions are articulated and documented, including input from all members of the team. The goal of these four elements is an approach to planning and placement that "[ensures] . . . high outcomes" and "[cultivates] the [student's] unique gifts, talents and interests" (Safire & Dugan, 2021, p. 29).

Actions to Take

- Use the questions in Table 5.1 to develop a 504 or IEP plan and determine placement.
- Use the questions, data, and decisions in Table 5.2 to consider the student's profile, identify measurable changes that represent an improved fit between the child and schooling, and identify the data that could be collected and shared to show that improvements are happening. These actions prepare teams to collaborate in developing IEP and 504 plans.
- Use the questions, data, and decisions in Table 5.3 to develop the plan and determine placement during the meeting scheduled for this purpose.
- Use the "strategies during meetings" in Figures 5.2 through 5.6 to engage all team members in responsive processes and interactions during 504 and IEP team meetings: strategies for welcoming team members, strategies for starting a responsive team meeting, strategies to support teams with identifying questions, and strategies for data collection.
- Use the "strategies to support decision-making" in Figure 5.7 to engage all team members in equitable processes for responsive decision-making: seeking consensus; documenting agreements, observations, and questions; exploring unresolved problems; and documenting decisions and confirming unresolved questions.

Tools to Use

Abbreviated Section 504 and IEP Eligibility Determination Agenda	
Abbreviated IEP Planning and Placement Agenda	

Visible Note-Taking Tool (Example)	
How Responsive Was Our Team? (Survey)	
Strengthening the Team Checklist	See Appendix
504 Planning and Placement	
IEP Planning and Placement	
Detailed 504 Planning Agenda	
Detailed IEP Planning Agenda	
Tool for Responsive Teaming: Organizing Data	
Facilitated IEP Team Meeting by the Region 13 Education Service Center in Austin, Texas	

(Continued)

(Continued)

Agreements, Wonderings, and Questions Jamboard	
National School Reform Faculty Protocols by NSRF	
Exploring Unresolved Problems Tool	

CHAPTER 6: AFTER THE TEAM MEETING: IMPLEMENTING THE PLAN AND MONITORING PROGRESS

This chapter considered the essential post-meeting processes of implementing the plan and monitoring progress with a case study of Laurel's team.

Points to Remember

- What happens after the planning and placement meeting (Chapter 5) can vary greatly, even if the meeting went well. Responsive teams plan communication to preserve a sense of connection on behalf of the student, answer questions, address unresolved problems, and to nurture the relationship and the trust that began with the referral.
- After the planning and placement meeting, team members collaborate to implement the plan, resolve any problems, and monitor progress.
- Strategies to sustain responsive teaming after 504 and IEP team meetings include communication strategies, plan implementation strategies, problem resolution strategies, and progress-monitoring strategies.

- Table 6.3 compares Section 504 and IDEA regulations regarding plan implementation. Three key differences in implementing Section 504 and IDEA relate to (1) requirements for a written plan, (2) regulatory oversight, and (3) relationships to support implementation. We recommend a written Section 504 plan.
- High-quality implementation of a 504 plan or IEP requires *engaging all team members* and *supporting team members and others* who will implement the plan.
- Despite the responsive team's efforts toward strong collaboration and communication during the planning and placement process (Chapter 5), disagreements and misunderstandings will arise. These differences become *problems* when they interfere with the team's ability to design and implement a plan that all team members believe will improve the fit between the student and schooling. We consider a problem to be resolved when team members perceive the decisions and actions to be "win-win" solutions that work for everyone (e.g., Fisher et al., 1991).
- We distinguish between *problems* and *questions*. Problems refer to a present situation that needs to be resolved now. Solving a problem is urgent. Some questions refer to implementation: the *who, what, when,* or *how* of an accommodation, modification, or service. Other questions seek to understand a circumstance in ways that go beyond our current understanding. These questions cannot be answered—for example, "What will happen to my child (who needs daily care) when I die?" Some questions about a circumstance should not be asked (e.g., "Did that child bring a gun to school because Dad is a member of the NRA?"); instead, these wonderings can be expressed in ways that promote compassion, understanding, and relationship.
- Section 504 and IDEA due process provisions differ. Due process is an important tool to resolve a problem as quickly as possible after the team has tried unsuccessfully to achieve a resolution.
- Team members laid the groundwork for monitoring and reporting progress during the planning and placement process (Chapter 5) when they asked, "How will we know the plan is working? What are the measurable changes we will see? What data will show access, progress, or an

improved fit between the child and schooling?" Answers to these questions led the team to make decisions about monitoring the student's success, generally defined as access to the general education program and schooling, and progress toward challenging educational outcomes. The purpose of progress monitoring is to track the student's success in meeting challenging IEP goals or challenging 504 outcomes.

- Section 504 and IDEA define progress monitoring of student access to, and progress in, the general education program differently.

Actions to Take

- Use the communication strategies summarized in Table 6.2 to plan and engage communication that nurtures relationships, trust, and a sense of connection as team members collaborate to implement the plan, resolve problems, and monitor progress.
- Use the responsive approach in Table 6.4 to get signatures on a 504 plan or IEP.
- Use the strategies in Figure 6.2 for engaging all team members and supporting team members and others who will implement the plan.
- Use the questions, data, and decisions in Table 6.5 to guide the efforts of everyone involved in implementing a plan with fidelity.
- Use the strategies for problem resolution recommended for IEP and 504 team processes.
- The responsive approach in Table 6.8 describes an approach to progress monitoring that is made concrete in the "Strategies to Consider" section. Use these strategies to implement responsive progress monitoring.

Tools to Use

Visible Note-Taking Tool (Example)	

Communication Preferences Chart	
Home-School Contact Log	
Signed/Unsigned Documents Tracker	
Ensuring Access to the IEP or 504 Plan and Understanding Its Implementation	
Implementing the IEP or 504 Plan With Fidelity	
Provider Service Delivery Log	
Work Sample Cover Sheet	
Jamboard for Celebrating Progress	

(Continued)

(Continued)

Maze Passage Generator From Intervention Central	
Student Reflection Logs	
Social Skill Autopsy	
Better Jokes Plan	
Venn Diagram Exemplar	
Peer Dialogue Sheet	

CHAPTER 7: ADDITIONAL OPPORTUNITIES FOR RESPONSIVE TEAMING: REEVALUATIONS, INDEPENDENT EDUCATIONAL EVALUATIONS, AND MANIFESTATION DETERMINATIONS

This chapter considered the responsive team's approach to reevaluations, independent evaluations, and the manifestation determination process. The chapter ends with a case study of Elijah's team applying strategies during a manifestation determination meeting.

Points to Remember

- The process of conducting reevaluations and considering independent evaluation affords many opportunities for responsive teams to strengthen relationships and engage in inquiry.
- Reevaluations occur as the routine work of responsive 504 and IEP teams. Independent evaluations typically occur when there are questions or disagreements about the district's evaluations. A manifestation determination (MD) meeting occurs only when there has been a serious disruption in the fit between the student and schooling. Regardless of the decisions that are made during these meetings, it is important to maintain and strengthen the connection between success at school and the student. In addition, there's likely a need to restore relationships and support among adults on the team as well, particularly in the case of independent evaluations and manifestation determinations.
- Teams that are assembled for reevaluations, independent evaluation review, or manifestation determination need to notice several conditions that could affect the team's process. Team members may have different understandings about what these processes entail. They may not know what's required for a compliant review of an independent evaluation or manifestation determination. They may not agree about what the outcomes of such a process should be for a particular student. Teams should also be aware that there are significant disparities in the rates of identification and service models, as well as in severity of disciplinary action involving students of color, students with disabilities affecting emotional regulation, and students living in poverty.

Regarding Manifestation Determinations

- A responsive team brings a mindset to school discipline that seeks to understand the fit between the child and schooling. The team is seeking to support a better fit for all involved—not to punish, blame, or exclude a child from the learning community. A responsive approach is concerned with adequate opportunity to learn in the Tier 1 setting. We recommend that a responsive team engaged in a manifestation determination asks, "Has the child had adequate access to alternatives to disciplinary action within the school community that can meet the need(s) or teach the skill(s) suggested by the behavior?"

- Responsive teams need to consider alternative approaches to strengthening the fit between the student and the school discipline code. Removals often reinforce behavior that we're trying to replace. Research-based alternatives to removal include schoolwide positive behavioral incentive systems, individual behavior intervention plans, group contingency programs, and restorative justice initiatives.
- IDEA defines "manifestation determination." Manifestation determinations respond to two yes-or-no questions: (1) Is the conduct in question caused by the child's disability? (2) Is the conduct in question the result of lack of implementation of a plan?
- It's important for all team members to know the legal language that defines and describes manifestation determination before meeting together to answer the previous two questions. Table 7.1 summarizes regulations and guidance provided by Section 504 and IDEA regarding MD. Team members involved in disciplinary responses should be aware of legal requirements regarding placement determination and the provision of a free appropriate public education (FAPE). Team members should also understand and communicate prior to an MD meeting about the following legal provisions: composition of the team, continuation of services, behavioral supports, interim alternative educational settings (IASES), and appeal.
- A manifestation determination is required before a change in placement for a child with a disability. IDEA defines a change in placement as a removal that "would exceed 10 school days" within a school year. See 20 U.S.C. 1415(k)(1)(B) and (C).
- These protections can also extend to children who have not yet been evaluated. If parents, educators, or school staff have raised concerns about the child previously or if the child was referred for an evaluation, the child may be protected even if they haven't been found eligible under Section 504 or IDEA 2004.

- Brainstorming, dialogue, and thoughtful problem-solving support a responsive team's collaboration during a manifestation determination. Responsive teams know that the outcomes of a successful MD must be a better fit between the student and schooling so the behavior does not recur *and* the preservation of a respectful, collaborating team that will continue to partner in the future to support the student's success.
- A responsive team's MD includes three steps: (1) identify guiding questions for the manifestation determination as a team, (2) review all relevant information (data), and (3) make decisions and clarify agreements/disagreements.

Actions to Take

- If your school's response to disciplinary infractions relies on removals from the classroom, collaborate with your school's leadership team to investigate research-based alternatives such as those listed previously.
- Use the question formulation technique (QFT) to identify guiding questions with team members.
- Use the "strategies to consider" to facilitate the process of connecting specific data points to questions.

Tools to Use

500 Most Commonly Used Words in the English Language by Summer Boarding Courses International	
Using QFT With Adults Video by the Right Question Institute	
List of Brainstormed MD Questions	

(Continued)

(Continued)

End of Step #1: List of Brainstormed MD Questions—Prioritized	
Beginning of Step #2: List of Brainstormed MD Questions—Prioritized	
End of Step #2: List of Brainstormed MD Questions With Relevant Data Points	
Video of Students Engaging in the Question Formulation Technique by the Right Question Institute	

CHAPTER 8: LEADING TEAMS THROUGH REVIEWS AND CHANGES IN ELIGIBILITY

This chapter considered how a responsive team reviews the plan and revisits eligibility with a case study of Laurel's team.

Points to Remember

- As members of a responsive team prepare to review progress, reevaluate, or revisit eligibility, they keep in mind that the purpose of individualizing education for students with disabilities is to strengthen the fit between the child and schooling. If a child has been found eligible, individualized supports and services are necessary to provide access or support progress in school. Responsive team members can anticipate changes in what the child knows, understands, and can do. Responsive team members must also anticipate changes in the way schooling is provided.

- Meetings to accomplish reviews, reevaluations, and changes in eligibility happen frequently for educators and much less frequently for students, families, and team members from outside the school community. This difference matters for teams striving toward responsive and efficient processes.
- Change can cause uncertainty and anxiety. Responsive teams approach changes in the location of services, placement, and eligibility in ways that recognize feelings and support team members through necessary transitions.
- Table 8.1 summarizes Section 504 and IDEA regulations related to reviewing plans, reevaluating a student for a disability, and redetermining eligibility.
- Reviews are conducted to ensure that 504 plans or IEPs do not need to be altered in order to offer FAPE to a child with a disability.
- The regulations about when teams must offer reevaluations are different for Section 504 and IDEA. Under Section 504, reevaluations must happen when a change that could impact services occurs. For children with IEPs, reevaluations must occur at least once every three years.
- When a team reconvenes, it needs to review several items: student strengths (including progress data), current challenges (including any lack of progress as evidence in the data and parent/student concerns), updates to goals (for students with IEPs only), adjustments to adaptations (including accommodations, modifications, services), least restrictive environment (placement), and any other items required by state regulations.
- Reviewing progress and revisiting eligibility are activities that happen after the plan that a team has developed has been tried. When a team reviews, reevaluates, or even reconvenes to discuss disputes, it encounters many opportunities to improve plans and to strengthen relationships.
- There are many strategies that can be used to strengthen team collaboration and compliance during reviews, reevaluations, and changes in eligibility or times when

team members disagree. We encourage you to develop intentional routines around reconvening 504 and IEP teams. We also encourage you to care actively for people as part of the process of developing responsive team routines. We recommend 504 or IEP teams follow a step-by-step approach when they reconvene.

- Feedback and connection after reconvening a 504 or IEP team are critical.

Actions to Take

- Use the six steps provided in Figure 8.1 to reconvene a responsive team. Notice that most of the work of reviewing and reconvening happens before the team comes together to make decisions.
- Use the actions suggested to organize and share data before a reconvene (Step #1).
- Use the actions suggested to create a question-driven agenda before the meeting (Step #2).
- Use the actions suggested to gather and share norms before the meeting (Step #3).
- Engage team members in visible note-taking during the meeting (Step #4).
- Use the actions suggested to engage team members in consensus-based decision-making during the meeting (Step #5).
- Use the actions suggested to engage team members in reflection and feedback after the meeting (Step #6).

Tools to Use

Student Profile Template	
Question-Driven Agenda	

Proposed Norms for Team Meetings	
Examples of Visible Notes	
Visible Note for Student Strengths	
Writing With Symbols by Widgit	
Responsive Team Meeting Feedback Survey	

SO WHAT?

This book invites change. Responsive teaming offers practices, strategies, mindsets, and perspectives—related to the work of IEP and 504 teams and the people who come together on these teams—that are dramatically different from the frequent approaches in schools. Initiating change requires attention, explanation, and care for people. If you decide to start your journey toward responsive teaming or if you are inspired to energize the efforts you've already begun toward this end, there will be questions and concerns—perhaps pushback and complaints too. This is to be expected.

If you've read some of this book, you know that this work is not easy. You might also guess that it is not a "quick fix" for the difficulties that IEP and 504 teams typically face. The frequent cultures of public schools are not currently hospitable to responsive practice. Research teaches us that change takes time to embed and self-perpetuate; it also requires much persistence and nurture. So why travel the road of responsive practice?

We invite you down this road because teams must do the work they are mandated to do, and we have found that responsive teaming makes this work more satisfying for all team members. We have heard parents/guardians, students, teachers, and related service providers express that they have felt unheard, unsafe, unwelcome, disconnected, and generally disenfranchised as potential collaborators at the team table. We have heard and seen how responsive teaming has changed this experience for everyone involved, how it has made IEP and 504 teams more accessible and more satisfying.

We invite you down this road for children and their families. We opened Chapter 6 with Principal Marc Swygert's plea: "You are fighting for the lives of children. It is that important." Responsive teaming as we've described it in this book is an approach that addresses the research related to IEP and 504 teams. This research informs the strategies we've offered in each chapter. This means that adopting responsive practices can lead teams to the ultimate goal described by ESL teacher Miriam Robinson: "a collaborative plan . . . that will focus on what the student needs in order to help the student begin to (hopefully) succeed." Though we can make no guarantees, we can offer the likelihood that responsive teaming will strengthen the work of your IEP and 504 teams toward improved access and improved outcomes for the students served by these teams.

Appendix

SUMMARY OF IMPORTANT INFORMATION: SECTION 504

From Section 504 Regulations 34 C.F.R. 104

- Eligibility:
  - Eligible student: "To be protected under Section 504, a student must be determined to: (1) have a physical or mental impairment that substantially limits one or more major life activities; or (2) have a record of such an impairment; or (3) be regarded as having such an impairment" (Office for Civil Rights, 2020).
  - If necessary, review the following indicators:
    - Physical or mental impairment defined 34 C.F.R. 104.3(j)(2)(i)
    - Major life activity defined 34 C.F.R. 104.3(j)(2)(ii)
- Free appropriate public education defined under Section 504 should the student be found eligible for protections
  - Summarize and explain the requirements: 34 C.F.R. 104.33(a) and (b)
- Decisions that must be made by the team if the student is found eligible under Section 504
  - Educational setting considerations: 34 C.F.R. 104.34 (a), (b), and (c)
  - Placement considerations: 34 C.F.R. 104.35(c)
  - Nonacademic setting considerations: 34 C.F.R. 104.37 (all sections)
- Procedural safeguards requirements from 34 C.F.R. 104.36

SUMMARY OF IMPORTANT INFORMATION: IDEA 2004

Be sure to review or post the following information from state or federal regulations so that all team members understand the requirements for IEP development.

As you review these requirements, note corresponding sections of your jurisdiction's IEP form and explain the decisions that team members will make in order to complete each section:

- IEPs must offer a free appropriate public education (FAPE) to the child. Review the definition of FAPE.
- IEPs must offer services in the least restrictive environment (LRE) to the child. Review the definition of LRE and remind the team that any service that involves "removal" of a child from the settings in which their nondisabled peers are learning must be "justified" by the team using data.
- IEPs must include accommodations, modifications, and specialized instructional methodologies required by the child. Share the definitions of each of these terms.
- IEPs must include measurable annual goals and current levels of educational progress associated with each goal. Explain the elements of each measurable goal and describe the team's process for identifying how each goal will be measured (e.g., what data will be used to measure progress?).
- IEPs must include a description of service delivery. Explain how services will be documented and the team's role in determining frequency, duration, provider, and location of specialized instruction.
- IEPs must include a statement about how the student will participate in statewide and districtwide assessments. Explain the types of assessment and accommodations that the team will consider.
- If the child is transition-aged (the age requirement varies from jurisdiction to jurisdiction), a statement of needed transition services, measurable postsecondary goals, and other age-specific elements of transition planning are required. Explain what these terms mean in your jurisdiction if the child is transition-aged.

- Parental input and consent are required. Review the regulations and explain specific points at which parental consent is required.
- Procedural safeguards are protections in place for the parent and student. Offer the notice of procedural safeguards from your jurisdiction and remind the parents/caregivers of due process rights.

ESTABLISHING A RESPONSIVE TEAM CHECKLIST

Identifying Questions and Criteria

- ☐ What are the 10 most important questions or criteria (regulatory provisions, questions from guidance documents) that all team members should know, understand, and be able to consult during team meetings?
- ☐ Are these questions and criteria available for reference during meetings?
- ☐ Are these questions and criteria shared using words and images and in language that all team members can understand?

Looking at Data Together

- ☐ What data points are most commonly shared at IEP and 504 team meetings?
- ☐ Are these data points organized and presented in a way that every team member can understand and use?
- ☐ Is there any data that might be more meaningful for understanding and making decisions about the child's learning profile? If so, how could this data be collected, organized, and presented in a way that every team member could understand and use?

Making Decisions Using Facilitation and a Problem-Solving Approach

- ☐ When the team convenes for eligibility determination, planning/review, or placement determination, are all team members equal participants in the process? Would all team members agree with your answer to this question if you asked them? Why or why not?
- ☐ When the team convenes for a meeting, does the team look at data points and sort them together before sharing opinions, ideas, or decisions?
- ☐ When the team convenes, are meetings focused on celebrating strengths and progress by identifying specific data points that show progress? Are meetings

focused on identifying important elements of the student's learning profile and aligning claims about strengths and areas of need with specific data points?

- ☐ After the team convenes, do team members leave with a sense of accomplishment, a shared understanding about what was decided and why, and a clear understanding about the next steps in the team's partnership?

STRENGTHENING THE TEAM CHECKLIST

Before the Meeting

- ☐ Include a Post-it with the invitation that encourages people to come with ideas.
- ☐ Send a text to team members noticing a success of the student or of a team member.
- ☐ Ask team members for coffee orders, tea orders, or snack preferences; be sure to check on allergies and dietary restrictions too.
- ☐ Choose a photo or short video or write a short story telling a favorite thing about the child; bring this to share with the team.
- ☐ Call one or more members of the team and ask, "How are you feeling about our meeting?" Listen. Learn. Don't fix or suggest during the call . . . just care.

During the Meeting

- ☐ Listen to understand. As you listen, focus on what the other person is saying. That's all.
- ☐ Wait. Think. If you're not sure what to say, don't say anything. Silence is OK.
- ☐ Check in to be sure you have heard what was said. Use the other person's exact words.
- ☐ Ask a clarifying question if you're not sure—for example, "I'm not sure what you meant by ____." *or* "Can you tell me more about that?" *or* "Can you give me an example?"
- ☐ Ask a probing question to support the team—for example, "I hear you saying ____ ; can you show us some of the data that connects with this idea? We want to support you." *or* "I wonder if you've thought about ____. What do you think of this as another option?"
- ☐ Be clear. As Brené Brown says, "Clear is kind." Don't pretend you agree if you don't.
- ☐ Don't feel the need to fight—just say what you mean in simple, clear terms. Be sure to connect claims to data. That helps everyone.

After the Meeting Is Over and Before You Leave

- ☐ Find one specific person or decision that you're grateful for. Write it down. Share it with the team if you can.
- ☐ Find one specific thing that you feel confident is moving in the right direction. Write it down. Share it with the team if you can.

After You Leave the Meeting (Maybe in the Day or Week Afterward)

- ☐ Thank someone on the team for something specific they contributed. If you can thank a person who surprised you or with whom you don't totally agree, that's helpful. If not, that's OK.
- ☐ Share a question or concern with the team. Tell them what you need to help you answer the question or feel less anxious about the concern.

References

Algozzine, B., Horner, R. H., Todd, A. W., Newton, J. S., Algozzine, K., & Cusumano, D. (2014). Dora-II technical adequacy brief: Measuring the process and outcomes of team problem solving. In *Grantee Submission*. Grantee Submission.

ALLIANCE National Parent Technical Assistance Center at PACER. (2008). Fostering parent and professional collaboration. Research Brief. In *Technical Assistance ALLIANCE for Parent Centers*. Technical Assistance ALLIANCE for Parent Centers.

American Institutes for Research. (n.d.). Intensive intervention and special education. https://intensiveintervention.org/intensive-intervention/special-education.

Avendano, S. M., & Cho, E. (2020). Building collaborative relationships with parents: A checklist for promoting success. *TEACHING Exceptional Children, 52*(4), 250–260.

Beck, S. J., & DeSutter, K. (2020). An examination of group facilitator challenges and problem-solving techniques during IEP team meetings. *Teacher Education and Special Education, 43*(2), 127–143.

Board of Education of the Hendrick Hudson Central School District v. Rowley, 458 U.S. 176 (1982).

Bolhuis, E., Schildkamp, K., & Voogt, J. (2016). Data-based decision making in teams: Enablers and barriers. *Educational Research and Evaluation, 22*(3/4), 213–233.

Boscardin, M. L. (2007). What is special about special education administration? Considerations for school leadership. *Exceptionality, 15*(3), 189–200.

Brennan, W. J., & Supreme Court of the United States. (1987). *U.S. Reports: Honig v. Doe, 484 U.S. 305*. [Periodical]. https://www.loc.gov/item/usrep484305/.

Burgess, H., & Spangler, B. (2003). Consensus building. *The Beyond Intractability Project*. https://www.beyondintractability.org/essay/consensus_building.

Cadieux, C., Crooks, C., & King, C. (2019). Parents' experiences with an individualized intervention designed to strengthen the family-school partnership: The parents in partnership with educators (PIPE) program. *Exceptionality Education International, 29*(2), 1–17.

Center on Multi-Tiered Systems of Supports. (2021). *Multi-level prevention system*. https://mtss4success.org.

Chaisson, K., & Olson, M. R. (2007). The Section 504 process in middle school: Perspectives of parents, teachers and Section 504 coordinators. *Journal of the American Academy of Special Education Professionals*, Spr/Sum, 81–95.

Collier, M., Shenoy, S., Ovitt, B., Lin, Y.-L., & Adams, R. (2020). Educational diagnosticians' role in home–school collaboration: The impact of efficacy and perceptions of support. *School Community Journal, 30*(1), 33–58.

Crespo, I., Santos, A., Valassi, E., Pires, P., Webb, S. M., & Resmini, E. (2015). Impaired decision making and delayed memory are related with anxiety and depressive symptoms in acromegaly. *Endocrine 50*, 756–763. https://doi.org/10.1007/s12020-015-0634-6.

Cummins, J. (1984). *Bilingualism and special education: Issues in assessment and pedagogy*. College Hill.

deFur, S. (2012). Parents as collaborators: Building partnerships with school- and community-based providers. *TEACHING Exceptional Children, 44*(3), 58–67.

Dennis, R. E., & Giangreco, M. F. (1996). Creating conversations: Reflections on cultural sensitivity in family interviewing. *Exceptional Children, 63*(1), 103–116.

Deno, S. L. (2014). Reflections on progress monitoring and data-based intervention. In B. Cook, M. Tankersley, & T. Landrum (Eds.), *Special education past, present, and future: Perspectives from the field.* (pp. 171–194). Emerald.

Dunlap, G., & Fox, L. (2007). Parent-professional partnerships: A valuable context for addressing challenging behaviours. *International Journal of Disability, Development and Education, 54*(3), 273–285.

Endrew F. v. Douglas County School District Re-1, 137 S. Ct. 988 (2017). https://sites.ed.gov/idea/files/qa-endrew-case-12-07-2017.pdf.

Etscheidt, S. K. (2006). Progress monitoring: Legal issues and recommendations for IEP teams. *Teaching Exceptional Children, 38*(3), 56–60.

Etscheidt, S. L. (2016). Assistive technology for students with disabilities: A legal analysis of issues. *Journal of Special Education Technology, 31*(4), 183–194.

Feinberg, E., Beyer, J., & Moses, P. (2002). *Beyond mediation: Strategies for appropriate early dispute resolution in special education.* Unpublished manuscript. National Center on Alternative Dispute Resolution (CADRE).

Fisher, D., Frey, N., & Almarode, J. (2021). *Student learning communities: A springboard for academic and social-emotional development.* ASCD.

Fisher, D., Frey, N., & Rothenberg, C. (2011). *Implementing RTI with English learners.* Solution Tree Press.

Fisher, R., Ury, W., & Patton, B. (1991). *Getting to yes* (2nd ed.). Houghton Mifflin Harcourt.

Francis, G. L., Haines, S. J., & Nagro, S. A. (2017). Developing relationships with immigrant families: Learning by asking the right questions. *Teaching Exceptional Children, 50*(2), 95–105.

Geller, E. S. (2017). *Actively caring for people in schools: How to cultivate a culture of compassion.* Morgan James.

Gomes, M. F., & McVilly, K. R. (2019). The characteristics of effective staff teams in disability services. *Journal of Policy & Practice in Intellectual Disabilities, 16*(3), 191–200.

Goran, L., Harkins Monaco, E. A., Yell, M. L., Shriner, J., & Bateman, D. (2020). Pursuing academic and functional advancement: Goals, services and measuring progress. *Teaching Exceptional Children, 52*(5), 333–343.

Grupe, D. W. (2017). Chapter 26: Decision-making in anxiety and its disorders. In J. Dreher & L. Tremblay, Eds., *Decision neuroscience* (pp. 327–338). Academic Press. https://doi.org/10.1016/B978-0-12-805308-9.00026-9.

Hammond, Z. (2015). *Culturally responsive teaching & the brain: Promoting authentic engagement and rigor among culturally and linguistically diverse students.* Corwin.

Hoover, J. J., Erickson, J. R., Patton, J. R., Sacco, D. M., & Tran, L. M. (2019). Examining IEPs of English learners with learning disabilities for cultural and linguistic responsiveness. *Learning Disabilities Research & Practice, 34*(1), 14–22.

IDEA [website]. (n.d.). *About IDEA.* https://sites.ed.gov/idea/about-idea/.

IDEA [website]. (2017). Policy letter: March 6, 2002, to Texas Education Agency Division of Special Education Senior Director Eugene Lenz. https://sites.ed.gov/idea/idea-files/policy-letter-march-6-2002-to-texas-education-agency-division-of-special-education-senior-director-eugene-lenz/.

Individuals with Disabilities Education Act of 2004, 34 C.F.R. 300 (2006).

Jenkins, J., Schulze, M., Marti, A., & Harbaugh, A. G. (2017). Curriculum-based measurement of reading growth: Weekly versus intermittent progress monitoring. *Exceptional Children, 84*(1), 42–54.

Jones, B. A., & Peterson-Ahmad, M. B. (2017). Preparing new special education teachers to facilitate collaboration in the individualized education program process through mini-conferencing. *International Journal of Special Education, 32*(4), 697–707.

Jones, J. C., Hampshire, P. K., & McDonnell, A. P. (2020). Authentically preparing early childhood special education teachers to partner with families. *Early Childhood Education Journal, 48,* 767–779. https://doi.org/10.1007/s10643-020-01035-7.

Klingner, J. K., & Edwards, P. A. (2006). Cultural considerations with response to intervention models. *Reading Research Quarterly, 41*(1), 108–117.

Klingner, J. K., & Harry, B. (2006). The special education referral and decision-making process for English language learners: Child study team meetings and staffings. *Teachers College Record, 108,* 2247–2281.

Kowalski, E., Lieberman, L., Pucci, G., & Mulawka, C. (2005). Implementing IEP or 504 goals and objectives into general physical education. *Journal of Physical Education, Recreation & Dance, 76*(7), 33–37.

Kurz, A., Elliott, S. N., & Roach, A. T. (2015). Addressing the missing instructional data problem: Using a teacher log to document Tier 1 instruction. *Remedial and Special Education, 36*(6), 361–373.

Lake, J. F., & Billingsley, B. S. (2000). An analysis of factors that contribute to parent–school conflict in special education. *Remedial and Special Education, 21,* 240–251.

Leithwood, K., Seashore L. K., Anderson, S., & Wahlstrom, K. (2004). How leadership influences student learning. http://www.wallacefoundation.org/KnowledgeCenter/KnowledgeTopics/CurrentAreasofFocus/Education Leadership/Pages/HowLeadershipInfluencesStudent.aspx.

Lesh, J. J. (2020). IEP 101: Practical tips for writing and implementing individual education programs. *Teaching Exceptional Children, 52*(5), 278–280.

Lo, L. (2012). Demystifying the IEP process for diverse parents of children with disabilities. *Teaching Exceptional Children, 44*(3), 14–20.

Lopez, S., McWhirter, A. C., Rosencrans, M., Giuliani, N. R., & McIntyre, L. L. (2019). Father involvement with children with developmental delays. *Global Education Review, 6*(1), 40–62.

Madigan, J. C., & Scroth-Cavataio, G. (2011). IDEA 2004: Building collaborative partnerships and effective communication between administrators, special and general educators, and multi-disciplinary professionals. *Principal Leadership,* 26–30.

Malhotra, D. (2016). *Negotiating the impossible: How to break deadlocks and resolve ugly conflicts (without money or muscle).* Berrett-Koehler.

Malone, D. G., & Gallagher, P. (2009). Transition to preschool special education: A review of the literature. *Early Education and Development, 20*(4), 584–602.

Menlove, R. R., Hudson, P. J., & Suter, D. (2001). A field of IEP dreams: Increasing general education teacher participation in the IEP development process. *TEACHING Exceptional Children, 33*(5), 28–33.

Militello, M., Schimmel, D., & Eberwein, H. J. (2009). If they knew, they would change: How legal knowledge impacts principals' practice. *NASSP Bulletin, 93*(1), 27–52.

Mind Tools Content Team. (n.d.). Win-win negotiation: Finding solutions that work for everyone. *Mind Tools.* https://www.mindtools.com/CommSkll/NegotiationSkills.htm.

Moses, M., Gilchrest, C., & Schwab, N. C. (2005). Section 504 of the Rehabilitation Act: Determining eligibility and implications for school districts. *Journal of School Nursing, 21*(1), 48–58.

Mueller, T. G., & Vick, A. M. (2019a). An investigation of facilitated individualized education program meeting practice: Promising procedures that foster family–professional collaboration. *Teacher Education and Special Education, 42*(1), 67–81. https://doi.org/10.1177/0888406417739677.

Mueller, T. G., & Vick, A. M. (2019b). Rebuilding the family–professional partnership through facilitated individualized education program meetings: A conflict prevention and resolution practice. *Journal of Educational and Psychological Consultation, 29*(2), 99–127.

Nagro, S. A., & Stein, M. L. (2016). Measuring accessibility of written communication for parents of students with disabilities: Reviewing 30 years of readability research. *Journal of Disability Policy Studies, 27*(1), 13–21.

National Center on Intensive Intervention. (n.d.). *Using academic progress monitoring for individualized instructional planning (DBI professional learning series module 2).* https://intensiveintervention.org/resource/using-academic-progress-monitoring-individualized-instructional-planning-dbi-training.

National Center on Response to Intervention. (2012). *RTI implementer series: Module 2—Progress monitoring training manual.* https://nanopdf.com/download/rti-implementer-series-module-2-progress-monitoring-training-manual_pdf.

O'Connor, E. A., Yasik, A. E., & Horner, S. L. (2016). Teachers' knowledge of special education laws: What do they know? *Insights into Learning Disabilities, 13*(1), 7–18.

Office for Civil Rights (OCR). (1997). *Letter to Durheim*, 27 IDELR 380.

Office for Civil Rights (OCR). (2016). *Parent and educator resource guide to Section 504 in public elementary and secondary schools.* U.S. Department of Education. https://www2.ed.gov/about/offices/list/ocr/docs/504-resource-guide-201612.pdf.

Office for Civil Rights (OCR). (2020, January 10). *Protecting students with disabilities: Frequently asked questions about Section 504 and the education of children with disabilities.* https://www2.ed.gov/about/offices/list/ocr/504faq.html.

Office of Special Education Programs. (n.d.). *Identification of specific learning disabilities.* U.S. Department of Education. https://sites.ed.gov/idea/files/Identification_of_SLD_10-4-06.pdf.

Office of Special Education and Rehabilitation Services (OSERS). (2019, August 30). *A guide to the individualized education program (archived information).* https://www2.ed.gov/parents/needs/speced/iepguide/index.html.

Peabody College, Vanderbilt University. (2021a). How can school administrators support implementation of high-quality IEPs? Page 5: Implementing the IEP. *Iris Center.* https://iris.peabody.vanderbilt.edu/module/iep02/cresource/q2/p05/#content.

Peabody College, Vanderbilt University. (2021b). How can school administrators support implementation of high-quality IEPs? Page 6: Monitoring IEP fidelity and student progress. *Iris Center.* https://iris.peabody.vanderbilt.edu/module/iep02/cresource/q2/p06/#content.

Powers, K., & Mandal, A. (2011). Tier III assessments, data-based decision making and interventions. *Contemporary School Psychology, 15*, 21–33.

Program on Negotiation. (2019). Overcoming cultural barriers in negotiation: Cross-cultural communication techniques and negotiation skills from international business and diplomacy. *Harvard University.* https://www.pon.harvard.edu/freemium/new-free-report-overcoming-cultural-barriers-in-negotiation/.

Right Question Institute. (n.d.). *What is the QFT?* https://rightquestion.org/what-is-the-qft/.

Rispoli, K. M., Lee, G. K., Nathanson, E. W., & Malcolm, A. L. (2019). The parent role in school-based teams for adolescents with autism spectrum disorder. *School Psychology, 34*(4), 458–467.

Rossetti, Z., Sauer, J. S., Bui, O., & Ou, S. (2017). Developing collaborative partnerships with culturally and linguistically diverse families during the IEP process. *Teaching Exceptional Children, 49*(5), 328–338.

Safer, N., & Fleischman, S. (2005). Research matters: How student progress monitoring improves instruction. *Educational Leadership, 62*(5), 81–83.

Safir, S., & Dugan, J. (2021). *Street data: A next-generation model for equity, pedagogy and school transformation.* Corwin.

Schimmel, D., & Militello, M. (2008). Legal literacy for teachers. *Principal Leadership, (9)*4, 54–58.

Scott, T. M., McIntyre, J., & Liaupsin, C. (2004). An examination of functional behavioral assessment in public school settings: Collaborative teams, experts, and methodology. *Behavioral Disorders, 29*(4), 384–395.

Section 504 of the Rehabilitation Act of 1973, 34 C.F.R. 104 (1973).

Shapiro, E. S. (2008). Best practices in setting progress monitoring goals for academic skill improvement. In A. Thomas & J. Grimes (Eds.), *Best practices in school psychology v* (pp. 141–158). National Association of School Psychologists.

Shaw, S. F., & Madaus, J. W. (2008). Preparing school personnel to implement Section 504. *Intervention in School and Clinic, 43*(4), 226–230.

Shogren, K., & Ward, M. (2018). Promoting and enhancing self-determination to improve the post-school outcomes of people with disabilities. *Journal of Vocational Rehabilitation, 48*, 187–196.

Sinai-Gavrilov, Y., Gev, T., Mor-Snir, I., & Golan, O. (2019). Seeking team collaboration, dialogue and support: The perceptions of multidisciplinary staff members working in ASD preschools. *Journal of Autism and Developmental Disorders, 49*(11), 4634–4645.

Spencer-Iiams, J., & Flosi, J. (2021). *Leading for all: How to create truly inclusive and excellent schools.* Corwin.

Spiel, C. F., Evans, S. W., & Langberg, J. M. (2014). Evaluating the content of individualized education programs and 504 plans of young adolescents with attention deficit/hyperactivity disorder. *School Psychology Quarterly, 29*(4), 452–468.

Sullivan-Walker, M. E., Rock, M. L., & Popp, P. A. (2017). Meeting the needs of students with disabilities experiencing homelessness: Federal, community, and educator roles. *Preventing School Failure, 61*(2), 155–162.

Summer Boarding Courses International. (n.d.). 500 most common words in English. https://summerboardingcourses.com/blogs/500-most-common-words-in-english/.

Technical Assistance ALLIANCE for Parent Centers. (2008). *Fostering parent and professional collaboration.* PACER Center.

TED. (2018, January 2). *Get comfortable with being uncomfortable|Luvvie Ajayi* Jones [Video]. YouTube. https://www.youtube.com/watch?v=QijH4UAqGD8.

University of Colorado. (2015). Consensus building techniques. https://drive.google.com/file/d/1JA1N9TKScpAwwUYM5OvxeNi_gfnW8Vx3/view.

University of Waterloo. (n.d.). Effective communication: Barriers and strategies. *Centre for Teaching Excellence.* https://uwaterloo.ca/centre-for-teaching-excellence/teaching-resources/teaching-tips/communicating-students/telling/effective-communication-barriers-and-strategies.

U.S. Department of Education. (2017). *Questions and answers (Q&A) on U. S. Supreme Court case decision* Endrew F. v. Douglas County School District Re-1. https://sites.ed.gov/idea/files/qa-endrewcase-12-07-2017.pdf.

U.S. Department of Education Office for Civil Rights. (2010). *Free appropriate public education for students with disabilities: Requirements under Section 504 of the Rehabilitation Act of 1973.* https://www2.ed.gov/about/offices/list/ocr/docs/edlite-FAPE504.html#:~:text=The%20Section%20504%20regulation%20requires,severity%20of%20the%20person's%20disability

U.S. Department of Education Office for Civil Rights. (2016). *Parent and educator guide to Section 504 in public elementary and secondary schools.* https://www2.ed.gov/about/offices/list/ocr/docs/504–resource-guide-201612.pdf

U.S. Department of Education Office for Civil Rights. (2020, January). *Protecting students with disabilities: Frequently asked questions about Section 504 and the education of children with disabilities (FAQ 30).* https://www2.ed.gov/about/offices/list/ocr/504faq.html

U.S. Department of Education Office for Civil Rights. (2021, September). *Back to school binder.* https://www2.ed.gov/about/offices/list/ocr/docs/back-to-school-binder-elementary-secondary-sept-2021.pdf.

U.S. Department of Education Office of Special Education and Rehabilitation Services. (2016). *Dear colleague letter on the inclusion of behavioral supports in Individualized Education Programs.* https://sites.ed.gov/idea/files/dcl-on-pbis-in-ieps-08-01-2016.pdf.

U.S. Department of Education Office of Special Education Programs. (2000). *Guide to the individualized education program.* https://www2.ed.gov/parents/needs/speced/iepguide/index.html#:~:text=The%20IEP%20creates%20an%20opportunity,each%20child%20with%20a%20disability.

Vanderbilt University. (2021). *Special education resource project: What is curriculum-based measurement?* https://my.vanderbilt.edu/spedteacherresources/what-is-curriculum-based-measurement/.

World Class Instructional Design and Assessment (WIDA). (2015). *Focus on: SLIFE: Students with limited or interrupted formal education.* https://wida.wisc.edu/sites/default/files/resource/FocusOn-SLIFE.pdf.

Yell, M. L. (2012). *The law and special education* (3rd ed.). Pearson.

Yell, M. L., Bateman, D., & Shriner, J. (2020). Developing and implementing educationally meaningful and legally sound IEPs. *Teaching Exceptional Children, 52*(5), 344–347.

Yell, M. L., Collins, J., Kumpiene, G., & Bateman, D. (2020). The individualized education program: Procedural and substantive requirements. *TEACHING Exceptional Children, 52*(5), 304–318.

Yell, M. L., Thomas, S. S., & Katsiyannis, A. (2012). Special education law for leaders and administrators of special education. In J. B. Crockett, B. S. Billingsley, & M. L. Boscardin (Eds.), *Handbook of leadership and administration for special education* (pp. 69–96). Routledge.

Zirkel, P. A. (2020). An updated primer of special education law. *Teaching Exceptional Children, 52*(4), 261–265.

Index

CORWIN
A SAGE Publishing Company